LIBERAL VIRTUES

Liberal Virtues

*Citizenship, Virtue, and Community in
Liberal Constitutionalism*

STEPHEN MACEDO

CLARENDON PRESS·OXFORD

Oxford University Press, Walton Street, Oxford OX2 6DP

Oxford New York Toronto
Delhi Bombay Calcutta Madras Karachi
Petaling Jaya Singapore Hong Kong Tokyo
Nairobi Dar es Salaam Cape Town
Melbourne Auckland

and associated companies in
Berlin Ibadan

Oxford is a trade mark of Oxford University Press

Published in the United States
by Oxford University Press, New York

First published in hardback and paperback 1990
First issued in Clarendon Paperbacks 1991
Paperback reprinted 1992

British Library Cataloguing in Publication Data
Macedo, Stephen
Liberal virtues.
1. Political ideologies: Liberalism
I. Title
320.51
ISBN 0-19-827872-1

Library of Congress Cataloging in Publication Data
Macedo, Stephen, 1957–
Liberal virtues / Stephen Macedo.
p. cm.
Includes bibliographical references.
1. United States—Constitutional law—Interpretaton and
construction.   2. Democracy.   I. Title.
KF4550M2   1990   342.73—dc20   89–77322
ISBN 0-19-827872-1

Typeset by Wyvern Typesetting Ltd, Bristol
Printed and bound in
Great Britain by Biddles Ltd
Guildford and King's Lynn

FOR MY FATHER AND
GRANDMOTHER, AND THE
MEMORY OF MY MOTHER

Acknowledgements

A number of friends, teachers and colleagues have read, discussed, and commented upon sections of this book over the last few years. I have benefited enormously from their insights and suggestions, and can only apologize where I have not had the good sense to take full account of their advice.

In Oxford, Mimi Bick, Chris Eisgruber, John Gray, Chandran Kukathas, and Emilio Pacheco read and commented on early drafts. Ronald Dworkin's careful supervision for a term was extremely valuable. Last but not least, without the unfailing encouragement, stimulation, and judicious guidance of Steven Lukes, I would have floundered long ago.

In Princeton, Joseph Carens, John Diulio, Robert George, Jennifer Nedelsky, and Bernard Yack read and commented helpfully on large sections. Discussions with Armando Bengochea, Carole Pateman, Adam Sloane, and Dennis Thompson were very valuable. The sections on constitutionalism and American politics are indebted to the early guidance and continued sage advice of Jeffrey K. Tulis. Much of the substance and the spirit of my argument are deeply indebted to Sotirios A. Barber. Finally, Amy Gutmann and Walter F. Murphy were truly exemplary supervisors of the doctoral dissertation on which this work is based. They were patient, careful, and insightful in reading and commenting upon several drafts, and provided just the right mix of guidance, encouragement, and threats. No graduate student could ask for more.

Walter Grinder and Jeremy Shearmur of the Institute for Humane Studies gave me important comments on early drafts. The support of the Institute has been absolutely invaluable over the years, especially the Claude Lambe Fellowship which enabled me to spend a year in Oxford. I owe a great deal to the people at IHS.

At Harvard, Mark Peterson, H. W. Perry, Jr., and Shannon C. Stimson provided advice on particular chapters. John Rawls and Leif Wenar coped patiently with versions of Chapter 2. I have learned a good deal from Joshua Henkin, Robert Katz, and David Patent, undergraduates whose theses dealt with topics related to the subject of this book, and from conversations and seminars with a number of Harvard's brilliant graduate students and undergraduates. I have benefited greatly from seminars and conversations with Harvey C. Mansfield, Jr. Judith N. Shklar has been everything one could wish for and more in a colleague: she read over the entire manuscript, offering gentle criticisms, important suggestions, practical advice, and invaluable support, for which I am deeply grateful.

Jack Crittenden read and commented helpfully on Chapters 6 and 7. William Galston and Charles Larmore provided insightful comments on a version of Chapter 2 at a symposium sponsored by the Institute for Humane Studies.

Hannes Gissurarson, Randy Krozsner, and Scott Wayland have patiently suffered through innumerable speeches and harangues on subjects related to this book. For their indulgence I am beholden to them, and to others. For my stubbornness I can only apologize, as I do to any whose ideas I unfairly criticize in this book. I hope the occasional sharp statement will be taken to signal only intellectual respect.

Several important studies have been constantly in the back of my mind as I have put this work together. I would like to acknowledge them here, as their influence remains implicit in the text: Don Herzog's *Without Foundations: Justification in Political Theory* (Ithaca, 1985), Nancy Rosenblum's *Another Liberalism: Romanticism and Reconstruction in Liberal Thought* (Cambridge, Mass., 1987), and Rogers M. Smith's, *Liberalism and American Constitutional Law* (Cambridge, Mass., 1985).

Opportunities to present and discuss parts of my argument at sessions arranged by the Hastings Center, the Hayek Society of Oxford, the Institute for Humane Studies, the Politics Department at Princeton, and the Harvard Government Department, are gratefully acknowledged.

Several of the main arguments of Chapters 1–4 were originally presented in 'Liberal Virtues, Constitutional

Community', *The Review of Politics*, v. 50 (1988). Portions of Chapter 2 appeared as 'The Politics of Justification', *Political Theory*, 18 (1990). Some of the material in Chapter 5 was first presented in *The New Right v. The Constitution* (Washington, DC: Cato Institute, 1987), 2nd edn. Permission to use this material is gratefully acknowledged.

In the final stages of manuscript preparation, David Bernhardt laboured tirelessly on my footnotes and citations, and Dwayne Bey saved me from traps laid by my computer. Henry Hardy of Oxford University Press has been patient and accommodating throughout the publication process.

A generous grant from the H. Smith Richardson Charitable Trust allowed me to complete this book. I am very grateful to the Trustees, to R. Randolph Richardson, President of the Smith Richardson Foundation, and to Dr Michael S. Greve, former Program Officer.

S.M.

Cambridge, Massachusetts
9 July 1989

Contents

Introduction

In 1942 Gordon Hirabayashi, a final-year college student in Washington state, became subject to a wartime curfew imposed on Japanese Americans on the West Coast. At first Hirabayashi went along, but after a week of dashing back to his hall of residence from the library or the coffee shop he stopped and thought, in his own words,

Why the hell am I running back? Am I an American? And if I am, why am I running back and nobody else is? I think if the order said *all* civilians must obey the curfew, if it was just a nonessential restrictive move, I might not have objected. But I felt it was unfair, just to be referred to as a 'non-alien'—they never referred to me as a citizen. This was so pointedly, so obviously a violation of what the Constitution stood for, what citizenship meant. So I stopped and turned around and went back.[1]

At first, nothing happened to Hirabayashi as a result of what he considered his 'expression of freedom'.[2] Then came the exclusion orders and Hirabayashi and his family were ordered to evacuate the West Coast. For young Hirabayashi compliance meant violating his principled belief in the injustice and unconstitutionality of the exclusion order. Non-compliance could, however, lead to indefinite separation from his family and possible imprisonment.

My mother said that she gave me moral support but she wanted me to come with the family to the camp. I know you're right and I admire this stand of yours, she said, but we don't know if we'll ever see each other again. In that period, I didn't know what was going to happen to me, and I didn't know what was going to happen to them, where they were going, how far away and for how long. Everything was just a total blank, full of anxiety. So she said, It's a matter of life and death. Why stick to a principle? Stick with us. She used

---

[1] Peter Irons, *The Courage of Their Convictions* (New York, 1988), 53.
[2] Ibid.

everything—tears and everything. And I couldn't do it. So when I wrote my statement [explaining his reasons for refusal to the FBI] it was only me.[3]

In 1965 Susan Epperson was teaching biology at Little Rock, Arkansas's Central High School when she was asked to participate in litigation to help overturn the state's ban on the teaching of the theory of evolution. She was torn. Epperson believed in the scientific method but was also a Christian, and she felt that teachers should strictly obey the law to set a good example for students. She objected to the law because it 'supported one particular religious viewpoint in state-supported schools', but was also afraid, 'Afraid there would be people who would hate me, and people who would say nasty things, people who would say that I wasn't a Christian. But I decided that that wasn't sufficient reason to say no.'[4]

Gordon Hirabayashi was convicted of violating the wartime curfew and exclusion orders. He spent time in various gaols and work camps and waited forty years to have his convictions overturned. Susan Epperson won her case.

To some people, liberal principles of freedom and equality mean a good deal, enough to justify risking unpopularity, separation from family, incarceration, or worse. Free government needs its heroes, individuals prepared to make great sacrifices on behalf of liberal values, and it has had them. Freedom also requires the more modest but still important contributions of a wide range of common citizens: tolerance and respect for the rights of others, self-control, reflectiveness, self-criticism, moderation, and a reasonable degree of engagement in the activities of citizenship.

Liberal politics stands, first and foremost, for individual freedom and rights, the rule of law, limited and accountable government. Liberal political thinkers have focused their main energies on justifying and explaining these core ideas and institutions. As a consequence, free government has come under a barrage of criticism for neglecting positive political ideals of citizenship, virtue, and community. For many,

---

[3] Irons, *The Courage of Their Convictions*, 54–5.
[4] Ibid. 226, 224.

liberalism lacks luster, it appears uninspiring, and not worthy of enthusiastic defence. A variety of critics, known as communitarians or civic republicans, advance complaints that focus on the lack of positive liberal ideals. These tend to pull up short when it comes to advancing workable alternatives to liberal politics, and they sometimes seem to stand only for a platform of 'anything but liberalism!' Citizenship, virtue, and community are, nevertheless, important ideals, well worth caring about and arguing over. Liberalism deserves a defence based on these ideals, and this book aims to help provide it.

The phrase 'liberal virtues' will seem, to some, at best an oxymoron and quite possibly a dangerous invitation to government interference, political perfectionism, and paternalism. Government ought not to try make people virtuous, liberals tend to say, it ought only to provide for equal freedom, order, security, and a few other widely acceptable public goods. I largely agree. We can oppose government intrusiveness and paternalism while allowing that there are attitudes and capacities that liberals ought to have and develop, and that when people do have and develop them a liberal regime will flourish. Liberal politics depends on a certain level and quality of citizen virtue, which is in many ways promoted by life in a reasonably just and tolerant, open liberal regime.

Liberal citizens typically possess reflective capacities, enjoy certain rights and privileges, and fulfil some basic political duties. But what attributes and character traits should citizens of a pluralistic liberal polity aspire to? Status-associated words have, as C. S. Lewis remarked, often become associated with the virtues (or vices) appropriate to a particular status, rank, or role. Words, according to Lewis, 'implying superior status can become terms of praise; those implying inferior status, terms of disapproval. Chivalrous, courteous, frank, gentle, generous, liberal, and noble are examples of the first; ignoble, villain, and vulgar, of the second'.[5]

A word like nobility begins to take on its social-ethical meaning when it refers not simply to a man's status but to the manners and

---

[5] C. S. Lewis, *Studies in Words* (Oxford, 1960), 21, and see Joel Feinberg's interesting discussion, 'The Ideal of the Free Man', in James F. Doyle, ed., *Educational Judgments: Papers in the Philosophy of Education* (London, 1973), 143–69.

character which are thought to be appropriate to that status. But the mind cannot long consider the manners and that character without being forced on the reflection that they are sometimes lacking in those who are noble by status and sometimes present in those who are not. Thus, from the very first the social-ethical meaning, merely by existing, is bound to separate itself from the status meaning. Accordingly, from Boethius down, it becomes a commonplace of European literature that the true nobility is within, that villanie, not status, makes the villain, that there are 'ungentle gentles' . . .[6]

In describing liberal virtues we are not thereby ascribing legal obligations to liberal citizens. Liberal virtues, even if not found in all or even many liberal citizens, are those forms of excellence appropriate to citizens of liberal regimes and conducive to flourishing in the kind of society liberalism creates. An account of virtues may criticize and not only reflect the actual behaviour of role holders, but should avoid wholly utopian or unrealistic expectations.

Unfortunately, 'liberal' has become a term of abuse in the American political lexicon, and so my employment of it could be seriously misleading. By 'liberal' I do not mean the ideology and programme of the left wing of the Democratic Party, I mean, rather, the great political tradition in which the American Founding was a seminal moment, I mean the tradition of John Locke, John Stuart Mill, and John Rawls. By 'liberal' I mean those political values like individual freedom and responsibility, and institutions such as the rule of law and the separation of powers, that have guided and informed the practice of constitutionalism in America and elsewhere. In much of the West, 'conservatives' speak often of individual liberty and responsibility and thereby profess their allegiance to liberalism.

Liberal justice and respect for the liberal rights of all moral persons ought to, I will argue, guide the political arrangements of a liberal polity. Moral persons are all who possess certain reflective capacities: the capacity for a sense of justice, and the capacity to form a plan of life.[7] (I generally follow John

---

[6] Lewis, *Studies*, p. 22.

[7] See John Rawls's discussion of the two 'moral powers' of persons in 'Kantian Constructivism in Moral Theory', *Journal of Philosophy*, 77 (1980), 525. Ronald Dworkin endorses a similar view by according rights to those who can 'make plans and give justice', *Taking Rights Seriously* (Cambridge, Mass., 1977), 182.

Rawls and Ronald Dworkin here, and discuss these matters at greater length in Chapter 5.) Liberal justice and rights, I shall argue, structure and partly determine the ends, goals, and visions of the good life that liberal citizens pursue.

I agree with William Galston that liberal justice and rights are not as independent of visions of the good life as liberal theorists have sometimes assumed or claimed.[8] I shall, however, try to avoid the theoretical debate about whether 'the right' is prior to 'the good' or vice versa, and will not adopt Galston's neo-Aristotelianism or base my defence of liberalism on a 'full theory of the good latent in liberal practice'.[9] The language of liberal justice and rights, the logic of respect for persons, and the practice in our politics of public justification, can serve as the organizing focuses of positive liberal ideals; from that base I will try to generate liberal virtues and a rejoinder to the communitarians.

This book aims to display, from one perspective at least, the ideals and demands implicit in basic liberal and constitutional institutions and practices (such as law, judicial review, and civil disobedience). It also takes up the defence of the modern liberal political thinking on which the communitarians focus their criticisms. Why, one might ask, should non-theorists be interested in liberal moral ideas? One good reason is that the theory and practice of liberal constitutionalism are closely connected. Liberal principles are frequently invoked to justify political decisions or to reform actual political practices. Citizens often profess an allegiance to the basic tenets of liberal political morality, tenets that importantly define the 'American ethos': a vision of what this regime stands for at its best.[10] Sharpening our understanding of the moral requirements and ideals to which liberals aspire is of more than academic importance.

It has long been a truism that 'the American political

[8] See William A. Galston, 'Defending Liberalism', *American Political Science Review*, 76 (1982), 621–9, and *Justice and the Human Good* (Chicago, 1980). Galston provides a telling critique of Kant, but not of all 'Kantian' political moralities.
[9] Galston, 'Liberalism', p. 627.
[10] The phrase is from Herbert McClosky and John Zaller, *The American Ethos: Public Attitudes toward Capitalism and Democracy* (Cambridge, Mass., 1984); the evidence marshalled in ch. 1 shows that professions of support for liberal-capitalist values (in the abstract at least) are widespread.

tradition is basically a liberal tradition' and that this tradition is the 'basis' of that country's 'national identity'.[11] As sociologist Robert Bellah and his associates conclude, Americans are drawn from different traditions but,

> beneath the sharp disagreements, there is more than a little consensus about the relationship between the individual and society, between private and public good. This is because, in spite of their differences, they all to some degree share a common moral vocabulary, which we propose to call the 'first language' of American individualism in contrast to alternative 'second languages', which most of us also have.[12]

It is, however, reasonable to ask to what extent liberal practice is capable of approaching the ideals and sustaining the virtues identified in theory. To what extent are citizens capable, not simply of mouthing liberal platitudes, but of acting on liberal principles?

Twentieth-century America has extended suffrage to women, civil liberties to blacks, many procedural rights to those accused of crimes, and extensive constitutional protections to speech, the press, religious practice, and various forms of privacy. Property rights and economic liberties are subject to more and more extensive regulation than they once were, but liberals themselves disagree on these issues perhaps more than on any other. Much important liberal ground remains to be won (and some that has been won is threatened) but progress has been made: American political practices and attitudes have become markedly more liberal in recent decades. The dominant trend, as McClosky and Brill argue, seems to be toward greater toleration and respect for liberal rights.[13]

The majority of Americans today profess a strong commitment to the basic liberal values of tolerance and respect for the rights of those with whom they disagree, but many are incapable or unwilling to apply abstract liberal values to

---

[11] Clinton Rossiter, *Conservatism in America: The Thankless Persuasion* (New York, 1962), 67, and Samuel Huntington, *American Politics: The Promise of Disharmony* (Cambridge, Mass., 1981), 23.

[12] Robert Bellah *et al.*, *Habits of the Heart* (New York, 1986), 20.

[13] Herbert McClosky and Alida Brill, *Dimensions of Tolerance* (New York, 1983), 416–22, and see McClosky and Zaller, *Ethos*, pp. 40–1.

concrete cases. Large majorities, for example, support the freedom to assemble to discuss political ideas, but only one in four Americans would allow a civic auditorium to be used by gay liberationists and only a tiny minority would open it to a revolutionary group advocating violent overthrow of the government.[14]

Among the factors encouraging greater toleration for diversity and support for liberal norms are secularization, urbanization, education, political participation, and greater exposure to the media.[15] 'Opinion élites' (intellectuals, educators, journalists, the clergy and the politically active) are markedly more liberal than the population as a whole when it comes to concrete cases in which the rights of unpopular minorities are at stake, and younger generations have become markedly more libertarian than their elders. Education and understanding are good for liberalism, and even political theory can sometimes hope to contribute to these in some modest way.

Much of my argument will be designed to show that liberals need not and should not support many of the practices and ideas that are attacked by critics of liberalism. Liberal rights are not based on disagreement or self-interest but on moral principles justifying the equal right to freedom. Liberal practice need not, and often does not, resemble the unattractive caricature assembled by communitarians. Liberal ideals are prefigured (albeit far from perfectly) in many existing attitudes and practices—articulating and defending these ideals is one way of responding to the communitarians. And articulating positive liberal ideals points the way toward liberal communities that are both more liberal and better communities.

The questions to be pursued in the chapters that follow are: what are the ideals and practices that form the moral core of liberalism? Can liberal politics generate an ideal of citizenship and civic virtue? Can liberal society support an ideal of human flourishing, a set of liberal virtues, and a vision of liberal community? And to what extent are these liberal ideals at home in the American constitutional polity?

Chapters 2 and 3 are fundamental to the constructive

---

[14] McClosky and Brill, *Dimensions of Tolerance*, p. 123.
[15] Ibid. 416–22.

portion of my argument. Those whose main interest is political theory may find it convenient to skip through (or over) Chapters 4 and 5. Those interested primarily in American constitutionalism may choose to forgo Chapters 6 and 7.

1

The Flight from Liberalism

INTRODUCTION

Liberalism embraces individuality, religious and social diversity, and commercial energy, by enshrining toleration and personal liberty as core political values. It protects personal liberties by imposing procedural and substantive limits on the ways that persons or governments can interfere in the lives of others. Benjamin Constant's depiction of 'the liberty of the moderns' is apt:

it is the right to be subjected only to the laws, and to be neither arrested, detained, put to death or maltreated in any way by the arbitrary will of one or more individuals. It is the right of everyone to express their opinion, choose a profession and practice it, to dispose of property, and even to abuse it; to come and go without permission, and without having to account for their motives or undertakings. It is everyone's right to associate with other individuals, either to discuss their interests, or to profess the religion which they and their associates prefer, or even to occupy their days or hours in a way which is most compatible with their inclinations or whims. Finally it is everyone's right to exercise some influence on the administration of the government, either by electing all or particular officials, or through representations, petitions, demands to which the authorities are more or less compelled to pay heed.[1]

The personal liberties at the heart of liberalism include freedom of conscience, of religious practice, and freedom of association (whether public, private, or intimate), the right to choose one's occupation or trade, freedom of speech, of discussion, of the press, of literature and the arts, of movement and travel. Liberal citizens must have access to

[1] Benjamin Constant, 'The Liberty of the Ancients Compared with that of the Moderns: Speech Given at the Athenee Royal in Paris', in *Political Writings*, ed. Biancamaria Fontana (Cambridge, 1988), 310–11.

independent courts and to 'due process' to contest charges made against them by other persons or by the state. Liberalism stands for constitutionally limited government and for the rule of law, which regularizes the exercise of political power by requiring that laws be made in advance of any prosecutions, according to known procedures, with publicity and a requisite degree of generality. Liberalism stands for equality before the law, for equal citizenship, and for the right of all persons to respect for their liberal rights. The Declaration of Independence, the Constitution of the United States, and the Declaration of the Rights of Man and Citizen are among the great liberal achievements. John Locke, John Stuart Mill, and John Rawls all figure prominently in the liberal pantheon.

Ideally, liberals are not simply committed to liberal principles and institutions, they are committed to them in a certain way. How should liberals be committed to liberal justice? What sorts of considerations should lead liberals to revise their political commitments? What should an argument for liberal politics be like? In the chapters that follow I shall suggest what seems to me the best way of being committed to liberal politics: the way of those committed to reflecting on politics from a public moral perspective. Liberal ideals of citizenship, virtue, and community, are, in part, products of a conception of the best way of being committed to liberal justice.

The basic commitment of an argument for liberalism such as that of John Rawls's *A Theory of Justice* is captured in the fact that it is a reasoned argument capable of being widely recognized and accepted as such: its assertions are supported with reasons, it anticipates objections and counter-arguments and meets them with good reasons, it attempts fairly to consider competing theories, and the grounds upon which one might take issue with the argument are clear. The argument is *public* in that it is assumed that everyone is capable of contributing reasons and objections, the best arguments might come from anywhere, and a view that can be justified publicly to all is the goal.[2] The argument is *moral* in that it calls upon us to

---

[2] John Rawls, *A Theory of Justice* (Cambridge, Mass., 1970), 16, and see Dworkin's discussion of Rawls, *Rights*, ch. 6, esp. pp. 162–3. Dworkin's basic value of 'equal concern and respect' is especially relevant at the level of moral justification,

consider principles of justice from an impersonal point of view, one capable of discerning reasons that should be acceptable to everyone concerned: everyone counts, no one can simply be left out of account or sacrificed for the sake of the rest. The argument is philosophical and *critical* in that it is not meant simply to mirror existing judgments and practices or to smooth out a few inconsistencies; it criticizes and tests the justifiability of existing views. The argument is Socratic.[3] Liberals, at their best, are determined to support principles of justice that can be publicly justified as the best available, all things considered.[4] These observations are not true of all liberal theories, and they are true of some non-liberal theories.

That *A Theory of Justice*, for instance, offers a public moral argument may appear to be a rather trite observation. Rawls might, however, have composed not a public argument but a threatening manifesto: 'Either concede to the two principles of justice or my friends and I will make trouble.' Instead of articulating moral reasons to support his political principles, he might have appealed to the 'gut reactions' or feelings of an 'average' citizen, as Lord Devlin appeals to the 'feeling of disgust' of 'the man on the Clapham omnibus' in order to justify prohibiting homosexuality.[5] He might have appealed to intimations, like Michael Oakeshott, or poetry, history, and the arts, as Richard Rorty suggests. Rawls might have relied on wit, sarcasm, irony, and hyperbole to deflate his opponents. He could have based his political appeals on those personal attachments and allegiances which 'constitute' our identities, as Michael Sandel advocates. He might have invoked scriptural interpretation or direct revelation from God or a personal faith. He might, alternately, have tried to

---

where it stands for the impartiality of a moral point of view. The moral requirement of showing concern and respect for persons capable of reflection is not itself derived from a contractual argument, like that of Rawls's original position; it is, rather, what compels us to undertake this kind of argument, see Dworkin, *Rights*, pp. 180–2.

[3] Rawls, *Theory*, p. 49.

[4] I eschew the label 'contractualism' because it seems to me to emphasize agreement at the expense of criticism and truth. Nevertheless, I generally accept Rawls's notion of reflective equilibrium, *Theory*, pp. 19–21, and T. M. Scanlon's understanding of contractualism, 'Contractualism and Utilitarianism', in A. Sen and B. Williams, eds., *Utilitarianism and Beyond* (Cambridge, 1984), 103–28.

[5] Patrick Devlin, 'Morals and the Criminal Law', in *The Enforcement of Morals* (London, 1965), 1–25.

convince a majority, or a powerful minority, that 'justice as fairness' would make them better off. Or Rawls might simply have asserted a preference for his two principles without providing any reasons at all. Political opinions are sometimes expressed in these ways, and in any number of other ways as well.

Political arrangements are often sustained by power, religious conviction, interest, preference, and sheer inertia, rather than by reasoned reflection; they are not always supported, or capable of being supported, by reasoned arguments, or at least not by publicly stated, openly debated, and widely accessible arguments. It may be that no political arrangements could be supported by reasoned arguments alone. It is not my purpose to suggest that the vitality of liberal politics is wholly dependent on liberal theory. My purpose, in the chapters that follow, is to examine the ideal of politics prefigured in liberal political theories that are committed, at base, to public justification, a commitment that informs many actual liberal practices.

This liberal response to the communitarians will explore the ideal of politics captured in the notion of liberalism as a public morality. In this ideal, liberal values are affirmed by both public officials and citizens as expressions of our moral duties toward one another, as the best answer to the question, 'what is the right way for us to live?' Critical reflection is a public commitment, a commitment, most fundamentally, to a way of deliberating publicly about what our political arrangements should be. Constitutional institutions are forums that structure and sustain this ongoing debate. A just liberal society has more than justice to recommend it: within such a society we can discern positive liberal ideals of community, of virtue, and of human flourishing. A community governed by liberal justice is attractive as a community, and not only as a place where liberal rights are not violated.

Individuality and social pluralism, liberty, legality, rights, limited government, and public reasonableness—let us take these, for now, as the central features of liberalism. Let us also defer a more thorough exploration of liberal politics and proceed, with this thumbnail sketch in hand, to the concerns of the communitarians.

THE COMMUNITARIAN CRITIQUE OF LIBERAL POLITICS

For its defenders, liberal individualism is a liberating achievement and an adventure, but the ideal has never been without its detractors. From both sides of the political spectrum critics have often railed against the allegedly detrimental effects of liberal individualism on public life, shared values, community, and the virtue of citizens. These criticisms have often focused on the liberal market order and the harmful consequences of capitalist economic relations. The growing prominence of the communitarian critics of liberalism has, however, shifted attention away from capitalist economics and towards the social consequences of liberal rights, law, and justice. The communitarians charge that liberal politics sacrifices fraternity, social solidarity, and citizen virtue to individual rights. Liberals, say the communitarians, neglect the shared projects and goals that would make citizens more than isolated and self-interested 'atoms'. Let us examine the central concerns of the most prominent communitarians.

According to Alasdair MacIntyre, the depth and pervasiveness of moral disagreement in liberal societies is hardly appreciated by defenders of liberal individualism: the radical disparateness of our moral beliefs renders our political practices indefensible. Contemporary moral discourse consists of 'interminable' and irresolvable clashes of 'incommensurable' rival arguments and traditions.[6] Utilitarian moral arguments contend with others based on human rights and we have, says MacIntyre, no good reason for preferring one position to another; we have no 'objective and impersonal' moral standards so our arguments are merely 'emotivist', or expressive of merely personal preferences and partisan feelings.[7] 'Moral pluralism' is too 'complacent' and imprecise a way of regarding our predicament; lacking any common, impersonal standards of reasonableness or justification, we lose the ability to distinguish 'manipulative and non-manipulative

---

[6] Alasdair MacIntyre, *After Virtue* (Notre Dame, Ind., 1981), 8, and see *Whose Justice? Which Rationality?* (Notre Dame, Ind., 1988), esp. chs. 1 and 20. I rely mainly on MacIntyre's earlier and widely cited book.

[7] MacIntyre, *After Virtue*, pp. 67–8, 9, 17.

social relations'.[8] Assertions of will and power masquerade as rational arguments. While liberals celebrate pluralism and diversity, MacIntyre depicts modernity in Hobbesian terms: rival groups have no shared moral standards so there is no way of fairly resolving their disputes; everyone uses 'good' and 'evil' as suits his interests.

The dire consequences of moral arbitrariness are exacerbated, for MacIntyre, because the 'modern self' is a set of 'open possibilities' with 'no necessary social content and no necessary social identity', it can 'be anything, can assume any role or take any point of view'. Modern liberal morality, says MacIntyre, calls upon us to pass judgment 'from a purely universal and abstract point of view that is totally detached from all social particularity', local allegiances, social practices, and inherited norms, roles, and traditions of behaviour. Detached from any fixed station in a stable social structure, modern man is hopelessly adrift, without bearings, compass, or appointed destination. We aimlessly plod out our lives in a world 'empty of objective standards of achievement'.[9]

If, for MacIntyre, we are adrift because detached or alienated from the common moral life we once had, we are also alone because our judgments and standards are merely personal and arbitrary. Liberal individuality has loosened the bonds between citizens that come from 'a common allegiance to and a common pursuit of goods' and has put nothing in their place. We have no understanding of, let alone any devotion to, a common set of virtues that would give meaning and direction to our lives and make our polity a moral community. For communitarians like MacIntyre, diversity and individuality alienate men from inherited standards, shared norms, and one another. Aimless, arbitrary, isolated, manipulated . . . all that keeps liberal individuals from plunging into a war of all against all is an imposed 'bureaucratized unity'.[10]

MacIntyre locates the root of the problems of liberal modernity in the loss of a common *telos*: shared, public standards for a good life. What liberals need, then, is to revive

---

[8] MacIntyre, *After Virtue*, p. 22.
[9] Ibid. 30–1, 119, 109.
[10] Ibid. 146, 236.

a pre-modern, loosely Aristotelian framework, in which politics is understood as the pursuit of shared human ends. Only in this way can we avoid what lies at the end of all modern pathways: the Nietzschian will to power. So for MacIntyre, Aristotle is 'the protagonist against whom I have matched the voices of liberal modernity'.[11]

So far so good. As MacIntyre himself admits, however, we have no readily available account of the good life that all should pursue. One might look to widely shared standards, or conventional notions of good and bad. But like many others, MacIntyre takes a critical stance toward social practices and conventions; he is not prepared to endorse any and all that arise: some practices 'simply are evil'. Moreover, MacIntyre is half-hearted in his desire for greater agreement about the ends and purposes of human life, and ambivalent about the value of organizing politics around a single conception of what is good in life. He notes 'the place in our cultural history of deep conflicts over what human flourishing and well-being do consist in and the way in which rival and incompatible beliefs on that topic beget rival and incompatible tables of the virtues'. He recognizes that conflict among goods may itself be good, that competition among goods may constitute a discovery procedure: it is 'sometimes only through conflict that we learn what our ends and purposes are'. And so, at one point, MacIntyre makes the utterly liberal concession, 'the good life for man is the life spent in seeking for the good life for man'.[12]

MacIntyre's understanding of liberal modernity combines an exaggerated, Hobbesian picture of radical disagreement, with a suspicion of large-scale political power and a nostalgia for the pre-modern moral community as romantic as it is ambivalent and selective. His final note, not surprisingly, is one of despair. He envisages 'coming ages of barbarism and darkness' and sees our only hope in the 'construction of local

---

[11] Ibid. 110–11, 137. MacIntyre has no apparent use for Aristotle's 'élitism'.

[12] Ibid. 152–3, 186, 204, This is also, of course, Socrates' vision of the philosophical life: 'no greater good can happen to a man to discuss human excellence every day . . . an unexamined life is not worth living,' Plato, *Apology of Socrates*, in *Euthyphro, Apology, Crito*, trans. F. J. Church, revised and introduced by R. D. Cumming (Indianapolis, Ind., 1956), 45.

forms of community within which civility and the intellectual and moral life can be sustained through the new dark ages'. With luck, we will be delivered by a new 'St Benedict'.[13] Some luck.

At this darkly drawn but rather ambivalent depiction of the liberal condition let us leave MacIntyre. His analysis is especially rich, his tone particularly shrill, and his conclusions almost humorously dire, but his general preoccupations are shared by the other communitarian critics of liberalism.

Michael Sandel, another prominent communitarian critic, takes as his object of attack 'deontological liberalism', which is organized around the idea that 'conceptions of the good are diverse, . . . that man is a being whose ends are chosen rather than given'.[14] Like MacIntyre, Sandel criticizes certain features of the liberal personality: the 'distance' between moral persons considered as reflective choosers and the ends and attachments they choose, the separateness of liberal individuals themselves, and their 'openness' or lack of a received or fixed identity. For Sandel, the liberal personality is not sufficiently 'situated' in a social context, the identities of liberal citizens are not 'constituted' deeply enough by social values and shared ends. Modern liberal theory, says Sandel, 'fails to take seriously our commonality'.[15]

Sandel, like MacIntyre, traces the roots of our alienation to the fact that liberal modernity is 'a universe empty of *telos* . . . a world ungoverned by a purposive order'.[16] While the communitarians do not urge the revival of Aristotelian metaphysics or cosmology, they generally do want to re-establish closer identifications between men and their political communities and to shift the focus of politics away from the protection of liberal rights and freedom to the pursuit of shared ends and ideals. Sandel's prescription for the ills of liberalism is to transcend liberal justice in deeper forms of 'constitutive' community, that is, in common attachments

[13] MacIntyre, *After Virtue*, 245.
[14] Michael Sandel, *Liberalism and the Limits of Justice* (Cambridge, 1982), 116.
[15] Ibid. 54–65, 174.
[16] Ibid. 175.

and allegiances deep enough to engage 'the identity as well as the interests of the participants'.[17]

Sandel offers, again like MacIntyre, no substantive picture of the common ideals from which communitarianism would take its bearings. Without some substantial vision of a common political good communitarianism appears to be a rather empty yearning for a golden age of togetherness and harmony, a longing spurred on by dissatisfaction with liberalism rather than the discovery of a preferable alternative. The militaristic Spartan polis appealed to Rousseau, but it is hard to imagine today's communitarians paying the price of Spartan virtue; some version of the Christian commonwealth seems more at home in America. There are, indeed, many who would like to restore closer ties between Church and State (*their* Church and our common state). This would be a sure prescription for conflict, and communitarians have not, in any case, converged on any recognizable orthodoxy.

We are left to wonder exactly what is the communitarian alternative to liberal law, rights, and freedom. We lack a convincing account of human ends and purposes and so, from a philosophical standpoint, we seem to be at a dead end. And yet, most members of real communities are not philosophers. Why should we regard the philosophical quest as a route to community rather than a steep and winding detour? Perhaps we should avoid philosophical sidetracks and look instead to democratic politics and popular conventions as paths to community.

We might locate community in the value of preserving whatever moral consensus particular communities have achieved. Sandel seems sympathetic to this suggestion: 'communitarians', he says, 'would be more likely than liberals to allow a town to ban pornographic bookstores, on the grounds that pornography offends its way of life and the values that sustain it.'[18] From the right, conservative communitarians argue that a society has a right to 'sustain' its identity in the face of minorities claiming the right to live differently. Unless positive action is taken against moral 'permissiveness', the

---

[17] Ibid. 182.
[18] Michael Sandel, 'Introduction', *Liberalism and its Critics* (Oxford, 1984), 6.

argument goes, moral ties that bind the members of a community will loosen, the community will disintegrate, and its members will drift apart and become isolated 'atoms'. Lord Patrick Devlin puts it this way:

Without shared ideas on politics, morals, and ethics no society can exist . . . if, having based it [society] on common agreement, the agreement goes, the society will disintegrate. For society is not something that is kept together physically; it is held together by the invisible bonds of common thought. If the bonds were too far relaxed the members would drift apart.[19]

The flaw in Devlin's 'disintegration thesis' is that it is rather difficult, as H. L. A. Hart points out, to distinguish the claim that a community will disintegrate unless its morality is enforced by law from the 'conservative thesis' which holds that a community should be defended from change.[20] That is, in becoming more permissive a society may not be disintegrating at all, nor its members drifting apart. It may simply be changing and acquiring a new, more liberal morality.

The case has not been made, for instance, that extending the right of intimate privacy from heterosexuals to homosexuals would lead to 'social disintegration'. If liberal societies have a robust capacity for coherence amid change and permissiveness, then Devlin would have to accept liberal norms. Conservatives like Devlin tend, however, to assume that social cohesion is quite fragile, often on the basis of merely anecdotal evidence.

'What makes a society', Devlin says, 'is a community of ideas, not political ideas alone but also ideas about the way its members should behave and govern their lives.' Devlin's conservative communitarianism has been cited approvingly by former US Attorney-General Edwin Meese and by New Right scholar and jurist Robert H. Bork. Bork interprets the judicial effort to protect individual rights to read pornography or to express opinions in strong language as the enforcement,

[19] Devlin, *Enforcement*, p. 10.
[20] H. L. A. Hart, 'Social Solidarity and the Enforcement of Morals', in *Essays in Jurisprudence and Philosophy* (Oxford, 1983), 250–62.

not of a liberal public morality, but of 'moral relativism'.[21] Contrary to liberal judges, Bork would allow legislatures to enforce the majority's view of good conduct in spheres often considered private. Rejecting the core liberal values of toleration and privacy, Bork would treat violations of the majority's view of good conduct as 'moral harms' against the community at large.

In order to shield the enforcement community morality from judicial intervention on behalf of individual rights, Bork distinguishes between the 'common sense of the community', which includes its practices and traditions, and what he calls 'abstract and philosophical' arguments, or the 'universalistic style of legal thought' propounded by 'theorists of moral abstraction'.[22] Bork wishes to vest political authority not in good arguments of political morality (which are bound to be somewhat abstract) but in the 'common sense of the people'. Individual rights are, for Bork, obstacles to the community's right (more accurately, the right of whoever has won a set of political conflicts) to oppose what it considers permissiveness and to impose on the whole polity a more exacting identity.

As opposed to the idealistic communitarianism of MacIntyre, Devlin and Bork are sceptical about abstract ideals and are content to allow the law to enforce popular morality. Bork, in particular, seems untroubled by the old spectre of majority tyranny. There are philosophers who, like Devlin and Bork, disparage the political authority of abstract, philosophical arguments about rights in favour of the inherited practices, conventions, and 'shared meanings' of the polity. The liberal ideal that I wish to defend aspires to critical reflection and public justification, so we should pause carefully to consider the arguments of those who would disparage the public authority of critical thought.

The connection between political practice and critical reflection is not a merely 'philosophical' issue: liberal, legal, and political institutions aim not only to protect freedom but to give good reasons to those who dissent, fostering a never-ending exercise in public justification. In confronting real

---

[21] Robert H. Bork, *Tradition and Morality in Constitutional Law: The Francis Boyer Lecture* (Washington, DC, 1984), 3.
[22] Ibid. 3, 6, 7.

political problems liberals, at their best, seek justifications for the exercise of power that do more than mirror received practices or social consensus. The revolt against philosophy, if successful, could undermine political practices, such as judicial review, that depend on the participants' confidence in the value of reason-demanding and reason-giving.

THE CONVENTIONALIST CRITIQUE OF LIBERALISM

Michael Walzer rightly contends that judicial review is especially concerned with the reasonableness of legislative acts, and so 'judges are the most likely instruments of philosophical reformation'.[23] The authority of law, Walzer argues, is 'a function of popular will and not of reason. . . . The people are the successors of gods and absolutist kings, but not of philosophers. They may not know the right thing to do, but they claim a right to do what they think is right (literally, what pleases them).'[24] Philosophical justification is one thing, and political authority is altogether different: 'Democracy has no claims in the philosophical realm, and philosophers have no special rights in the political community.'[25]

Ironically, Walzer's preferred political arrangements depend crucially upon both philosophy and judicial review. The people's 'claim to rule' rests not simply on their power but on the quality of an argument: 'Rousseau's argument', which presumably is a good one. Walzer's democracy is not, furthermore, mere majoritarianism: he would have judges enforce 'twin bans on legal discrimination and political repression', ensuring that the democratic process remains open and inclusive.[26] But if the democratic process must in these ways pass philosophic muster, then authority does not depend on

---

[23] Michael Walzer, 'Philosophy and Democracy', *Political Theory*, 9 (1981), 388.

[24] Ibid. 383.

[25] Ibid. 397. It may be significant that the American public has expressed vastly more confidence in the Supreme Court than it does in Congress. In a July 1987 Gallup Poll, 54% of those questioned expressed a 'high level of confidence' in the Supreme Court, a figure just below the support registered for organized religions (57%) and the military (63%), and well above Congress (41%), *Gallup Report*, no. 253 (October 1986), 2–13.

[26] Walzer, 'Philosophy', p. 383, 391, Walzer endorses the theory of judicial review of John Hart Ely's *Democracy and Distrust* (Cambridge, 1980).

popular will alone, and democracy and critical reasonableness are not distinct.

Social criticism, Walzer says, should be 'interpretive', it should involve 'criticism from within' or 'imminent critique'. It should not seek the simply best city, but rather 'the best city for the Spartans'. And yet, while Walzer emphasizes the importance of loyalty to local traditions and practices, he also acknowledges a 'universal moral code', a set of prohibitions on 'murder, deception, betrayal, gross cruelty' that are justified everywhere.[27] The localistic and anti-philosophical veneer of Walzer's argument is thin: it barely masks a general moral *theory* of liberal democratic politics which is every bit as 'philosophical' as its competitors.

Walzer's political vision contains prohibitions that are universal and values that are abstract and general. Indeed to point out the importance of belonging is to highlight the value of communal loyalties as such, rather than the special worth of one's own community. A reflective, 'cosmopolitan' communitarian (as opposed to the partisan of a particular community) would take seriously the rights of other communities, he would respect outsiders and not only members of his own community; he would, in these ways, embrace liberal norms.[28] By heaping scorn on the judiciary and philosophy, however, Walzer risks pandering to thoughtlessness, wilfulness, and popular tyranny.

Political conflicts typically involve clashes among and within communities. Politics is not mainly foreign relations, there are plenty of 'outsiders' inside our pluralistic polities ('the wogs begin long before Calais,' as Clifford Geertz has said).[29] Debates over issues like pornography are precisely debates over the best understanding of the way of life of our communities. In order to make any headway in understanding why justifications that go beyond references to local practices

[27] Michael Walzer, *Interpretation and Social Criticism* (Cambridge, Mass., 1987), 64, 12, 24.
[28] I have benefited from the insightful discussion of Walzer in Robert Alan Katz, 'Communitarianism and the Limits of Intercommunal Respect: A Moral Argument with Historical Illustrations Drawn from the Case of Israel', Senior Thesis in Government (Harvard, 1987).
[29] Clifford Geertz, 'The Uses of Diversity', *Tanner Lectures on Human Values*, 7, ed. Sterling M. McMurrin (Cambridge, 1986), 262.

and traditions are important, we must come to grips with the multi-communal nature of modern political life.

Walzer's embrace of local meanings is half-hearted: he cannot really resist the pull of a broad, self-critical moral perspective. Others are more consistent than Walzer in eschewing reliance on philosophical reflection.

For Michael Oakeshott, politics ought not to pursue 'abstract "justice" . . . or some other abstract "principle" ', politics ought to be 'the pursuit of intimations'.[30] And these intimations may be studied in the history and the 'legend' of one's political culture. From the point of view of philosophy, says Oakeshott, political culture will look like

a history of the incoherencies philosophers have detected in common ways of thinking and the manner of solution they have proposed, rather than a history of doctrines and systems. . . . Political philosophy cannot be expected to increase our ability to be successful in political activity. It will not help us to distinguish between good and bad political projects; it has no power to guide or to direct us in the enterprise of pursuing the intimations of our tradition.[31]

Oakeshott regards political knowledge as historical, particular, and embodied in the practices and traditions of an ongoing, if ever-fluid, way of life. Political knowledge is what experienced practitioners have, it cannot be articulated in rules, principles, and theories, without vital loss or 'abridgement'. Political philosophy, by contrast, should be regarded as practically impotent.

The animating feature of Oakeshottian politics is the primacy of the inarticulate knowledge of practices and traditions over technical, self-conscious, 'rule-book' knowledge. The great error of our times is the error of rationalism: the 'conversion of habits of behavior, adaptable and never quite fixed or finished, into comparatively rigid systems of abstract ideas'.[32] And Oakeshott leaves no doubt that among the errors of rationalism is 'the self-conscious pursuit of formulated

---

[30] Oakeshott, 'Political Education', in *Rationalism in Politics and Other Essays* (London, 1969), 134.

[31] Ibid. 130, 132.

[32] Oakeshott, 'Rationalism in Politics', in *Rationalism*, p. 21.

moral ideals'.[33] Practical politics can do without the aspirations of moral philosophy.

Since Oakeshottian politics takes its bearings from the fluid practices and traditions of a particular way of life, one might expect that its motto for political action would be 'go with the flow'. As the time changes, that is, one might expect an Oakeshottian conservative to change with them. And yet we find in Oakeshott's political writings, especially the most recent, lucid articulations of the classical liberal ideal of the rule of law, of pre-welfare state minimal government: political arrangements concerned only to protect the freedom of people to pursue a variety of self-chosen purposes, goals, and projects. Oakeshott abhors the politics of the 'mass man' ('helpless, parasitic, and able to survive only in opposition to individuality', in short, a dependent), of social planning, and the pursuit of collective ends beyond the protection of liberty.[34] The intimations that Oakeshott pursues, even now, are those of nineteenth-century classical liberalism, which he extols as 'the most civilized and least burdensome conception of a state yet to be devised'.[35]

By virtue of his own disparagement of articulated critical principles and ideals, however, Oakeshott cannot offer a moral defence of classical liberalism once its practice has been abandoned and its intimations supplanted. Neither can he offer a moral critique of the turn that contemporary politics has taken once it has persisted long enough to acquire practices and intimations of its own. As habits, expectations, and practices grow up around the welfare state, or any political innovation, the basis for Oakeshottian criticism disappears. Through sheer persistence, ideologies may become institutionalized, rationalism itself acquires intimations to pursue, and the conscientious Oakeshottian should either pursue them or remain silent. Oakeshottian conservatives might continue

---

[33] Oakeshott, 'The Tower of Babel', in *Rationalism*, p. 77. See also Oakeshott's criticisms of Hayek in 'Rationalism'.

[34] Oakeshott, 'The Masses in Representative Democracy', in William F. Buckley, ed., *Did you Ever See a Dream Walking?: American Conservative Thought in the Twentieth Century* (Indianapolis, Ind., 1970), p. 122.

[35] Oakeshott, 'The Rule of Law', in *On History and Other Essays* (Oxford, 1983), 164, see also *On Human Conduct* (Oxford, 1975), part 2, 'Civil Association'.

to advocate old intimations, practices, and conventions against new ones, but without good reasons for preferring the old to the new (reasons that do more than refer us to brute preferences for particular conventions) he will appear at best idiosyncratic, at worst merely obstinate or reactionary, and in either case increasingly irrelevant.

The fact is that old intimations, conventions, and practices do persist alongside new ones, and new ones arise all the time. The central difficulty for politics as the pursuit of intimations is the ideological complexity of modern states. At some point in Britain's past, it may have been possible for a relatively homogeneous and unified ruling class, unselfconsciously nurtured by a particular understanding of practical political life, to pursue shared intimations taken as given.[36] With the right sorts of education and oversight it is even possible that such an élite might govern in the interests of all.[37] But in today's democratic and pluralistic polities no set of intimations is 'given': conventions, traditions, and practices compete for our allegiance. The complexity of our political culture means that we could not be governed by Oakeshottian intimations even if we wanted to: this ideologically rudderless conception of politics could work only until people start arguing about which direction to take.

It does no good at all, in the face of political conflict, to say 'pursue your intimations'—whose intimations? Those of rural Christians or urban yuppies? Our problem is precisely that people have widely different senses of how to settle the controversies surrounding affirmative action, gay rights, and pornography. If we want to try and settle questions of political morality in a justified manner, we must go beyond conflicting intimations and invoke articulable, publicly defensible reasons and principles that all ought to be able to accept. And so,

[36] We could say that Oakeshottian politics is possible in political conditions analogous to those of 'normal science' in Thomas Kuhn's terminology, see *The Structure of Scientific Revolutions*, 2nd edn. (Chicago, 1970). There is too much disagreement in pluralistic societies for them to be like Kuhnian normal science writ large, but our disagreements are not radical enough for us to be in a position analogous to Kuhn's 'revolutionary' periods.

[37] For one such proposal see Plato's *Republic*, trans. Allan Bloom (New York, 1968).

Oakeshott's attempt to undermine the practical reliance on articulable values and principles fails.

Political conflicts do not arise because isolated individuals, perverted by philosophy, abandon practices and upset stable ways of life to pursue abstraction for its own sake. Conflicts arise because traditions, practices, and communities are numerous, overlapping, fluid, and complex. Conventionalists like Oakeshott misdescribe the setting of political conflict and fail to understand that the pursuit of good reasons is one of our time-honoured practices. The notion that theory and practice are distinct rests on a misunderstanding of our practices.

Richard Rorty's pragmatic variation on an Oakeshottian theme provides another lesson in the futility of trying to separate theory and practice. Rorty's main purpose is to debunk philosophical theories that claim to adjudicate in advance what counts as reliable knowledge.[38] But in his zeal to subvert the sovereign claims of metaphysics and epistemology Rorty sweeps too broadly: he undermines the practice of self-critical, moral reason-giving in political deliberation, a deep practice the resort to which is a response to the plurality of the conventions, practices, and intimations competing for our attention in politics.

Rorty's anti-foundationalism clearly means to eschew the quest for the sorts of 'very evident and very certain demonstrations' that Descartes sought (demonstrations modelled on geometric proofs).[39] We can agree with Rorty that the best answers to questions of political morality depend on a variety of complex considerations that we grapple with in public arguments, not on the application of a rigid and austere method yielding only 'certain and indubitable' truths. We do not reflect on political issues by 'purging' the mind and setting aside all opinions and prejudices. Rather, we subject the ideas we have to critical scrutiny by considering alternative views carefully, playing one position off against another, and judging on the basis of available evidence.

[38] Richard Rorty, *Philosophy and the Mirror of Nature* (Princeton, N.J., 1979), see part 2, 'Mirroring', esp. pp. 155–64.
[39] René Descartes, *Meditations on First Philosophy*, trans. Laurence J. Lafleur (Indianapolis, Ind., 1960), see the 'Letter of Dedication'.

Rorty seems consistently to travel well beyond the dismissal of Cartesian foundationalism, and to imply that the proper working standard of political justification is community agreement.[40] Rorty attacks those 'intellectuals' who marginalize themselves by upholding abstract theories and 'general principles' instead of the traditions and practices of their community.[41] Rational behaviour, he says,

is just adaptive behavior of a sort which roughly parallels the behavior, in similar circumstances, of the other members of some relevant community. Irrationality, in both physics and ethics, is a matter of behavior that leads one to abandon, or be stripped of membership in some such community.[42]

Truth, Rorty says elsewhere, is 'what our peers will, *ceterus paribus*, let us get away with saying'.[43]

That knowledge is generated, tested, and refined socially seems clear enough, and the emergence and enforcement of conventions can be *explained* in terms of the beliefs people actually accept. But it in no way follows that we can identify truth or justified belief with the verdict of any particular group, to do that is to ignore the distinction between justification and explanation.

To identify good moral reasons with those actually enforced by a particular community reduces morality to the maxim, 'If you want to get along, go along'. To say that moral criticism of a community is 'irrational' simply because the criticism is rejected and the critic ostracized is to identify the reasonable with what is accepted. To apply Rorty's view to political morality is to identify justice with the advantage of the stronger.[44] It is to assume that the group can never be wrong, and it is to completely miss the point of the political practice of moral criticism.

---

[40] I should emphasize that Rorty's focus is on theories of knowledge rather than on political and moral theory; one might accept much of his powerful discussion of the former without embracing his much more dubious remarks about the latter.

[41] Rorty, 'Postmodernist Bourgeois Liberalism,' *Journal of Philosophy*, 80 (October 1983), 587, criticizing Dworkin's political reliance on general moral principles.

[42] Ibid. 586.

[43] Rorty, *Mirror*, p. 176.

[44] As Thrasymachus argued in Plato's *Republic*, Bk. 1.

Rorty resists viewing the practice of moral criticism from the inside: inside a moral disagreement what counts is not an opinion poll but the quality of the available arguments and reasons. We ask all the time whether a particular community's judgment was based on reasonable, informed, defensible arguments, or on collective unreason, prejudice, or superstition, and we can answer such questions only by considering the quality of rival arguments, not by seeing who gains most support.

It would be hard to imagine a pattern of 'behaviour' less 'adaptive' than that of Socrates. For playing the philosophical gadfly, Socrates was not only stripped of membership in his community but put to death by it. Rorty's view implies that we should label Socrates not only irrational but immoral, and this without even examining the merits of his case. If the arbiter of morality is a process of individual adaptation and community rejection then Socrates' case could have no 'merits'. He failed to adapt.

That Socrates thought he was doing the 'right thing' is only, on Rorty's view, the ultimate irony.[45] That Socrates is often held out as a paradigm of virtue in our community (and not only by professional philosophers, but by statesmen like Martin Luther King) is evidence that Rorty radically mischaracterizes the place of philosophical criticism in our political practices.[46]

Rorty connects his conception of morality with communitarian politics by quoting Sandel's remark that the 'moral force' of our 'loyalties and convictions' consists 'partly in the fact that living by them is inseparable from understanding ourselves as the particular persons we are—as members of this family or community or nation or people, as bearers of this history, as sons and daughters of that revolution, as citizens of

---

[45] Oakeshott's discussion of Plato's 'cave analogy' is similar in spirit to Rorty's position here, see *Human Conduct*, pp. 27–31. Discussions with three sympathetic interpreters of Rorty, Scott Wayland, Bernard Yack, and Randy Kroszner, have been very helpful to me.

[46] King invoked Socrates in his 'Letter from Birmingham City Jail', in Hugo Adam Bedau, *Civil Disobedience: Theory and Practice* (New York, 1969), 75, as does 'Publius' in Alexander Hamilton, John Jay, and James Madison, *The Federalist Papers*, ed. Clinton Rossiter (New York, 1961), nos. 55, 63. Hereafter, I refer to the *Federalist Papers* by number only and will often refer to their authors collectively as Publius.

this republic'.[47] But Rorty would go even further than Sandel. 'I would argue', he says,

that the moral force of such loyalties and convictions consists *wholly* in this fact, and that nothing else has *any* moral force. There is no 'ground' for such loyalties and convictions save the fact that the beliefs and desires and emotions which buttress them overlap those of lots of other members of the group with which we identify for purposes of moral or political deliberations, and the further fact that these are the *distinctive* features of that group, features which it uses to construct its self-image through contrasts with other groups.

Rorty goes on to say that moral justification

is mostly a matter of historical narratives . . . rather than of philosophical metanarratives. The principal backup for historiography is not philosophy but the arts, which serve to develop and modify a group's self-image by, for example, apotheosizing its heroes, diabolizing its enemies, mounting dialogues among its members, and refocusing its attention.[48]

Overlapping, distinctive identifications, supported by historiography and the arts, are the proper materials for public morality according to Rorty.

Standards of political morality must, certainly, be debated and applied publicly, and they will inevitably be rooted in the practices of some community (or in 'our community' characterized at one level of abstraction or another). Once we recognize, however, that our pluralism makes us 'multi-communal', and not simply 'communitarian', the critical questions must be recast: which communal standards should we apply? Which group of our peers has the best argument?

Neighbourhoods are parts of cities, cities are parts of states, and states parts of the nation. Churches, families, and a host of other associations cut across all political divisions. All are communities, in some sense, and they often come into conflict. During the American Civil Rights movement some Southerners argued that they could take care of their own and that they did not need a lot of Northerners (outsiders to their

---

[47] Rorty, 'Postmodernist', p. 586, quoting Sandel, *Limits*, p. 179. Elsewhere, Rorty emphasizes the importance of encouraging the philosophical and intellectual 'identification with our community', 'Habermas and Lyotard on Post-Modernity', *Praxis International*, 4 (1984), 41.

[48] Rorty, 'Postmodernist', pp. 586–7, emphasis in original.

way of thinking) coming down and telling them how to live. Whose community standards should have been enforced? Whose practices? Whose conventions? Those of states or that of the nation? It is hard to see how conventionalists could settle this issue. From a liberal public moral perspective we could begin to distinguish good reasons from mere prejudice, stereotype, and ignorance. We would acknowledge the moral personhood of blacks, insist on respect for their rights, and include them within a reformed political community.

Communitarians might favour those communities with relatively high levels of consensus. But the lack of actual dissensus is not sufficient to establish the moral quality of a community. In some Southern communities before the Civil Rights movement blacks went along, whether from fear or ignorance, with injustice. Not only men have thought that every woman's place is in the home. Passive acceptance does not alter the moral viciousness of systematic discrimination. Injustice is no less objectionable when it succeeds in stamping out criticism.

The problem of disagreement that frustrates conventionalists like Rorty might be solved by political subdivision. Why assume, after all, that current political boundaries are necessarily coextensive with communities of shared meanings?[49] As the bloody history of nationalist movements vividly shows, one could apply the most sophisticated arts of the gerrymanderer and still be hard pressed to discern contiguous territories, of any substantial size, which are not checkerboards inhabited by persons with different cultural and religious identities. And within a vast country like the United States, no political view is so far-fetched that some do not profess it (consider Lyndon Larouche). If our basic political commitment is to respecting the integrity of communities of shared meanings, then we may be committed to a task of endless political subdivision.

Liberal regimes like the United States are not as radically divided as MacIntyre claims: he emphasizes the apparent

[49] Sandel discusses this problem, *Limits*, pp. 145–7. Walzer only suggests that political boundaries are more likely than others to embrace shared meanings, *Spheres of Justice* (New York, 1983), 28–9.

irresolvability of meta-ethical disputes (between, for instance, utilitarianism and rights-based moralities) but neglects the fact that Americans share basic commitments to abstract liberal values and a common language of political morality in which to argue out their disagreements. Prohibitions on murder, theft, fraud, and bribery are widely accepted, as is the value of representative institutions and of many basic civil and political rights. While America has more dissensus than the conventionalists suppose, she has less than MacIntyre fears. Disagreement makes arguments about political morality necessary; agreement often suffices to make them constructive. Private citizens are not simply 'left to their own devices' to deal with moral disagreement; on the contrary, liberal institutions from courts to legislatures to universities debate the fundamentals of political morality.[50]

Because standards of political morality must be public, and because morality is something that we learn, advocacy of any reasoned political position is advocacy of, in effect, the reasons of a 'community'. But we move between many different communities, and the political community itself is a dynamic array of communities, not a single homogeneous community. It is our 'multi-communality', and not some metaphysical separation between mind and nature, that spawns and exercises the critical capacities of individuals.

We cannot say in advance that the conventions or reasons of any particular community, let alone any political community, will be the best ones; the best reasons can be determined only by actually judging the relative merits of the alternatives before us. And debates over political morality are occasions when communities engage in self-criticism, old communities may re-form or be torn apart, and new ones emerge. It is true that the best reasons of public morality will always be the reasons of a community, but since communities are diverse, overlapping, and fluid, the idea of community does not help us identify, in advance, the best reasons of political morality.[51]

Anti-theoretical conventionalism and morally criterionless anti-foundationalism may appear, at first, to be allies of

[50] See MacIntyre's puzzling claims in *Whose Justice?*, pp. 2–3.
[51] See John Dewey, *The Public and Its Problems* (Chicago, Ill., 1954), 24–9, who tries to get critical leverage out of the idea of a relevant community.

communitarian politics. But those who invoke tradition, convention, or social practice really provide no help to any political position so long as the very diversity of traditions, conventions, and practices is the root of our predicament.

Defending the central political role of abstract moral arguments does not place philosophy above our practices and traditions, it emphasizes the importance of one of our practices and traditions. Unlike Bork and Rorty, Oakeshott at least admits the 'predominantly rationalistic' character of the American polity, the prominent place of 'abstract principles' in US politics, and the status of the Declaration of Independence as 'one of the sacred documents of the politics of Rationalism'. Rorty appears to believe that American politics has been thoroughly pragmatic and anecdotal all along: ' "No taxation without representation" ', he says, 'was not a discovery about the nature of Taxation, [*sic*] but an expression of distrust in the British Parliament of the day.'[52] So much for the 'unalienable Rights' of the Declaration, and a sizeable portion of America's constitutional tradition.

It is almost as though Rorty, having dismissed the absolute pretensions of Platonic philosopher kings, sees no alternative but to embrace a criterionless populism, a caricature of Jacksonian democracy, whose partisans dismissed the learned John Quincy Adams on the grounds

> That not to know of things remote
> From use, obscure and subtle, but to know
> That which before us lies in daily life,
> Is the prime wisdom.[53]

Rorty's inarticulateness about better and worse in political morality is matched by the indistinctness of the dividing line he posits between arguments that are acceptably practical, pragmatic, and literary, and those that are too philosophical. Plato is out and Doonesbury is in. But where do Locke's *Second Treatise* and Mill's *On Liberty* fall? What of the *Federalist Papers*, the Declaration of Independence, and the American Constitution? What about the opinions of the US Supreme

[52] Richard Rorty, *Consequences of Pragmatism* (Brighton, 1982), Introduction, p. xxxvii, and compare Oakeshott, 'Rationalism', pp. 26–8.
[53] Milton, *Paradise Lost*, VIII, 192–5, and see Richard Hofstadter, *Anti-Intellectualism in American Life* (New York, 1963), 160.

Court or the political speeches of Abraham Lincoln and
Martin Luther King? There is a broad swath of practically
orientated liberal political theory and reflective, morally self-
critical liberal practice which together form a political tradition that is arguably America's best. There is enough overlap
between serious thinking about political morality and American political practice to make any simple dichotomy quite
untenable.

Rorty asserts that 'the political discourse of the democracies, at its best, is the exchange of what Wittgenstein called
"reminders for a particular purpose"—anecdotes . . . and
predictions. . . .'[54] But what Rorty means by 'best' here is
quite unclear—he is radically inarticulate about what makes
political practices better and worse. Eschewing universal,
timeless, and transcendent standards is one thing, but Rorty
fails to articulate even working standards of right and wrong
for the here and now, based on the best reasons currently
available.[55]

Rorty assumes rather easily that democracies are at their
'best' when telling anecdotes. He implies that moral reasons
and arguments really do not, in practice, 'pay their way' or
have much 'cash value'. But Rorty's own depiction of how
practical moral issues get resolved is quite bizarre.

Deciding which beings are to be included in the liberal
community as bearers of rights is itself a difficult question of
political morality. Mature, reflective, responsible adult

[54] Rorty, 'Postmodernist', p. 587, and see 'Habermas and Lyotard', p. 41, where
Rorty commends 'the history of concrete social engineering which made the contemporary North Atlantic culture what it is now'.
[55] Rorty's standards of evaluation are mysterious. He disclaims subjectivism and
relativism, and thinks that by 'playing vocabularies and cultures off against one
another, we produce new and better ways of talking and acting—not better by
reference to a previously known standard, but just better in the sense that they come to
seem clearly better than their predecessors,' *Pragmatism*, p. xxxvii. We should, Rorty
says, listen to someone's account of himself but not accept that account uncritically,
ibid. 200–2. Fine, but if we reject someone's self-interpretation in politics we must
articulate reasons for doing so or stand accused of arbitrariness. Rorty says that the
Enlightenment is 'better' than religion, and that 'the pragmatist is betting' that what
succeeds Enlightenment science will be better still, ibid. p. xxxviii. Better in terms of
some standard not yet available? Perhaps, but until that standard is available, we must
apply the best standards of political morality we have. Rorty occasionally invokes the
idea of utility as a standard, but not systematically, see for instance ibid. pp. xix and
xli.

citizens clearly count (nowadays) as full members—they are bearers of the full range of liberal rights. Children have some rights (they may not be sold into slavery or mistreated in various ways), but because they are still developing basic capacities of judgment, reflection, and responsibility they are not allowed to enter into contracts or vote in elections. There are, of course, many hard questions: do foetuses have a right to life? Do animals have rights of any sort?

Rorty disparages the whole project of looking for moral reasons to justify judgments of inclusion and exclusion in the categories of liberal rights-holders. Of the altered status of 18-year-olds compared with 4-year-olds, Rorty says, 'what has happened is a shift in a person's relations with others, not a shift inside the person which now *suits* him to enter such new relationships'. The judgment involved in distinguishing those in their late teens from infants might be 'injudicious' but not 'mistaken'. 'The community', says Rorty, is the source of 'epistemic authority', and philosophy 'cannot, by supplying a loftier critical point of view, reinforce or diminish the confidence in our own assertions which the approval of our peers gives us'.[56]

Between 4-year-olds and 18-year-olds there are relevant differences providing good reasons for withholding and granting rights. No 4-year-olds, but most 18-year-olds, attain levels of judgment and responsibility that justify the possession of a range of liberties: to leave home, engage in sexual intercourse, marry, have children, make contracts, and so on. Our judgments about the threshold of adulthood change, but not arbitrarily. Opinion in the USA as to the capacity of 18–20-year-olds to consume alcohol responsibly has shifted as drunk-driving contributes to more traffic fatalities. As to the political rights of 18-year-olds, it is no coincidence that the voting age in America was lowered toward the end of the Vietnam War: if 18-year-olds are mature enough to fight and die for their country can they justly be denied the franchise? The political activities of college students during the War may have helped to convince many of their elders that 18-year-olds are astute enough to vote (it may have convinced others of just

[56] Rorty, *Mirror*, pp. 187–8.

the opposite). There is plenty of material here for reasoned judgments of political morality. None of the factors I have cited pinpoints a simple threshold of adulthood, but all point to relevant considerations that sound judgments will take account of. One may still 'feel confident' of one's opinion without having reflected critically on these factors, but such confidence will be unjustified.

Rorty sees no point or benefit in articulating and criticizing reasons for ascribing rights. We extend forms of respect to babies and 'the more attractive sorts of animals' (he mentions koala bears), because they arouse our sympathy while other 'beings' (Rorty mentions flounders, spiders, pigs, and photoelectric cells) do not:

Pigs rate much higher than koalas do on intelligence tests, but pigs don't writhe in quite the right humanoid way, and the pig's face is the wrong shape for the facial expressions which go with ordinary conversation. So we send pigs to slaughter with equanimity, but form societies for the protection of koalas. This is not 'irrational', any more than it is irrational to extend or deny civil rights to the moronic (or fetuses, or aboriginal tribes, or Martians).[57]

Or blacks, or women? Personhood, says Rorty, is just a matter of 'being one of us'.[58] And morality, for Rorty, is just the way we do things around here, like it or lump it.

It does not take a professional philosopher to see that reasons are required to justify distinctions between pigs and koalas, or between Caucasians and aborigines. We do not need metaphysics or epistemology to argue that if aborigines feel pain, and are capable of reflection, choice, and resentment, then we have reasons for respecting their rights, reasons whose force is not dependent upon the assent of any particular group. Moral reasons need not, as Rorty assumes, simply mirror public opinion, and they often do not. We have good reasons for rejecting the claim that blacks are subhumans or that 'a woman's place is in the home'. Liberal politics at its best is a matter of demanding, offering, and testing public moral arguments and reasons.

Moral reasons publicly offered to justify political decisions

[57] Rorty, *Mirror*, pp. 189–90.
[58] Ibid. 382 n. 24.

now are apt to be relied upon or invoked by others later, who claim that the same reasons justify their claims or support their grievances: if white males have the vote, why not let blacks and women have it too? Blacks and women are reflective, capable of forming political judgments, and their interests, like those of white males, are at stake in politics every day. Those who disagree should provide reasons for their disagreement, reasons they would be prepared fairly to extend to relevantly similar cases.

Where we have no good reason for the distinctions and discriminations we draw, we have anomalies or inconsistencies calling, not for bland acceptance, but for further reflection and perhaps revisions in our thinking. Public, articulate consistency in the application of reasons justifying our political arrangements is a basic, perhaps the basic, requirement of liberal fairness: articulate consistency expresses our respect for the dignity of others capable, like ourselves, of giving and accepting reasons. We aspire to moral articulateness and consistency not because we make a 'philosophical' fetish of abstraction, but because we seek publicly to respect our common reasonableness, and we recognize that the only alternative to the fair and consistent application of moral reasons is arbitrariness, mere wilfulness, and tyranny.[59]

CONCLUSION

Walzer, Bork, Oakeshott, and Rorty are united by a common opposition to 'philosophical vanguards' armed with the products of reflection, and bent on imposing the rule of abstract principles on polities which, they claim, could do much better without them. Walzer claims to be looking for principles of justice for people with a 'firm sense of their own identity', for 'individuals like us . . . who are situated as we are, who share a culture and who are determined to go on sharing it'. He proceeds by asking, 'What choices have we already made in the course of our common life? What understandings do we

---

[59] See Dworkin's excellent discussion of articulate consistency as a central feature of political morality in *Rights*, ch. 6, esp. pp. 162–3.

(really) share?'[60] For Walzer and others, the opposition to a
philosophical vanguard translates into a circumscription of the
role of judicial review.

Debates over the political authority of 'philosophy' rage
among philosophers and among political practitioners. Conservative critics of judicial review argue that moral theory is
no more than the way 'intellectuals' register their personal
preferences. As Chief Justice William H. Rehnquist puts it,
'Many of us necessarily feel strongly and deeply about our
own moral judgments, but they remain only personal moral
judgments until given the sanction of law.'[61] And Bork has
argued that 'Every clash between a minority claiming freedom
and a majority claiming power to regulate involves a choice
between the gratifications of the two groups'.[62] With no
principled way, for Bork, to discriminate between different
kinds of gratification, the majority should have its way.
Political or moral theory does not, proponents of New Right
jurisprudence claim, help us articulate common standards of
reasonableness. Political authority comes from the will of the
people, through elections, and through their ratified instrument, the Constitution. Constitutional limits on popular
authority (such as rights) should be interpreted narrowly
because we must not assume that the people gave up more of
their power than they clearly intended to do. The power of
judges should be confined to enforcing only those rights and
limits on popular power clear in the constitutional text and
originally intended by the framers.

Criticisms of the practical role of philosophy tend to col-
lapse, I have argued, into forms of conventionalism which, far
from leaving our political practices intact, would undermine
some of our most valuable and cherished practices. Defenders
of liberalism have themselves sometimes fled from philosophy. Consider the old 'end of ideology' notion that, as
Daniel Boorstin put it, 'We must refuse to become crusaders
for liberalism, in order to remain liberals'. America is great

    [60] Walzer, *Spheres*, p. 5.
    [61] William H. Rehnquist, 'The Notion of a Living Constitution', *Texas Law
Review* 54 (1976), 704.
    [62] Robert H. Bork, 'Neutral Principles and Some First Amendment Problems',
Indiana Law Review, 47 (1971), 9.

because it has no political theory; having a political theory and trying to impose it on others is un-American.[63] I'm OK, you're OK.

Underlying Boorstin's view, like Rorty's, is a self-congratulatory embrace of 'the way we do things around here'. Liberals are sometimes like that but not, I think, at their best. We do better to recognize that political theory is a useful critic that has a central place in our practices, and that in politics we should try to live up to the demands of reflective self-criticism.

To be fair, the 'end of ideology' movement took off in the heyday of the Cold War when American self-confidence may have frightened many academics. The anti-ideologists may have intended their argument to be therapeutic, as does Rorty.[64] Unfortunately, the prescription rests (nowadays, at least) on a misdiagnosis. Liberals would do far better, I shall argue, to embrace a public and moderate form of reflective justification.

Claims about the proper style of political discourse could have important institutional implications. If 'reasonableness' is just a matter of accurately reflecting shared practices and commonly accepted standards, why not entertain a strong presumption in favour of the reasonableness of representative legislatures? A conventionalist conception of reasonableness could, in other words, contribute to the feeling common among constitutional commentators that judicial review is basically an 'anomalous institution' needing to be carefully circumscribed.[65]

Communitarian criticisms of liberalism could, I have argued, push us into the embrace of populism or conventionalism and away from the search for good reasons. Liberal practice, at its best, refuses to banish critical moral thinking. Liberal citizens exercise their critical capacities by making judgments among various standards and claims (all communal in one way or another), and they do this in politics and not only in their free time.

One important source of sustenance for liberal constitutionalism is a belief in the worth of treating other people reasonably;

[63] Daniel Boorstin, *The Genius of American Politics* (Chicago, Ill., 1965), 189, 1.
[64] See Rorty, *Mirror*, pp. 5–6.
[65] See below, ch. 5.

this belief helps explain and justify our commitment to the rule of law and to judicial review: one law applies to citizens and public officials alike, and individuals have the right to challenge elected officials to defend their interpretation of that law in court. Together, the US Constitution (properly interpreted) and judicial review (vigorously exercised) help insure that Americans are governed by more than mere power, preference, or convention; when functioning properly these liberal institutions embody a basic commitment to public reasonableness.

Liberal ideals of citizenship, virtue, and community can be located in an ideal of liberal constitutionalism sustained by a basic political commitment to public reasonableness. Philosophy is not a distinct, parallel system to 'ordinary' thinking, 'its very problems', as Popper says, 'are enlargements of the problems of common sense knowledge'.[66] We must search for good reasons and strong arguments because modern states are not 'communities of shared meaning' in any simple sense, they are associations of more or less reasonable people who agree on some things and disagree on others, whose reasonableness we wish to respect and whose allegiance we hope thereby to engage.

[66] Karl R. Popper, *The Logic of Scientific Discovery* (New York, 1968), 22.

2

Liberalism and Public Justification

What does liberalism stand for? What does it mean to be a citizen of a liberal, constitutionalist regime? How can we live up to the demands that such a regime imposes on us? To answer these questions requires an effort in critical, moral, self-interpretation: what do we stand for at our best?[1] What in our practices and ways are we proud of?

Part of the answer to these questions, and perhaps the part that springs most quickly into our minds, is that as citizens of liberal, constitutional regimes, we enjoy certain rights, we are free to choose along a fairly wide spectrum, and the security of our persons and property is protected. We receive, in other words, certain political goods at reasonable (or at least acceptable) cost: paying our taxes, obeying the law, voting now and then. The benefits of private citizenship are not to be sneezed at: they place certain basic human goods (security, prosperity, and freedom) within the grasp of nearly all, and that is nothing less than a fantastic human achievement.

The defence of liberalism could rest on the benefits of private citizenship, but there is more to be said. There is another more active and demanding dimension to liberal citizenship, vital though perhaps subordinate. By exploring the active, public side of liberalism we can do more than merely deflect communitarian and republican concerns, we can distil liberal conceptions of virtue and community that constitute positive rejoinders to republican and communitarian criticisms; we can, as well, better understand what

---

[1] I am thinking here on the approaches to constitutional interpretation of Ronald Dworkin, *Law's Empire* (Cambridge, Mass., 1986), and Sotirios A. Barber, *On What the Constitution Means* (Baltimore, Md., 1984).

the liberal polity requires of its citizens to flourish or even survive.

My response to liberalism's critics takes the form of a critical interpretation of liberalism in general, and American constitutionalism in particular. My aim is a vision of liberal practices that is realistically utopian: one that fits our practices and expectations about human behaviour closely enough to be realistic, but that distils from those practices a core of moral ideals worth striving toward.[2]

LIBERALISM AS PUBLIC REASONABLENESS

Liberalism stands for peace through toleration, law-bound liberty, and a rights-orientated conception of justice. Less often noted, perhaps, is that liberal constitutionalism attempts to combine liberal freedom with reasoned self-government. Liberal institutions provide the settings for ongoing efforts to formalize, clarify, contest, justify, refine, and extend liberal principles.

The conviction that other people should be treated reasonably, that the application of power should be accompanied by conscientious and open efforts to meet objections with reasons, is an important source of sustenance for liberal constitutionalism. This aspiration to public reasonableness helps explain and justify our commitment to the rule of law and to judicial review: one law applies to citizens and public officials alike, and individuals have the right to challenge elected officials to defend their interpretation of that law in a court insulated from political pressure.

Liberalism sets itself against arbitrary government in all its forms. The essence of the liberal ideal of the rule of law, as Lon Fuller aptly observed, is its commitment to a form of power which is 'horizontal' and reciprocal rather than 'vertical' and managerial: self-governing citizens and government officials all subject to the same law, not a law-making sovereign and subjects receiving law.[3] The moral core of this order is a

---

[2] See Rawls, 'The Idea of an Overlapping Consensus', *Oxford Journal of Legal Studies* 7 (1987), 18–22.

[3] Lon L. Fuller, *The Morality of Law* 2nd edn. (New Haven, Conn., 1969), 232–42.

commitment to public justification: the application of power should be accompanied with reasons that all reasonable people should be able to accept. Tocqueville captures the spirit of public justification nicely; even under the old regime in France, he argued,

the courts were largely responsible for the notion that every matter of public or private interest was subject to debate and every decision could be appealed from; as also for the opinion that such affairs should be conducted in public and certain formalities observed. Obviously incompatible with the concept of a servile state, such ideas were the only part of a free people's education furnished by the old regime. Even the administration had borrowed much from the terminology and usages of law courts. The King felt it incumbent on him always to justify his edicts and set forth his reasons for them before making them effective; decisions of the court were preceded by lengthy preambles. . . . [P]ublic debate was the order of the day and everyone had the right of expressing his opinion. All these customs and procedures were so many obstacles to royal despotism.[4]

In a liberal regime, criticism of the government is accepted and even encouraged, and liberal citizens expect to be answered with reasons rather than mere force or silence. 'Liberals demand', as Jeremy Waldron puts it, 'that the social order should in principle be capable of explaining itself at the tribunal of each person's understanding.'[5]

Liberal, democratic politics is about justification, but not about any kind of justification at all. Liberal political justification, even in an ideal form, should be understood politically— this chapter considers why and how.

In a liberal political community, no one is above needing publicly to justify the exercise of political power. Contrast James I's defence of absolutism, a defence that turned crucially on the assertion that the king is ordained by God to judge and

---

[4] Alexis de Tocqueville, *The Old Regime and the French Revolution*, trans. Stuart Gilbert (Garden City, NY, 1955), 117, on how governmental immunity from prosecution promotes popular servility and public despotism, see Part 2, chs. 4 and 11, and A. V. Dicey's *The Law of the Constitution* (Indianapolis, Ind., 1982), chs. 5 and 7.

[5] Jeremy Waldron, 'Theoretical Foundations of Liberalism', *Philosophical Quarterly*, 37 (1987), 127–50.

not be judged by his subjects: 'The wickedness of the king can never make them that are ordained to be judged by him to become his judges.'[6] The king's coronation oath is directed to God, James insisted, and only God can judge the king:

Kings are justly called Gods; for they exercise a manner of resemblance of Divine power upon earth. . . . They make and unmake their subjects; they have the power of raising up and casting down; of life and death; judges over all their subjects and in all cases, yet accountable to none but God. They have the power to exalt the low things and abase the high things and to make of their subjects like men at chess.[7]

Opposition to the practice of public justification comes in a great variety of forms, not all of them sinister. Among the reasons advanced against the proposed American Constitution during the ratification debates, was its creation of federal jurisdiction over suits brought by individuals against the state governments. According to the Anti-Federalist Brutus: 'It is improper, because it subjects a state to answer in a court of law, to the suit of an individual. This is humiliating and degrading to a government, and, what I believe, the supreme authority of no state ever submitted to.'[8]

The controversial German legal theorist Carl Schmitt ridiculed the liberal commitment to public discussion: 'making a decision', on many essential issues, 'is more important than how a decision is made.'[9] The bourgeoisie is the 'discussing class', said Schmitt, and that is its weakness: 'a class that shifts all political activity onto the plane of conversation in the press and parliament is no match for social conflict.'[10] 'Dictatorship

---

[6] James I, 'The Trew Law of Free Monarchies: Or the Reciprock and Mutuall Duetie Betwixt A Free King, and His Naturall Subjects', in *The Political Works of James I*, intro. by Charles Howard McIlwain (Cambridge, Mass., 1918), 66.

[7] James I, 'A Speach to the Lords and Commons of the Parliament at White-Hall', 21 Mar. 1609, in *Works*, pp. 307–8.

[8] 'Brutus', letter XIII, in *The Complete Anti-Federalist*, ii, ed. Herbert J. Storing, pp. 428–33. I am indebted to a paper by Donald R. Brand, 'In Defence of Sovereign Immunity', presented at the Program for Constitutional Government, Harvard University, 6 Oct. 1989.

[9] Carl Schmitt, *Political Theology: Four Chapters on the Concept of Sovereignty*, trans. George Schwab (Cambridge, Mass., 1988), 55–6; Schmidt is, at this point, describing de Maistre's view of sovereignty, but with evident sympathy.

[10] Ibid. 59.

is the opposite of discussion', and was destined, Schmitt supposed, to triumph over it.[11]

By affirming the public role of justification, contemporary liberal philosophy often seems to have fashioned a grand alliance with political practice. Ronald Dworkin famously calls for a 'fusion of constitutional law and moral theory'.[12] The best arguments establish individual rights and the right to win hard cases. 'Hercules', Dworkin's ideal judge, 'will not submit to popular opinion in hard cases', but neither will reflective citizens.[13] The liberal fusion of moral theory and political practice holds out the promise of a morally elevated politics. But for this fusion to be at all plausible, the project of justification must be made accessible to people as we know them.

On the contemporary American political scene, New Right moral sceptics mock the liberal aspiration to public justification. Consider Robert H. Bork's contrast between the new constitutional commentary and the old:

The older commentators, secure in their common-sense, lawyers' view of the Constitution, wrote prose that is clear, straightforward, muscular, and unphilosophical. Such commentary was accessible and useful to practicing lawyers as well as to scholars. Modern theory is not. Its concepts are abstruse, its sources philosophical rather than legal, its arguments convoluted, its prose complex.[14]

'As for philosophers', as Francis Bacon put it, 'they make imaginary laws for imaginary commonwealths, and their discourses are as the stars, which give little light because they are so high.'[15] The complexity and abstruseness of moral philosophy, Bork suggests, makes it inaccessible to lawyers (and, *a fortiori*, citizens) and easily manipulable for political purposes; its presence in judicial reasoning is, moreover, an insult to common sense.

Moral philosophy could, if not adapted to the needs of liberal democratic politics, become a source of mystification

[11] Ibid. 63.
[12] Dworkin, *Rights*, p. 149.
[13] Ibid. 129.
[14] Robert H. Bork, foreword to Gary L. McDowell, *The Constitution and Contemporary Constitutional Theory* (Cumberland, Va., 1985), p. vi.
[15] Francis Bacon, *The Advancement of Learning* (London, 1974), Bk. 2, sect. 23.49.

and tyranny. Indeed, Hercules, Dworkin's ideal judge, might appear to be a superhuman figure endowed with powers of reason far beyond those of mere mortals handing down rulings and opinions from Olympus. This would be a mistake: Dworkin deploys a specifically public conception of justification that anticipates worries about moral reasoning's abstruseness and inaccessibility. Liberals should, Dworkin argues, seek principles that we and our successors will find 'easy to understand and publicize and observe; principles otherwise appealing are to be rejected or adjusted because they are too complex or are otherwise impractical in this sense'.[16]

Public justification is a liberal attempt to establish practices of critical reasonableness among people whose capacity for reason is limited. And so, liberals typically seek justifications that are widely acceptable to reasonable people with a broad range of moral and philosophical commitments and interests.[17] The aim is reasonable agreement: to be both reasonable and agreeable in a widely pluralistic society. As Rawls asks, 'given the fact of pluralism—the fact that a plurality of conflicting comprehensive religious, philosophical and moral doctrines are affirmed by citizens in a modern democratic society—how can we design our defense of [liberalism] so as to achieve sufficiently wide support for such a regime?'[18]

This chapter articulates and defends an approach to liberal public justification. The goal is a process of reasoning that is publicly accessible, but genuinely justificatory, one that forms a plausible part of our actual practices without forsaking critical reasonableness. One danger of such an approach, as we shall see, is that widely acceptable reasons will be embraced in spite of the fact, or even *because*, they mask the true nature of the liberal regime.

In the quest for reasonable consensus amidst diversity, liberals have a tendency to minimize the broad and deep

---

[16] Dworkin, *Rights*, p. 166.

[17] Representatives of liberal contractualism include Rawls, Scanlon, and Nagel (see Nagel, 'Moral Conflict and Political Legitimacy', *Philosophy and Public Affairs*, 16 (1987), 215–40), and Bruce A. Ackerman (see *Social Justice in the Liberal State* (New Haven, Conn., 1980) and 'Why Dialogue?' *Journal of Philosophy*, 86 (1989), 5–22). There are, of course, important differences among these writers.

[18] John Rawls, 'The Priority of Right and Ideas of the Good', *Philosophy and Public Affairs*, 17 (1988), 275.

implications of liberal politics. Reticence in spelling out the controversial implications of liberalism could lead to the embrace of a liberal false consciousness. Beginning from a desire to respect reasonable persons, public justification could become liberal hoodwinking, and 'political' liberalism could come to rest on a noble fib.

Liberal public justification cannot avoid controversy: it engages and seeks to shape our deepest and most personal values. Liberals should acknowledge their partisanship and the practical impossibility of perfect convergence on common principles of justice. A workable conception of public justification will embrace the virtue of principled moderation, a virtue that allows us to aspire to public justification while accepting the infirmities of the human condition.

LIBERAL PUBLIC JUSTIFICATION

Most of us spend at least some time trying to justify ourselves to ourselves and to others. We argue and disagree about what is the right thing to do, both in politics and in private life. The experience of moral self-examination and deliberation, of wondering about the quality of our reasons for acting as we do, is not an unusual experience. Philosophy carries on in a more sustained and careful way the project of critical reflection that we all participate in at least occasionally.

And yet, while we all have our philosophical moments few of us make a career of it. Most people are not even amateur philosophers, and much that counts as academic philosophy is far beyond the reflective capacities of the average citizen. If the practice of liberal public justification stands simply for the political authority of philosophy it might contribute to the tyranny of a few philosophical types (not professors to be sure, but perhaps judges). Public justification avoids a direct confrontation between philosophy and liberal democratic politics by shaping and moderating the aims of both. The question is how this adjustment can occur without either distorting our politics beyond recognition or substituting populist rhetoric for reflective and critical thought. How can justification go public and remain importantly justificatory?

Public justification regards certain kinds of reasons as politically authoritative: moral reasons that can be openly presented to others, critically defended, and widely shared by reasonable people. The reasons must be impersonal or *moral*: good reasons for others as well as oneself, not mere references to narrow interests or self-interest. They must be *general* reasons, ones we are prepared to extend to relevantly similar cases. The reasons must be *public* in the sense of being widely and openly accessible; appeals to inner conviction or faith, special insight, secret information, or very difficult forms of reasoning, are ruled out. Public justification must, finally, be *critical* in that objections have been sought out and reasonable alternatives confronted or anticipated.[19]

At the most basic level public justification has dual aims: it seeks reflective justification (good reasons) but it also seeks reasons that can be widely seen to be good by persons such as they are. These dual aims are pursued together so that, politically speaking at least, there is no independent standard against which a political theory can be judged.[20] Public justification does not work down from a prior, purely philosophical standard; participants aim at a system of principles that all can see to be reasonable (not one that only a few will regard as true or best).[21]

The dual aims of justification are consonant with the principled commitments of a liberal democratic society: by pursuing both together we respect not only the goodness of good reasons, but also the freedom and equality of citizens whose capacity for reason is limited and who espouse widely divergent comprehensive views.[22] Indeed, the goodness of good reasons, for a public moral theory, becomes entirely a function of their capacity to gain widespread agreement among reasonable people moved by a desire for reasonable

---

[19] This account is indebted to discussions in Rawls, *Theory*, pp. 130–6, Dennis F. Thompson, 'Representatives in the Welfare State', in Amy Gutmann, ed., *Democracy and the Welfare State* (Princeton, NY, 1988), and H. B. Acton, 'Political Justification', in Hugo Adam Bedau, ed., *Civil Disobedience: Theory and Practice* (New York, 1969).

[20] As Rawls puts it: 'The very content of the first principles of justice . . . is determined in part by the practical task of political philosophy'; 'Kantian Constructivism in Moral Theory', *The Journal of Philosophy*, 77 (1980), 543; see also p. 524.

[21] Rawls, 'Overlapping Consensus', p. 24.

[22] Ibid. 4–5.

consensus.[23] As Thomas Nagel puts it,

we should not impose arrangements, institutions, or requirements on other people on grounds that they could reasonably reject (where reasonableness is not simply a function of the independent rightness or wrongness of the arrangements in question, but genuinely depends on the point of view of the individual in question to some extent).[24]

Why public justification? We acknowledge, first of all, the permanent fact of pluralism: reasonable people disagree not only about preferences and interests, but widely and deeply about moral, philosophical, religious, and other views. While acknowledging pluralism we, secondly, respect as free and equal moral beings all those who pass certain threshold tests of reasonableness: we respect those whose disagreement with us does not impugn their reasonableness.[25] We try to distinguish, finally, between intractable philosophical and religious issues and other problems that are both more urgent (at least from a liberal perspective) and easier to grapple with.[26] We urgently need agreement on certain practical problems: securing basic liberties and establishing fair principles of distribution.[27] There are reasonable and widely acceptable answers for only a few questions of political justice, as Rawls says, and 'political wisdom consists in identifying those few, and among them the most urgent'.[28]

Public justification embodies a complex form of respect for persons: it respects both our capacity for a shared reasonableness, but also 'the burdens of reason'.[29] People disagree for a variety of reasons which do not impugn their reasonableness or undermine their claim to respect. Public justification offers

---

[23] Persons, that is, with the two 'moral powers' ('the capacity for an effective sense of justice' and 'the capacity to form, revise, and rationally pursue a conception of the good') described by Rawls in 'Constructivism', p. 525.

[24] Nagel, 'Moral Conflict', p. 221.

[25] I have benefited from an excellent unpublished paper by Amy Gutmann, 'A Liberal Public Philosophy', presented at the Conference on Liberalism and the Good, sponsored by Georgetown University, 3–5 Nov. 1988, Washington, DC.

[26] On the notion of urgency, see Scanlon, 'Preference and Urgency', *Journal of Philosophy*, 72 (1975), 655–69.

[27] Rawls, 'Overlapping, Consensus', pp. 16–17.

[28] Ibid. 16.

[29] Rawls, 'The Domain of the Political and Overlapping Consensus', *New York University Law Review*, 64 (1989), 233–55, 235–8.

a way of accepting the infirmities of reasonable citizens. Moral arguments are, as Rawls reminds us, complex and the relevant evidence is often difficult to assess and weigh appropriately. The concepts of political morality are inherently vague. Our judgments are inevitably somewhat subjective—shaped, that is, by the totality of our personal experiences which are bound to differ from one person to another. In morality our deepest convictions, habits, desires, and interests are at stake; 'most people', as Aristotle recognized, 'are bad judges concerning their own things.'[30] Moral values are diverse and different ones weigh in on both sides of moral issues. Particular political institutions cannot embody all values: we must make hard choices and be selective.[31]

It should be no surprise that reasonable and reasonably conscientious people will disagree about their conclusions. The burdens of reason make convergence on common political principles difficult; they also make it reasonable to accept and try to live with a range of reasonable disagreement on many political questions.

Public justification as I have described it plays a representative role, mediating, in effect, between philosophy and the citizenry, representing philosophy to citizens and citizens to philosophy.[32] The public conception avoids excessively subtle and complex forms of reasoning, preferring arguments that not only are sound 'but such that they can be publicly seen to be sound'.[33] Public justification respects the 'constraints of simplicity and availability of information', moderating the

---

[30] Aristotle, *Politics*, trans. Carnes Lord (Chicago, Ill., 1984), Bk. 3, ch. 9, p. 97; Aristotle's remarks on the limits of precision and demonstration in ethics are also relevant, *Nichomachean Ethics*, trans. Martin Ostwald (Indianapolis, Ind., 1962), Bk. 1, chs. 3 and 5, pp. 5–6, 8–9.

[31] This account is drawn from Rawls, 'Domain'.

[32] Political justification does not apply a general moral theory like utilitarianism to the basic structure of society. All of this largely coheres with the description of 'reflective equilibrium' developed in *Theory*, see Sections 9 and 87. Rawls's more explicit emphasis on political theory's dual aims helps show that it would be wrong to charge Rawls with making merely social or conventional standards absolute. Allan Bloom said that, for Rawls, conflicts between individual belief and social consensus must always be resolved 'in favor of society'; see 'Justice: John Rawls vs. The Tradition of Political Philosophy', *American Political Science Review*, 69 (1975), 661–2. Rawls does not rule out the possibility of real or objective standards of morality.

[33] Rawls, 'Overlapping Consensus', n. 2 above, p. 21; and see 'Constructivism', pp. 537, 561.

aims of philosophy so as to insure the wide accessibility of the relevant forms of reasoning and evidence: these should be not too difficult and (if possible) not too deeply at odds with firmly held and not unreasonable views.[34]

With its significantly public standard of reasonableness, liberalism fosters trust and promotes co-operation.[35] And it expresses the need to perform certain urgent tasks without waiting to settle deep and intractable disputes.

Public justification embodies the philosophical impetus toward critical reflection in a qualified form. These qualifications may strike us at first as odd, and indeed as inconsistent with certain aspects of our political culture. Through the institution of judicial review (which interprets and extends our most basic working political principles) our culture elevates the political authority of courts, whose authority flows from their capacity to recognize good reasons and make good arguments. ('Judicial review', Michael Walzer charges, 'is the crucial institutional device through which the philosophical conquest of politics takes effect.'[36]) That culture also respects the academy and frequently appeals to its authority in politics (appointing professors to important positions, citing their works, relying on what is taken to be sound scholarship, especially in court opinions but also elsewhere).[37]

But the expertise of academics gives them no automatic political authority in a liberal democratic society. Academics may gain authority by framing political arguments that can be widely appreciated and endorsed as good. In judicial

---

[34] Rawls, 'Priority', p. 258; and also 'Not Metaphysical', pp. 225, 230. Rawls argues that the political conception of justice needs a 'companion agreement on guidelines of public inquiry and rules for assessing evidence. Given the fact of pluralism, these guidelines and rules must be specified by reference to the forms of reasoning available to common sense, and by the procedures and conclusions of science when not controversial', 'Overlapping Consensus', p. 20, and see also p. 16. And notice the remarks in *Theory* to the effect that the construction of the original position relies only on general facts that are widely acceptable; see sect. 26, esp. pp. 158–9.

[35] Rawls 'Overlapping Consensus', p. 21. Complex arguments should be avoided, in part, because they generate suspicion.

[36] Michael Walzer, 'Flight From Philosophy', a review of Benjamin Barber, *The Conquest of Politics*, *New York Review of Books*, 36 (2 Feb. 1989), 43.

[37] See Sotirios A. Barber's excellent discussion, 'Judge Bork's Constitution', in Walter F. Murphy and C. Herman Pritchett eds., *Courts, Judges and Politics*, 4th edn. (New York, 1986).

proceedings, moreover, evidence must be openly presented and debated before a jury of average people rather than experts. For judges, as Benjamin N. Cardozo put it, 'the thing that counts is not what I believe to be right. It is what I may reasonably believe that some other man of normal intellect and conscience might reasonably look upon as right.'[38] Judges and other public officials should try to discern interpretations of the fundamental law whose reasonableness can be widely seen.[39]

The public conception of justification construes the ends and means of justification in a way that accords with our broader commitment to respecting the freedom and equality of persons. Having done so, it honestly acknowledges the substantive characteristics of *public* moral justification: it does not aim to identify what are simply the best reasons, where best is a function of only the quality of the reasons as reasons leaving aside the constraints of wide accessibility.[40]

Given a polity with a widespread capacity for reasonableness and a general commitment to liberal principles, it seems to me right to say that the best political justifications will be public in the manner described.[41] And yet, the concessions that public justification makes to accessibility should not be confused with other, more political and problematic concessions that some liberals might be disposed to make in the face of disagreement and controversy.

THE POLITICS OF JUSTIFICATION

Liberals have a tendency to minimize what they stand for and to evade their ultimate commitments. 'The question is', asks

---

[38] Benjamin N. Cardozo, *The Nature of the Judicial Process* (New Haven, Conn., 1949), 89.

[39] Which is not something that Ronald Dworkin puts much emphasis on. It also should be clear that this paragraph helps answer Michael Walzer's concerns about the anti-democratic tendencies of liberal political theory, see 'Philosophy and Democracy'.

[40] See Rawls, 'Independence', p. 14.

[41] This is an important qualification. Public justification might yield unacceptable results in some circumstances. This may parallel Aristotle's claim that the practically best regime depends in part on particular circumstances, 'For by nature there is a certain [people] apt for mastery, another apt for kingship, and another that is political,

Rawls, 'what is the least that must be asserted; and if it must be asserted, what is its least controversial form?'[42] There may be good political reasons, in some circumstances, for coyness or even deception about what hangs on the resolution of a highly charged controversy. But a general theoretical reticence or evasiveness can lead to confusion and unfounded charges of political indecision or weakness and moral spinelessness. And so, Carl Schmitt: faced with the question, 'Christ or Barabbas, the liberal answers with a motion to adjourn the meeting or set up an investigative committee'.[43]

Liberalism was born a response to controversy, disagreement, and war—an element of caution is understandable. But liberalism is not, either as a theory or as a stable practice, based on disagreement or relativism or neutrality or compromise in the face of every controversy. Liberalism asserts and should stand by substantive and contestable conceptions of political morality. And for the purposes of my argument, we cannot recognize the distinctive ideals of liberal virtue and community without identifying the substance that permeates liberalism, shaping even its conception of public justification.

Some liberals try to argue that liberalism stands only for certain political arrangements and not for a broad and deep way of life. John Rawls has seemed to argue for the superficiality of liberal values, acknowledging the full implications of liberalism with decided reticence. This reticence, I shall suggest, is significant: it grows out of a desire for widespread agreement, but also flirts with a kind of liberal false consciousness. Using some of Rawls's later work as my foil here, I shall try to display the dangers of reticence and argue that liberals should be candid about their partisanships, open in their arguments, and explicit on the need for principled moderation.

Liberal public justification, I have argued, properly seeks principles and arguments that can widely be seen to be reasonable. That does not mean, however, that liberals can

and this is both just and advantageous', *Politics*, ed. Lord, p. 115; see Bk. 3, chs. 13 and 17 generally.

[42] Rawls, 'Overlapping Consensus', p. 8.

[43] Carl Schmitt, *Politische Theologie: Vier Kapitel zur Lehre von der Souveränität* (Munich and Leipzig, 1922), 78, quoted in Ellen Kennedy's introduction to *The Crisis of Parliamentary Democracy*, trans. Ellen Kennedy (Cambridge, 1985), p. xvi.

succeed in shaping positions that all will find agreeable: the most reasonable position in a public sense will still be one that religious fanatics and others (I will generally use religious fanaticism as an example for simplicity's sake) will find deeply objectionable. Public justification concedes something to reasonable disagreement, but it does not abandon substantive liberal values, and it cannot help but shape people's lives broadly and deeply and relentlessly over time.

Rawls argues that political justification should extend the principle of toleration to the ultimate questions of philosophy itself: liberals should avoid 'claims to universal truth, or claims about the essential nature and identity of persons' and instead secure a reasonable political consensus on the shared ground (or 'overlapping consensus') that exists in our polity.[44] Political justification 'deliberately stays on the surface', it seeks only 'to identify the kernel of overlapping consensus', the ideas 'likely to be affirmed by each of the opposing comprehensive moral doctrines in a reasonably just democratic society'.[45]

The liberalism of overlapping consensus avoids close links with 'comprehensive' moral ideals: ideals that include 'conceptions of what is of value in human life, ideals of personal virtue and character, and the like, that are to inform much of our nonpolitical conduct (in the limit our life as a whole)'.[46] Comprehensive conceptions are bound to be contested as merely partisan conceptions of the good life, while liberal politics accepts the fact of pluralism. As Charles Larmore puts it, 'We do better to recognize that liberalism is not a philosophy of man, but a philosophy of politics.'[47] And so,

we adopt a conception of the person framed as part of, and restricted to, an explicitly political conception of justice. . . . [P]ersons can accept this conception of themselves as citizens and use it when discussing questions of political justice without being committed in

[44] Rawls, 'Justice as Fairness: Political, Not Metaphysical', *Philosophy and Public Affairs*, 14 (1985), p. 223 and *passim*.

[45] Ibid. 246.

[46] Rawls, 'Priority', p. 252; religious and philosophical conceptions of morality, as opposed to a political conception, tend to be comprehensive. Rawls wants to distance his limited political conception from all comprehensive conceptions, whether friendly to liberalism (Kantian autonomy, Millian individuality) or not so friendly (perfectionism).

[47] Charles Larmore, *Patterns of Moral Complexity* (Cambridge, 1987), 129.

other parts of their life to comprehensive moral ideals often associated with liberalism, for example, the ideals of autonomy and individuality.[48]

It often seems, in his later work, as though Rawls is telling religious 'true believers' and others who would resist comprehensive ideals of autonomy or individuality that they can accept basic liberal rights and principles without revising the full set of their personal convictions.[49]

It is one thing to seek reasons that are widely accessible and acceptable, quite another to refuse to spell out the broad and deep implications that basic political principles and institutions have (however they are justified). Liberal political principles do not 'stay on the surface', and their consequences cannot be confined to a particular sphere of our lives.

Politics is the final recourse for people who cannot agree. People who disagree about religious beliefs or other commitments must regard common political principles as regulative of all their interactions with others. Liberalism requires, therefore, not merely an overlapping consensus but a consensus that practically *overrides* all competing values.[50]

The idea of an overlapping consensus does correctly suggest that specifically political values need not do all the work of supporting the liberal settlement for everyone or even most people.[51] The comprehensive moral and religious views of liberal citizens may provide a variety of values and interests which support, without forming a part of (or at least not an official part of), the shared political framework: for example,

---

[48] Rawls, 'Not Metaphysical', p. 245; and Larmore, 'Liberalism . . . does not require an individualistic image of man; its individualism can be strictly political', *Patterns*, p. 126.

[49] 'Each of the different comprehensive philosophical, religious, and moral doctrines accepts justice as fairness in its own way . . . from within its own point of view. . . . [T]hey recognize its concepts, principles, and virtues as theorems, as it were, at which their several views coincide'. Rawls, 'Not Metaphysical', p. 246. Liberal principles are accepted as 'theorems', Rawls says, that is, not as self-evident axioms, but as demonstrable by reasoned argument.

[50] Rawls allows that 'the political conception of justice' expresses 'values that normally outweigh whatever other values oppose them . . .': 'Overlapping Consensus', p. 16.

[51] 'Deep and unresolvable differences on matters of fundamental significance is permanent': Rawls, 'Constructivism', p. 542.

religious convictions that prize, on religious grounds, free and open argument in a pluralistic environment. Shared liberal values need not themselves be strong enough to override all competing ones so long as the weight, as it were, of liberal and supporting (or pro-liberal) values is enough to outweigh all competing (or anti-liberal) values and interests. Nevertheless, the success and stability of liberal politics depends on people's private beliefs and commitments becoming importantly liberalized—becoming, that is, supportive of liberal politics.

Liberalism provides wide bounds within which people are free to settle on their own religious beliefs, aesthetic values, and so on. And yet, basic liberal principles (of respect for persons and their rights, for example) wash across and seep into the whole of our lives, not determining all our choices but limiting them all and structuring and conditioning our lives as a whole. Illiberal forms of private association are strictly ruled out. Many other interests and commitments, while not strictly ruled out, are bound to be discouraged by the free, open, pluralistic, progressive, and (arguably) commercialistic nature of a liberal society.

Liberals do not assume that personal beliefs and interests support free institutions. In John Locke's 'Letter Concerning Toleration', for example, the liberal flag was planted deep within the bounds of people's comprehensive values. True enough, Locke denies that the 'care of men's souls' is committed to civil authority and emphasizes the distinction between public and private realms. Nevertheless, Locke's argument for liberal toleration appeals directly to, and depends upon, a certain kind of private character: he appeals to 'all Men that have Souls large enough to prefer the true Interest of the Publick before that of a Party'.

Locke deploys a variety of arguments for toleration: that salvation depends on an inner faith that cannot be coerced, a distinction between the essential and the non-essential in Christian doctrine, the suspicion that intolerance is a mere cloak for power, a social compact argument for political legitimacy, and the claim that oppression not liberty leads to violence and rebellion. In short, we find a repertoire of religious and political arguments that were, by Locke's time, largely familiar if not yet widely accepted. By crossing the public/private boundary in some of the arguments he adduces for toleration, Locke directly engages and tries to shape deeply personal religious concerns—a dangerous strategy, perhaps, but one that is unavoidable. Liberal institutions such as law and rights require the willing support of liberal citizens. For that support to be forthcoming and for a liberal state to flourish liberal values must be internalized by citizens.[52]

These remarks may seem jejune, but people's private commitments in a liberal society do not become liberal accidentally. Public institutions shape private attitudes, and vice versa. If people are not prepared to accept the constraints and formalities implicit in the rule of law or the electoral process, for example (if bribery and other forms of corruption are rampant) these liberal institutions cannot survive. Liberal polities often take care, in shaping educational institutions and in other ways (such as promoting commerce), to encourage its citizens to adopt a range of commitments that support the liberal political settlement. It is easy for us to take the success of liberalism for granted, but only because liberal institutions have been at work for so long.

The notion that liberalism rests on an overlapping consensus might also suggest that political norms somehow stay on the surface, giving rise to no deep claims about the kind of persons liberalism takes us to be. Rawls claims that embracing liberal justice 'no more commits us to a metaphysical doctrine about the nature of the self than our playing a game like Monopoly commits us to thinking that we are landlords engaged in a desperate rivalry, winner take all'.[53] But liberal justice requires us to be a certain sort of person all the time.[54] We do not 'play' at being just now and then, as we occasionally play Monopoly.

---

[52] For an excellent discussion of the ways in which liberal due process and elections help shape character broadly and deeply, see George Kateb, 'Remarks on the Procedures of Constitutional Democracy', J. R. Pennock and J. W. Chapman, eds., *Nomos XX: Constitutionalism* (New York, 1979), 215–37.

[53] Rawls, 'Not Metaphysical', pp. 238–9.

[54] Rawls may, here, be responding to Bernard Williams's assertion that 'ground projects' giving our lives basic point and meaning are properly beyond the reach of impersonal moral criticism, see 'Persons, Character, and Morality', in *Moral Luck* (Cambridge, 1983), and his remarks on moral integrity in J. J. C. Smart and Bernard Williams, *Utilitarianism: For and Against* (Cambridge, 1973), pp. 108–18. Or he may

We can, no doubt, often distinguish between the public and private identities of liberal citizens: politically speaking, Saul of Tarsus setting out for Damascus is the same as the St Paul who arrives there.[55] Nevertheless, liberalism is certainly not compatible with all deep views of human personality, rather, it presupposes the widespread existence of certain deep character traits.[56]

It cannot be right to argue, as Rawls does, that liberal citizens may 'regard it as simply unthinkable to view themselves apart from certain religious, philosophical, and moral convictions, or from certain enduring attachments and loyalties'.[57] Liberalism elevates impartial standards of respect for all persons; it implies that people should be capable of reflecting on the whole range of their particular commitments (friendships, family ties, business associations—though not on all of them all at once) for the sake of interposing impersonal standards of justice and honouring the equal rights of others.

Critical self-reflection is not required if our personal commitments are already liberal—but what guarantees that? The reflective capacities of liberal citizens, alert to possible conflicts between personal commitments and liberal rights, should be a central mechanism for preserving and advancing the cause of justice in a well-ordered society (which is, after all, a society in which citizens have an active 'capacity to understand, apply, and to act *from*' a sense of justice).[58] A liberal society could not be well ordered in which personal friendships, regional attachments, or group memberships typically took priority over respect for liberal rights. It could not be well-ordered if composed of people incapable of reflectively distancing themselves from personal commitments for the sake of considering possible conflicts with the basic requirements of liberal justice.

The extent to which liberal values constitute us as persons

be accepting Michael Sandel's insistence on the value of commitments that deeply constitute our identity, see *Liberalism and the Limits of Justice* (Cambridge, 1982).

[55] As Rawls remarks, 'Not Metaphysical', p. 242; and see Larmore, *Patterns*, p. 125, whose defence of liberal neutrality is quite lucid but unsuccessful.

[56] As Amy Gutmann argues in her excellent 'Communitarian Critics of Liberalism', *Philosophy and Public Affairs* 14 (1985), 308–21.

[57] Rawls, 'Not Metaphysical', p. 241, and 'Constructivism', p. 545; and see Larmore's critique of 'the myth of wholeness', pp. 114–30.

[58] Rawls, 'Not Metaphysical', p. 233, emphasis added, and see *Theory*, sect. 69.

becomes clearer when we consider the dynamic qualities of liberal public justification. Many basic liberal guarantees now seem pretty firmly settled in Western constitutional systems (due process, the right to criticize the government, a broad franchise, bars on slavery) and these might be taken as a hard core of rights whose fixity contributes to public trust and political stability. It cannot be claimed, however, that a constitution fixes 'once and for all, the content of basic rights and liberties'.[59] Constitutions often employ broad and open-ended phrases precisely to encourage moral progress through political argument.

The contours of every one of our most basic liberties remains a matter of lively disagreement.[60] The American Constitution did not so much settle as frame an ongoing debate about the bounds between individual liberty and government power. Indeed the Constitution itself announces, in the Ninth Amendment, that citizens have basic rights that are unenumerated and we are left to work them out for ourselves. The Constitution's amendment provision implies that the founders foresaw future public reflection and debate on their handiwork.

Public justification should be a never-ending commitment. Justice as fairness (for example) is hard to interpret, its implications are in many ways debatable and uncertain. It would be sheer hubris to think that we have, or ever will have, the whole political truth. We are searchers for the truth, 'still searching what we know not, by what we know, still closing up truth to truth as we find it', in Milton's words,

Truth indeed came once into the world with her divine Master, and was a perfect shape most glorious to look on: but when he ascended, and his Apostles after him were laid asleep, then strait arose a wicked race of deceivers, who as that story goes of the *Ægyptian Typhon* with his conspirators, how they dealt with the good *Osiris*, took the virgin Truth, hewd her lovely form into a thousand peeces, and

---

[59] Rawls sometimes seems to suggest that liberalism settles basic moral issues once and for all: 'a liberal conception meets the urgent political requirement to fix, once and for all, the content of basic rights and liberties, and to assign them special priority. Doing this takes those guarantees off the political agenda . . .'. 'Overlapping Consensus', pp. 19–20.

[60] The very existence of some basic rights (such as privacy and economic liberty) is sharply contested as a matter of constitutional law.

scatter'd them to the four winds. From that time ever since, the sad friends of Truth, such as durst appear, imitating the careful search that *Isis* made for the mangl'd body of *Osiris*, went up and down gathering up limb by limb still as they could find them. We have not yet found them all, Lords and Commons, nor shall we ever doe, till her Masters second coming; he shall bring together every joynt and member, and shall mould them into an immortall feature of lovelines and perfection.[61]

We are always learning and confronting new circumstances, discovering 'onward things more remote from our knowledge'.[62] We cannot honour our status as reasonable beings unless we remain open to discussions with others about our deepest political conceptions, whatever they may be. At the point at which the argument is closed, public reason is transformed into public dogma.

Liberalism establishes, for good reason, a process of public debate about itself among other things. 'He who knows only his own side of the case', as Mill observed, 'knows little of that.'[63] Liberals need dissenters from liberalism: unless we keep debating and remain open to new and better reasons we could have no confidence in the reasons we now think are good. Not surprisingly then, closing public debate on basic political issues is incompatible with our deepest ideals and our practice of respecting even subversive speech (while drawing a sharp line between speech and action).[64]

I do not mean to say that the question of slavery, for example, should be reopened. But the fact that race remains on the agenda means that the liberal understanding of this basic issue remains vivid and has a chance to grow and deepen and become pervasive. Since the process of public justification is dynamic and open, we can hope that liberal values will be tested, refined, and extended ever more fully throughout society.

---

[61] John Milton, *Areopagitica, Complete Prose Works of John Milton*, vol. ii, ed. Douglas Bush *et al.* (New Haven, Conn., 1969), 549–51. Milton's relevance here was suggested to me by Philip Hogan.

[62] Ibid.

[63] John Stuart Mill, *On Liberty*, ed. D. Spitz (New York, 1975), 36.

[64] See *Brandenburg* v. *Ohio* 395 US 444 (1969). Why protect the advocacy of violence? Because it is still advocacy. In dealing with the positions advocated by Klansmen, however, we tolerate but do not compromise; we allow them their say but do not budge.

Public justification is not a means only but also an end in itself: being a self-critical reason-giver is the best way of being a liberal and a good way (liberals must suppose) of living a life. The reflective, self-critical capacities we associate with public justification must, therefore, be regarded as *permanent* and ever-developing characteristics of liberal citizens at their best. With authoritative institutions and practices that take public justification seriously, the liberal can realistically hope for progress toward ever greater reasonableness.

In order to facilitate the public acceptance of basic liberal principles, liberals often seem to limit the reach and consequences of liberal principles in the ways we have seen.[65] I have argued, in effect, that liberalism constitutes a regime: liberal principles and goals shape our lives pervasively, deeply, and relentlessly; liberal institutions embody those principles and help us reach those goals.

At the end of the political day, liberals must be prepared to make judgments about what range of practices is to be permitted, and so, what range of beliefs is reasonable. Liberal political actors must, in settling practical problems, take stands on the largest questions of meaning and value in human life: when does the right to life begin and end? What range of religious and sexual practices should be permissible? Reticent liberals sometimes argue as though the largest moral questions can be avoided in politics. Rawls, for example, claims that liberals can avoid assessing the truth or falsity of deeply held personal views, such as religious beliefs or other aspects of people's comprehensive moral views: 'nor need we say that political values are intrinsically more important than other values and that's why the other values are overridden. Indeed,

---

[65] To a great extent, so far as Rawls's liberal theory is concerned, the modes of limitation that we have examined so far are more apparent than real—instances of reticence rather than a real refusal to acknowledge the full implications of liberalism. Rawls admits that liberalism shapes the lives of liberal citizens broadly and deeply, influencing 'people's deepest aspirations': 'Constructivism', p. 539. Indeed, he allows that the institutions established by liberal justice 'can have decisive long-term social effects and importantly shape the character and aims of the members of society, the kinds of persons they are and want to be': 'Constructivism', p. 538. A political conception of justice specifies, he says 'the form of a social world—a background framework within which the life of associations, groups, and individual citizens proceeds': 'Overlapping Consensus', p. 21 and 'Priority', pp. 262–8.

saying that is the kind of thing we hope to avoid, and achieving an overlapping consensus enables us to avoid it.'[66] Does it really? Can public justification avoid making some ultimate judgments about which religious beliefs, for example, are justified?

What does a liberal say about a range of religious beliefs that include ecumenical Catholicism, fundamentalist Protestantism, and sects that require holy war against non-believers? There are, says Rawls, 'no resources within the political view to judge those conflicting conceptions. They are equally permissible provided they respect the limits imposed by the principles of political justice.'[67] Underline 'provided': all religions compatible with liberalism will be respected, those not compatible will be opposed.[68] The liberal must in this way imply that religious convictions incompatible with liberalism are insupportable. Liberal political values occupy much of the same space as personal comprehensive ideals, religious and otherwise.

In making a self-conscious personal choice about whether to support liberal politics, it would be necessary to weigh liberal and pro-liberal values against the strongest competing package as one sees it. (Is the freedom to debate, choose, and live one's own way really more important than struggling to establish a common culture that supports piety and other-worldliness and punishes blasphemers? Is peaceful pluralism really more important than the ideal of Christian Unity?) In order to vindicate its overriding status, a liberal political morality will have to speak directly to illiberal personal ideals, arguing that these are false or less important than competing liberal values, or that they can be mended and made compatible with liberalism.

Rawls tries to avoid the issues of truth and ultimate importance by excluding from the political space, as it were, the comparison between political conceptions and conflicting comprehensive views: 'Of course, citizens must decide for

---

[66] Rawls, 'Overlapping Consensus', p. 17; and see 'Priority', p. 271: 'We need not establish the absolute importance of political good, only that it is a significant good within a political conception of justice.'

[67] Rawls, 'Overlapping Consensus', p. 9.

[68] Illiberal religions will be tolerated (so long as they go along with the regime) but prevented from acting on their illiberal beliefs.

themselves whether, in light of their comprehensive views, and taking into account the great political values realized by the political conception, they can endorse that conception with its idea of society as a fair system of social cooperation.'[69] Must political theory simply be silent at the crucial moment of deciding on the merits of liberalism?[70]

The reticent liberal employs a remarkable division of labour. First, there is the stage of theory construction, in which we leave aside the controversial elements of our comprehensive personal perspective—not because we believe them to be untrue, but because we recognize that reasonable people with whom we wish to form a political association reject these views.[71] The stage of construction is a search for reasonable argument. Only after construction is complete do we enter a second stage in which the question of acceptance comes to the fore, and that question re-engages the full set of our values (from which we have abstracted for the sake of construction but otherwise retained). At this second stage, then, our controversial religious and other personal convictions are re-engaged: the full import and character of the liberal construction can only now be gauged. Only now can we consider the full ramifications of living in a liberal regime, ramifications whose characterization is bound to be broad and contestable (can I really live with the kinds of attitudes and beliefs likely to be promoted by a liberal framework?) and so inadmissible at the stage of construction.[72]

[69] Rawls, 'Priority', p. 259, and for similar remarks see 'Domain', pp. 246 and 250.

[70] Consider what Rawls says in defending his list of 'primary goods' against the charge these 'are not what, from within anyone's comprehensive doctrine, can be taken as ultimately important: they are not, in general, anyone's idea of the basic values of human life': 'Priority', p. 258. Rawls argues that the primary goods are not intended as an account of what is of ultimate or basic importance: that question has no public answer, that is, no answer widely acceptable to reasonable people. It is precisely the sort of question which a 'political' theory seeks to avoid or to abstract away from. Questions of ultimate importance are filtered out by the requirement that the theory be publicly accessible and widely agreeable. And so, from the point of view of a 'political' conception, there exists no other space of values to which the index of primary goods is to approximate, for if there were, this would make the view at least partially comprehensive and hence defeat the aim of achieving an overlapping consensus given the fact of pluralism: ibid. 259.

[71] The idea of approximating to truth has, Rawls says, no role in 'political' justification: 'Constructivism', p. 561.

[72] One thinks, for example, of the resistance of the Amish to public high school education, a conflict the Supreme Court faced in *Wisconsin* v. *Yoder* 406 US 205 (1972).

Segmenting the process of justification keeps political philosophy, in its constructive role, from speaking directly to
contentious personal comprehensive views: only at the
second, extra-political stage of theory acceptance or rejection
would broad liberal values confront competing religious ones.
Only here would we weigh Brian Barry's claim that liberalism
rests on a 'Faustian vision' of life, exalting 'self-expression,
self-mastery and control over the environment, natural and
social; the active pursuit of knowledge and the clash of ideas;
the acceptance of personal responsibility for the decisions that
shape one's life'.[73]

Segmenting the process of justification, as the reticent
liberal would have us do, is an artificial way of avoiding direct
conflict between political and personal values and an unrealistic depiction of what public justification involves. The conflict is not really avoided but merely shifted off the political
agenda (and, presumably, out of political forums) by bracket-
ing the question of theory acceptance, making it private, and
leaving it aside until the public construction is complete. The
broader and deeper implications of liberalism remain, however, a matter of public concern: public justification should
have something to say about how the interface between
political and personal values is negotiated. Managing that
interface is, in a sense, *the* crucial political issue—an issue that
we cannot help addressing in public forums, an issue that (in
some of its aspects at least) we *should* address in public forums.

To accept the liberal settlement is to accept institutions,
ideas, and practices whose influence over our lives and our
children's lives will be broad, deep, and relentless: family life,
religious life, and all paradigmatically private associations take
on the colour of liberal values. In marriage, as Galston points
out, the rule is no longer 'till death do us part', but rather, 'till
distaste drive us apart'.[74] Nuns criticize their bishops and even
the Pope; authorities of all kind come into question. Certain
types will find the liberal culture hospitable (artiste,

---

[73] Brian Barry, *The Liberal Theory of Justice* (Oxford, 1973), 127.

[74] Galston, 'Comment on Stephen Macedo, "The Politics of Justification"',
Presented at a symposium on The Politics of Justification, Institute for Humane
Studies, George Mason University, Fairfax, Va., 21 Apr. 1989, p. 7; and see the
insightful discussion in Galston's 'Pluralism and Social Unity', *Ethics*, 99 (1989),
711–26.

entrepreneur, arguer, and playboy) and others (devout and simple) will find the going tough.

The personal moral convictions of citizens and other political actors should be engaged, as features of our public moral framework are worked out. Public justification involves not a rigid segmentation of public and private spaces of value, but a process of negotiation between shared public values and each person's entire set of values. When thinking about political morality none of us can entirely leave behind the baggage of our personal convictions. At each stage of the argument we seek principles that we can live with in our public and broader personal roles and capacities, as beings at once public and private.

Rawls reluctantly admits that a defender of liberalism cannot avoid steering into the shoals of religious controversy and other matters of deep disagreement:

in affirming a political conception of justice we may eventually have to assert at least certain aspects of our own comprehensive (by no means necessarily fully comprehensive) religious or philosophical doctrine. This happens whenever someone insists, for example, that certain questions are so fundamental that to ensure their being rightly settled justifies civil strife. . . . [T]he salvation of a whole people, may be said to depend on it. At this point we have no alternative but to deny this, and to assert the kind of thing we had hoped to avoid.[75]

The participants in theory construction have recourse to their comprehensive moral views as they go along. And so, for example, liberals must 'deny that the concern for salvation requires anything incompatible with' equal liberty of conscience.[76]

Public justification is a process of constructive negotiation in which the moves are partly determined by what we regard as reasonable assertions and compromises *from within* our comprehensive view, and not only from a public perspective. To accept the appropriateness of *public* justification is to agree to filter out reasons and arguments whose grounds are private (like religious faith), or too complex to be widely understood, or otherwise incapable of being widely appreciated by

---

[75] Rawls, 'Overlapping Consensus', p. 13.
[76] Ibid. 13.

reasonable people. But reasonable people will continue to disagree reasonably even in politics: public justification is somewhat porous. We all carry our comprehensive moral views throughout our lives, in all our roles and offices; our deepest convictions and commitments are at risk in politics and so they are shaping and being shaped by politics. Enough must be said by defenders of a political theory, therefore, to adjudicate at least the most serious conflicts between public principles and widely held personal views, and to tame or override the illiberal components of personal moral perspectives. The success of liberal public justification does not require the common embrace of one comprehensive set of answers to all the great religious, philosophical, and moral questions, but neither does it allow the separation of public and private spaces of value: liberalism requires that all private commitments have a certain form and fall within a certain range. Our differences will, hopefully, be narrowed and rendered manageable. More than that we cannot hope for.

JUSTIFICATION *v*. LOYALTY?

The stability of a liberal regime requires that the personal moral and religious views of many people will (when illiberal) be mended to support the liberal settlement. Ideally, this transition will take place via candid, open public arguments. This is important in part because the transitional stage does not break sharply with normal practice: personal and political views are bound to differ from one person to another, and public justification is, in any case, the way liberals should live. But there could be substantive and very political reasons for wanting to avoid addressing the most divisive political questions. Avoiding the risk of serious conflict could justify efforts to enlist loyalty in quiet and unobtrusive rather than open and articulate ways.

Public justification is not the only means of getting people to be liberals. Some people will become liberal without participating in or being directly influenced by anything like a public argument. Indeed, one might even suppose that some people are *more* likely to be liberals if they are not provoked to reflection by a public moral argument. There might, in other words, be a trade-off between candid public argument and liberal socialization.

Many people's comprehensive moral views are, Rawls asserts, rather loosely formulated and only partially thought through.[77] Some who go along with liberalism only as a *modus vivendi* or who might oppose it altogether will often fail to be fully conscious of the relation between liberal political principles and their broader personal values. As a consequence, liberal principles

> are more likely to win an initial allegiance that is independent of our comprehensive views and prior to conflict with them. Thus when conflicts do arise, the political conception has a better chance of sustaining itself and shaping those views to accord with its requirements. We do not say, of course, that the stronger the initial allegiance the better; but it is desirable, politically speaking, that it be strong enough to make an overlapping consensus stable.[78]

People may go along without understanding and eventually develop liberal convictions out of habit rather than from anything like a reasoned argument: 'many if not most citizens come to affirm their common political conception without seeing any particular connection, one way or the other, between it and their other views.'[79]

Unconscious socialization, the result of living in an open, pluralistic environment, can contribute to a liberal settlement.[80] In her fictionalized account of the life of the Emperor Hadrian, Marguerite Yourcenar depicts the frustrations of imposing the rule of law on semi-barbarous peoples accustomed to the reign of sect and clan warfare, bloodfeuds, and so on. Chided by friends for his laborious efforts in imposing laws and fair settlements on peoples used to nothing but war, Hadrian, then a judge in Egypt, asserted that:

---

[77] 'Normally we do not have anything like a fully comprehensive religious, philosophical, or moral view, much less have we attempted to study those that do exist, or to work out one for ourselves.' Rawls, 'Priority', p. 274.

[78] Ibid. 274–5.

[79] Rawls, 'Overlapping Consensus', p. 19.

[80] Rawls is not alone here; Larmore endorses the separation of '*citoyen* and *homme*' because it promotes 'a sort of institutionalized myopia', p. 125.

each hour of calm was a victory gained, though precarious like all victories; each dispute arbitrated served as precedent and pledge for the future. It mattered little to me that the accord obtained was external, imposed from without and perhaps temporary; I knew that good like bad becomes a routine, that the temporary tends to endure, that what is external permeates to the inside, and that the mask, given time, comes to be the face itself. . . .[81]

As a practical matter one might pin one's hopes on the unreflective spread of liberal practices and principles, especially if one were disposed to see self-critical reflection and open justification as politically provocative, potentially disruptive, and largely beside the point of liberal politics. '*The most dangerous party member*', said Nietzsche, is the one 'who, by his all-too-devout pronouncement of the party principles, provokes the others to apostasy'.[82] Political theorists have often, as Leo Strauss pointed out, deployed 'exoteric' versions of their theories: ones that sacrifice full disclosure in order to avoid confrontation and contention and smooth the way to a political settlement.[83]

Widespread, unreflective theory acceptance might be jeopardized by the open and candid defence of liberalism as a regime. Sacrificing philosophical candour and open argument in order to smooth the transition to liberal peace might well be justified, if there really is a tension between candour and allegiance (the deeper implications of liberalism will be offensive to some) and the need for allegiance to liberalism really is more urgent than the need for full disclosure and open public justification. Under some circumstances, in other words, open public justification may be a luxury, and promoting liberal false consciousness a pragmatic and prudential imperative.

Must liberals, in order to generate allegiance, exercise caution in spelling out and defending the full implications of

---

[81] Marguerite Yourcenar, *The Memoirs of Hadrian*, trans. Grace Frick (New York, 1981), 97.

[82] Friedrich Nietzsche, from *Human, All-Too-Human*, in *The Portable Nietzsche*, ed. Walter Kaufmann (New York, 1968), 58.

[83] Leo Strauss, *Persecution and the Art of Writing* (Ithaca, NY, 1989). The motivations of the Rawlsian and Straussian versions are importantly different. A Rawlsian version might be called *Disagreement and the Art of Writing*.

liberalism? Should philosophical types keep their big mouths shut?[84]

Compromising on the full disclosure of what liberalism stands for, shying away from open and candid public justification, entails high costs. First of all, while public justification is a form of respect for persons, failing to be candid is a form of disrespect. Only when arguments are advanced and defended openly does the search for widely accessible reasons express respect for the reasonableness of common citizens. The embrace of liberal false consciousness is moved not by principled respect or a desire to live by public reasons but by fear of conflict and despair at the incapacity for reasonableness.

Many practical problems cannot be settled without confronting the deep and divisive implications of a liberal public morality. Constitutional cases involving the First Amendment's free exercise of religion clause are a minefield or (depending on how you look at it) a goldmine of hard and deeply revealing questions at the tense interface of religion and politics. Just what are the assumptions and deep consequences, for example, of a public education that honours criticism and science but has no room for religion? Does that regime promote, in effect, a religion of secular humanism?[85] One could try, of course, to paper over and avoid hard questions by paying lip-service to the public/private distinction and a simplistic idea of liberal neutrality. These ideas have a certain currency but, even when sincerely deployed, they obfuscate what is at stake in political issues and so risk distorting our practices.[86]

There are other benefits of public justification that a lack of candour would threaten: public justification, by avoiding overly complex and esoteric arguments, fosters trust, but any

---

[84] This pointed formulation of the interrogative was suggested to me by Harvey C. Mansfield, Jr.

[85] See *Edwards* v. *Aguillard* 96 L. Ed. 2nd 510 (1987), which concerned a state act mandating balanced treatment for creation science and the theory of evolution.

[86] A case in point would be Justice Brennan's opinion in *Edwards*, ibid., which deployed the usual liberal arguments about keeping religion out of the public sphere without really acknowledging, as Justice Scalia points out in dissent, that this in effect promotes a scientific, man-centred world-view which is a direct alternative to other world-views, such as ones offered by religions.

lack of candour, should it become publicly known, would undermine that trust. And while avoiding problems might seem justified as a temporary measure, critical reflection might be hard to revive, especially under conditions of real popular consensus and after philosophical and popular culture have diverged.

Besides the costs of theoretical reticence there are positive benefits of stirring up a bit of controversy. My sense is that Mill was right in thinking that some internal opposition to a society's political morality is a good thing (as Yogi Berra put it: 'if the world were perfect, it wouldn't be'). Liberals in particular are apt to forget or minimize what they stand for, which could have contributed to the slow and limp response of Western intellectuals to Ayatollah Khomeini's call for Salman Rushdie's death. Confronting an occasional fanatic, grappling with a bit of divisiveness, reminds us of what in the world we stand for as liberals and that in that world liberal values are neither uncontroversial nor foregone conclusions.

Timidity and a too ready willingness to compromise can be as dangerous as intransigence and dogmatism, and it is not clear that divisiveness is now a greater danger than timidity. Draining liberalism of self-consciousness and partisanship cultivates allegiance that is blind and bland. We should pick our fights carefully but preserve our ability to recognize and fight the good fight. A certain boldness in the defence of liberalism may nowadays be a public service, since liberals typically are not deeply reflective about what their regime stands for.

Of course, domestic peace and tranquility and the many political goods unrelated to self-critical, reason-giving citizenship all might counsel in favour of papering over divisive questions. And let me add one additional consideration in favour of reticence: liberalism is an export-commodity and not only a good for domestic consumption.[87] There are places in the world where liberal values are decidedly on the defensive. To encourage the acceptance of liberalism, we might want to keep the price down by playing along with those who would minimize what it stands for.

---

[87] I owe this point to Paul Rosenberg.

My own disposition is to adopt the public conception of justification and to deploy it candidly: public reasonableness matters a great deal, it lies close to the core of our most honourable political practices and aspirations, as we shall see, and it should be compromised on none but the most pressing grounds. We should seek justifications that are reasonable and can be widely seen to be reasonable. Once justification has gone public, however, a good deal has been conceded to pluralism and the burdens of reason. We should be extremely reluctant to go further and avoid articulating what appear to be inescapable but possibly divisive implications of liberalism.[88] To do so would be to strike at the heart of the liberal aspiration to public justification, driving a wedge between critical reflection and political practice.

FOR A PRINCIPLED LIBERAL MODERATION

Lest my defence of 'open justifications openly arrived at' should appear naïve, let me introduce one final consideration. Public justification's acceptance of a certain amount of controversy needs to be set against a wider background that explicitly acknowledges the worth of moderation, a virtue that may serve as a more worthy surrogate for the reticence and evasiveness that implicitly characterize much liberal thinking.

The aim of liberal public justification is to respect diversity while forging a framework of common moral principles that all can understand, accept, and openly affirm before one another. The aim is a transparent, demystified social order, one capable, as Waldron puts it, 'of explaining itself at the

---

[88] I offer this recommendation tentatively. More thought needs to be given to the sorts of considerations Rawls points toward; the historical record and the ideas of practical men must also be examined. See, for example, the *Federalist* no. 37's meditation on the 'necessity of moderating still further our expectations and hopes from the efforts of human sagacity'. Indeed, the *Federalist Papers* exhibit a decided disingenuousness on certain divisive issues: see the treatment of federalism in no. 45, and the treatment of slavery might be another example. One Supreme Court justice riding the circuit in the early years of the republic preached the need for 'that salutary caution with which all public measures ought to be discussed': see Ralph Lerner, 'The Supreme Court as Republican Schoolmaster', in *The Thinking Revolutionary* (Ithaca, NY, 1987), 102.

tribunal of each person's understanding'. Rawls's political conception of justice aims at 'a publicly recognized point of view from which all citizens can examine before one another whether or not their political and social institutions are just'.[89] Achieving a common moral framework allows us to express in politics our common reasonableness, it allows us, in effect, mutually to recognize one another as equally reasonable moral beings.

The only way we can achieve a public moral framework while accepting the deep and permanent fact of pluralism is by putting aside not only the personal interests and religious beliefs, but also some philosophical and moral convictions that other reasonable people will reasonably disagree with. Participants in such a process must share a desire to affirm principles that are not simply justified (or true), but rather capable of being widely seen to be justified (or reasonable).

In the pursuit of reasonable public principles, Rawls seems to insist that we do not strike balances among the different comprehensive moral doctrines (religious and philosophical) that exist in society: to do so would be to abandon the hope of appearing before one another as free and equal, or fully autonomous, citizens.[90] Instead, we put those deep and difficult moral matters to one side, and search for mutually acceptable common ground. We do not accept, moderate, and balance enduring and ineliminable differences of belief and perspective, we seek a shared ground of publicly reasonable consensus.

It is unrealistic to hope for complete or perfect convergence on a shared moral framework. Complete convergence would require a very strong and sustained desire for public moral agreement, and a profound capacity for mutual moral understanding. The kind of common moral standpoint represented by Rawls's original position may be an ideal to be aspired for but, practically speaking, we cannot hope really to converge

---

[89] Rawls, 'Not Metaphysical', p. 229. The public role of political theory is to provide a 'shared point of view among citizens with opposing religious, philosophical and moral convictions': 'Constructivism', p. 542. A well-ordered society is one in which everyone 'accepts and knows that others accept' the same first principles of political morality: 'Constructivism', p. 521.

[90] Rawls, 'Priority', pp. 275–6; and see 'Constructivism', pp. 522, 527, 532.

on a common understanding of basic political principles.[91] We must be prepared, in political life, for a not unreasonable measure of moral opacity. People will be moved to peek, as it were, out from behind the veil of ignorance not only by self-interest but also by the variety of moral beliefs excluded by the drive for principles all reasonable people can accept.

Moderation is a virtue that comes to the fore when we acknowledge that after public reasonableness has done its work (or as much work as reasonable people are prepared to allow it to do), our moral perspectives will inevitably remain plural and divergent. Moderation allows us to accept the fact that a large and diverse group of reasonable people will never completely unite on precisely the same moral platform.[92] Even the best possible liberal settlement will have something of the character of a composite of irreducibly dissimilar parts.

It would be nice to think that all of us—rich and poor, libertarian and socialist, Catholic, Jew, Amish, and Jehovah's Witness—could stand before one another simply in our moral capacity; and, indeed, we should aspire to do so. But we must accept the fact that at the end of the political day reasonable people will continue to disagree and moral perspectives will remain divergent.[93] At that point, the most reasonable thing may well be mutually to moderate our claims in the face of the reasonable claims of others, to balance, and split at least some of our differences.

Liberal moderation builds on respect and goes beyond toleration. We respect persons and views that we regard as reasonable. Even when we cannot really respect a particular view (anti-Semitism, racism, and other views based on sheer prejudice) we may still tolerate its expression, partly because it

[91] Indeed, Rawls's own account of the burdens of reason suggests the same conclusion: 'To some unknown extent, our total experience, our whole course of life up until now, shapes the way we assess evidence and weigh moral and political values, and our total experiences surely differ': Rawls, 'Domain', p. 237.

[92] There are inklings of all this in Rawls: he implies a need for moderation and compromise by speaking not of perfect but 'sufficient' convergence ('Constructivism', pp. 561, 562, 564).

[93] It may even be valuable that we cannot put all of our distinguishing features aside when entering the political realm. It is probably no mistake that so many of the great Supreme Court cases have involved anarchists, Jehovah's witnesses, Christian Scientists, creationists, Japanese American, black Americans, etc.

is being expressed by a person: we wish to respect that person as a being capable of reason and we wish to respect speech (the vehicle of reason) as such. We tolerate the anti-Semite by allowing him to express his views, but we concede no ground to him: we do not accommodate the anti-Semite's views because we do not respect them; we do not compromise with those views, we approach them with resoluteness rather than moderation.

Moderation goes beyond toleration. There are, for example, many reasonable arguments on both sides of the abortion debate. The abortion question is so vexing, in a sense, precisely because there are weighty reasons on both sides, and it is easy to see how reasonable people can come down on either side. On policy issues like abortion, which seems to come down to a fairly close call between two well-reasoned sets of arguments, moderation would lead us not only to respect our opponents but to compromise with them, to find some middle ground which gives something to each side: legalized abortion, perhaps, but only up to a certain point in the pregnancy, and only with consultations that help insure that the decision to abort is carefully considered.[94]

The principled moderation I am defending is a liberal virtue justified by the respect owed to our shared reasonableness and the difficulty of occupying a common moral standpoint, of exercising our common capacity for reasonableness in the same way. Taking moderation seriously would lead us to qualify Dworkin's insistence that the party with the strongest case on balance (no matter how close a call) has a right to win. The best solution may sometimes be to give something to each side.[95] Moderation in the face of very strong competing cases offers a way of honouring not simply the best case but also the case that is very strong. In such instances there is a principled

---

[94] Amy Gutmann suggests this in her 'Public Philosophy'.

[95] In her recent book comparing the abortion laws of various nations, Mary Ann Glendon argues that European patterns, effectively giving something to both sides (respecting the woman's right to choose up to a point, but requiring consultations, etc.) are superior: see *Abortion and Divorce in Western Law* (Cambridge, Mass., 1987). We should resist the conclusion that principled moderation furnishes a general principle in favour of judicial deference: not all cases are like abortion. We need not assume that there are very strong arguments on both sides of most questions.

case for judicial statesmanship, for brokering of principles, but not for pragmatism or a blanket deference to legislatures.[96]

This liberal moderation is principled because it is grounded in the most basic commitments of public justification itself: respect for our common reasonableness. There are, of course, other varieties of, and grounds for, moderation. A pragmatic moderation would be guided by a strategic sense of what will maximize the realization of important values; a prudent moderation would embrace compromise in order to avoid conflict. Both of these forms of moderation temper public justification and undermine the kind of respect it embodies.

To accept a principled moderation is to admit that a mutually transparent political order is unrealizable. Explicitly embracing the value of moderation means that we represent citizens in public justification with their reasonable differences and disagreements (and some measure of partiality of perspective) intact. In this way we come to grips with the residual and realistically ineliminable moral diversity that (on my analysis) underlies liberal reticence without compromising on liberal respect for reasonableness.

I am not, I should emphasize, arguing that we should celebrate our inability to abstract away from some of our differences; we should acknowledge but not idealize our incapacity to achieve a common moral perspective. We should, rather, accept this limitation as a given feature of the human condition and adopt an attitude that allows us to cope with it constructively while striving to live up to realistic liberal ideals.

CONCLUSION

In a letter written in 1822 Jefferson declared: 'I trust that there is not a young man now living in the United States who will not die a Unitarian.'[97] Thomas Pangle interprets Jefferson as recognizing that in a liberal society,

---

[96] See Stanley C. Brubaker, 'Reconsidering Dworkin's Case for Judicial Activism', *The Journal of Politics*, 46 (1984), 503–19, an insightful account which, however, too hastily leaps for deference.

[97] Thomas Pangle, *The Making of Modern Republicanism* (Chicago, Ill., 1988), 83.

The only genuine truth, or objective validity, religion can evince is its tolerance, its refusal to press its theological pretensions too seriously or strenuously; the only genuine measure of the merits of a religion is its effectiveness in promoting peace, lawfulness, and the moral habits conducive to support for the rights of man.[98]

Jefferson's expectations about the emergence of a liberal religion in America may seem, in light of the upsurgence of religious fundamentalism, naïve. But one cannot help but be impressed by the contrast between America's 'true believers' and those in much of the rest of the world. Compare the violent reaction of many Muslims to Salman Rushdie's *The Satanic Verses* with the relatively tame response of Western Christians to the film, *The Last Temptation of Christ*. Not to mention the rather surprising moderation and general law-abidingness of Christian fundamentalists in the face of America's liberal abortion laws. If it seems that 'we are all Unitarians now', that is because of the success of liberalism in pervasively shaping a common culture, not because all religions are by nature liberal.

Liberalism counts on the active support of liberal religions, and the passive acquiescence of some others, but it is deeply at odds with certain religious faiths (from Augustinian Catholicism to Islamic fundamentalism) and many other ways of life. When liberalism succeeds in establishing itself that will be because liberal political values and those values that support liberalism come to be regarded as more important than competing packages of values. Liberalism will succeed and become stable and robust where persons, their largest moral views, institutions, and society as a whole, are liberalized.

The public conception of justification may seem to embrace the concerns of 'post-modernist' philosophers like Rorty who deny the availability of objective standards of truth.[99] While

---

[98] Pangle, *The Making of Modern Republicanism*, p. 83. Pangle may press a bit too hard here. Liberalism helps make religion liberal, but it need not deny that aspects of religious truth transcend politics.

[99] Rorty, for example, embraces and claims that Rawls adopts a form of pragmatism which 'makes it impossible to ask the question "Is ours a moral society?" It makes it impossible to think that there is something which stands to my community as my community stands to me . . .'. Richard Rorty, 'The Contingency of Community', *London Review of Books*, 24 July 1986, p. 13. Moral judgments, for Rorty, reduce to ways in which a society defines its identity and distinguishes itself from others: see 'The Priority of Democracy over Philosophy', in Robert Vaughn, ed., *The Virginia Statute of Religious Freedom: Two Hundred Years After* (Madison, Wis., 1988).

acknowledging the practical limits of reason, public justification does not embrace conventionalism, localism, or scepticism. Reason establishes the contours and substance of moderation: it is reasonable to want to live in accordance not only with reasonable principles but with principles that all can see to be reasonable. We have good reasons for tempering our expectations about the public efficacy of reason, not for abandoning our aspiration to govern ourselves reasonably.

Even where citizens share a desire to establish and support political institutions that can be commonly affirmed as reasonable, fully public justifications on controversial issues (ones that all reasonable people really do accept) will often be impossible to come by—we must reconcile ourselves to that. While it may fail to achieve a construction that all reasonable people can agree upon, public reflection can help us identify and rule out *unreasonable* options. It can, as well, help us narrow the gaps and negotiate the tensions among public and personal values.[100]

Because it respects public arguments and evidence, reasonable persons and the limits of reason as located in persons, public justification is distinctly liberal and democratic, substantive and partisan. Where liberals see respect for free and equal persons, some religious people are going to see 'secular humanism' and the hegemony of a way of thinking that owes a lot to science and the enlightenment but that is deeply at odds with some forms of religion. This cannot be avoided. Liberals offer true believers, like everyone else, a sphere of privacy and the opportunity to continue arguing. The liberal must, in the end, defend his partisanship and not evade it. If liberalism is justified that must be, in part at least, because of the superiority of justifications based on widely acceptable reasons and public arguments, and because reasonable people really are worthy of liberal respect.

It might be taken as a measure of the ultimate 'success' of liberalism that it has constituted our culture and personalities so deeply that we hardly notice what it stands for and what it stands against, and what we stand for and against. If, in taking firm hold on a society, liberalism induces a kind of forgetful-

---

[100] Again, this seems to me to be the impetus for Aristotle's defence of the mixed regime in Book 3 of the *Politics*.

ness about its own deepest implications, we might call that a 'political' success, a sleight-of-hand by which liberalism appears to be different things to different people and nothing very much to anyone. This merely 'political' success is, however, a failure of public justification.

In political practice, as I shall explain in the chapters that follow, something like a commitment to public justification has informed and ennobled liberal institutions. The American Constitution, for example, is an aspirational document that provides not only institutions to argue within, but ideals to strive for and argue about, 'standard maxims', as Lincoln remarked, like basic human equality, a maxim

for free society which should be familiar to all: constantly looked to, constantly laboured for, and even, though never perfectly attained, constantly approximated, and thereby constantly spreading and deepening its influence and augmenting the happiness and value of life to all people, of all colours, everywhere.[101]

The founding era, on this view, must be seen not as a completed act of liberal statecraft, but as the initiation of an ongoing project of publicly interpreting, questioning, debating, and reshaping, not just the details but (at least occasionally) the fundamentals of constitutional government. The task of liberal citizenship, as we shall see, is not only to enjoy private rights, but to struggle to complete the unfinished business of liberal construction.

Does the public conception of justification, discussed here, overcome the old opposition between politics and philosophy? That opposition is, in a sense, eased: philosophers are required to acknowledge that in politics extreme rigour must give way to accessibility, and non-philosophers gain respect on grounds of their shared reasonableness. Public justification politicizes philosophy while philosophizing politics, moderating but not denying the potentially divisive nature of critical reason.[102]

Public justification is a core liberal goal, one that informs

---

[101] *The Lincoln–Douglas Debates*, ed. Robert W. Johannsen (New York, 1965), 304; and see Barber, *Constitution*, p. 60 and *passim*, from which I draw the theme of the US Constitution as aspirational.
[102] Rawls, 'Overlapping Consensus', p. 24.

practical aspirations and political institutions that liberals can be proud of. But public justification is not our only political goal. We want the freedom to live our own lives, and so an intermittent release from political argument. We want peace, and more than that, we want comity or concord.

Comity is a political good that is not quite the same as moral consensus, as Richard Hofstadter explains:

Comity exists in society to the degree that those enlisted in its contending interests have a basic minimal regard for each other. . . . The basic humanity of the opposition is not forgotten; civility is not abandoned; the sense that a community life must be carried on after the ascerbic issues of the moment have been fought over and won is seldom far out of mind. . . .[103]

And in the first *Federalist*, Publius urged moderation as a means to comity even more forcefully:

So numerous indeed and so powerful are the causes which serve to give a false bias to judgment, that we, upon many occasions, see wise and good men on the wrong as well as on the right side of questions of the first magnitude to society. This circumstance, if duly attended to, would furnish a lesson of moderation to those who are ever so much persuaded of their being in the right in any controversy.

Comity, or concord, requires a gift for conciliation and a willingness to compromise. Liberal moderation furnishes good grounds for principled accommodation.

Grounds exist outside public justification and its aims for other forms of moderation (a prudent moderation, for example, in the face of rancour and imminent violence). We do well, however, to make room for a principled moderation at the most basic level, in our understanding of public justification. To do so allows us to define and defend a form of moderation whose justification grows out of the commitment to reasonableness itself, and so to extend moderation in the first instance on grounds that help draw people into the process of public reason. Principled moderation supports the hope for an ever more reasonable political order.

[103] Richard Hofstadter, *The Progressive Historians* (Chicago, Ill., 1979), 454.

3

Law and Liberal Citizenship

The moral lodestar of liberalism is, I have argued, the project of public justification, which melds the aims of philosophical criticism with those of liberal respect and democratic equality. It seeks a reflective moral standard that is accessible to people as we know them. Chapters 3–5 explain how liberal political institutions (judicial, legislative, and executive) all participate in the task of public justification, but in ways that distinctively combine that task with other political aims. Public justification politicizes philosophy; liberal political institutions carry further and specify that politicization, bringing justification to bear in the operation of politics.

No sovereign will commands ultimate authority in a liberal community of interpreters: no judicial, legislative, executive, or even popular body has the final say about what is constitutionally permissible. Decisions must be made but the political conversation is never closed. Every authoritative ruling or decision is open to challenge and overruling on the basis of better interpretations of the principles of political morality commonly acknowledged to be supreme: the guiding, limiting principles of liberal justice. Liberal law, properly understood, promotes a community of interpreters: a citizenry of self-critical reason-givers.

A polity characterized by many competing conceptions of the good life may seem to be the very antithesis of a consensual community. And yet, liberal justice overarches the diversity of liberal society informing its constitution and providing a public morality—a community property, publicly affirmed and constantly revitalized and updated in being applied to new circumstances. All citizens properly participate in liberal politics by acting in accordance with their own best understandings of the demands of liberal principles, by reviewing official acts in light of these understandings, and even by resorting to civil disobedience when circumstances demand. Liberal politics invites all citizens to participate in the process of making, testing, and refining law.

In thinking about a realistic liberal political ethic, we want to steer between moral Pollyannaism and cynicism. We should try to form expectations that may be hard to live up to but not impossible to approximate or that miss the point of actual liberal institutions. In practice we may not live up to the reason-giving and reason-demanding expectations of public justification. But our performance is not poor enough to warrant collapsing liberal expectations into the cynical view. The courtroom in particular is at once a political arena and a forum of principle, one that draws the limits of collective power while also injecting principles into our politics. As Cardozo put it,

The restraining power of the judiciary does not manifest its chief worth in the few cases in which the legislature has gone beyond the lines that mark the limits of discretion. Rather shall we find its chief worth in making vocal and audible the ideals that might otherwise be silenced, in giving them continuity of life and of expression, in guiding and directing choice within the limits where choice ranges.[1]

Articulating a legal framework capable of serving as a liberal means to the ends of citizenship, virtue, and community is the burden of this chapter. I begin by considering the resources of a legal framework in which principles of justice are interpreted by citizens and public officials alike. The public morality of liberal law helps provide the basis for an ideal of politics more broadly. In this way I hope to show that defects in the liberal self-image can be made over by resources implicit in liberalism itself.

LIBERAL PUBLIC MORALITY: LAW AND POLITICS

One could conceive of liberal self-government without the institutions of public education or public welfare or any

---

[1] Cardozo, *Judicial Process*, p. 94.

number of other enterprises that nearly all modern states actually engage in. But not law. It is simply impossible to imagine the politics of the 'great societies' of the modern world—large, open, commercial, and free—without widespread respect for general rules of conduct. Of all the institutions that support modern liberal societies none is more basic or central than that of law.

Liberalism stands for choice: the equal freedom of persons to choose religious beliefs and practices, an occupation, leisure pursuits, and so on. Law co-ordinates the free choices of unseen millions, and sets the terms for the 'anonymous collaboration' of modern mass society.[2] Law helps impart order to liberty by imposing on all free actions certain general conditions (if you want to make a contract get two witnesses) and limits (don't coerce, defraud, or harm others) that together create a system of mutual self-restraint harmonizing the freedom of each with the freedom of all. Substantially *liberal* law, as Lon Fuller puts it, 'does not tell a man what he should do to accomplish specific ends set by a lawgiver; it furnishes him with baselines against which to organize his life with his fellows.'[3] Liberal rules of law are, in Adam Smith's metaphor, like rules of grammar rather than precepts for 'what is sublime and elegant in composition'.[4] Liberal laws prescribe not a 'what' to say, but a 'how' to say whatever one chooses, imposing 'adverbial' conditions on the self-chosen actions of individuals.[5]

The rule of law requires that government act, in the main, through the promulgation in advance of reasonably general rules of conduct. In this way, law imposes on potentially arbitrary power regularized forms that promote predictability and individual security. Criminal proceedings must honour a due process containing elaborate requirements of official

[2] The phrase is Fuller's, *Morality of Law*, p. 22.

[3] Fuller, *The Principles of Social Order*, ed. Kenneth I. Winston (Durham, NC, 1981), 234.

[4] Adam Smith, *The Theory of Moral Sentiments*, ed. D. D. Raphael and A. L. Macfie (Oxford, 1979), 327, and see Fuller, *Morality*, p. 6, and Friederich Hayek, *Law, Legislation and Liberty*, vol. ii, *The Mirage of Social Justice* (Chicago, Ill., 1978), 12–15. I do not, by this comparison, mean to suggest that law is in any strong sense neutral with regard to the choices that people make or the preferences they have: liberal law is character and regime shaping.

[5] See Oakeshott, 'Rule of Law', *passim*.

restraint and fair play that guarantee a basic respect even for those charged with injuring others.[6] Before a man can be denied his life, liberty, or property, a case must be made in an independent and impartial court of law charged with insuring that justice is administered fairly and due process respected.

Law stands for a certain kind of order: the mutual observance of general, public rules and procedures. Liberal law not only establishes the ends and limits of power, it also provides a setting and structure for public justification. Indeed, the impartial, politically independent institution of the court provides a most promising setting in which to approach the reasoned reflection required by justification. The question is whether and how far public justification can be pursued via law without significantly impairing its ordering function.

Plato distinguished two ways of thinking about the law. It can, on the one hand, be kept short and simple: do this, don't do that. But shorter is not always better. On this first understanding, law would be like the doctor of a slave who 'gives his commands just like a headstrong tyrant and hurries off...'. Laws might, however, include not only general statements of what is required, but explanations addressed to the reason of those receiving laws. The second model makes law more like a doctor ministering to a free man, treating both illness and patient, 'from their beginning and according to nature, communing with the patient himself and his friends, and he both learns something himself from the invalids and, as much as he can, teaches the one who is sick. He doesn't give orders until he has in some sense persuaded....'[7] Tyranny is power without rhyme or reason, and law as rules precludes only the most egregious forms of arbitrariness: the 'lawful' ruler may opt for a draconian simplicity rather than the more complex, patient, and respectful mode of rule with reason-giving.

Legal positivism elevates the ordering function of law: the positivist's law aspires to be a clear and settled social standard of conduct, it shies away from the mystification and conflict that could result from conflating law and morality, rule and

---

[6] I draw here on Kateb's excellent essay, 'Remarks on the Procedures of Constitutional Democracy'.

[7] Plato, *The Laws*, trans. Thomas Pangle (Chicago, Ill., 1988), Bk. 6, p. 107.

critical reasoning. Legal positivists view the law as a system of rules whose validity is a question not of their substance but of adherence to an established and accepted form of enactment, which H. L. A. Hart calls the 'rule of recognition'.[8] A legal system exists when the laws are generally obeyed by citizens while judges and other public officials affirm the master rule as a normative standard.[9]

The authority of law, for the positivist, resides in its peremptoriness: law is not meant to initiate but to cut off conversation and deliberation.[10] As Hobbes put it: 'COMMAND is, where a man saith, *Doe this*, or *Doe not this*, without expecting any other reason than the will of him that sayes it.'[11] What the law is need not bear much relation to what the law ought to be: it does not follow from the mere fact that a rule is immoral that it is not a rule of law, and morally desirable rules are not necessarily legal.[12]

The point of positivism is to separate law and morals, to raise the law above moral conflict by distinguishing the question of legal validity from that of moral goodness. Emphasizing law's non-ideological and neutral qualities, positivists seek a law whose authority is compatible with any number of ultimate moral commitments: 'what is law is a matter of social fact, and the identification of law involves no moral argument'.[13] For positivists, indeed, the reasons why citizens obey the law are their own business.[14] The positivist's law is concerned, at base, not with moral reasons or debate but

---

[8] H. L. A. Hart, *The Concept of Law* (Oxford, 1961), 97–107.

[9] Hart, *Concept*, pp. 112–13.

[10] H. L. A. Hart, *Essays on Bentham* (Oxford, 1982), 243.

[11] Thomas Hobbes, *Leviathan*, ed. C. B. Macpherson (Harmondsworth, 1981), ch. 25, p. 303, and see Hart, *Bentham*, p. 253.

[12] See Hart, 'Positivism Law and Morals', in *Essays in Jurisprudence and Philosophy* (Oxford, 1983), 55. Hart does allow that a legal system must conform with a 'minimum content of natural law': see Hart, *Concept*, pp. 189–207.

[13] Joseph Raz, *The Authority of Law: Essays on Law and Morality* (Oxford, 1983), 38. I have benefited from the instructive discussion in Judith N. Shklar, *Legalism* (Cambridge, Mass., 1986), Introduction and Part I, esp. pp. 41–2.

[14] Hart, *Bentham*, p. 256; citizens must accept, but not necessarily believe in the moral legitimacy of the legal institutions, ibid. 268. Hart holds that legal and moral obligations are distinct, indeed that terms like duty and obligation have different meanings in the two contexts; Raz sees a closer connection between legal and moral obligation, see Hart, *Bentham*, ch. 6.

with common subscription to properly instituted rules of conduct.

The positivistic approach to law has definite advantages. There is much to be said for having a set of authoritative rules whose validity is distinct, to a great extent, from substantive judgments of moral value that are bound to be controversial. There is much to be said for emphasizing, as positivists do, the centrality to law of clarity, publicity, and obedience. To the extent that liberals fear controversy, and seek political institutions whose authority is independent of substantive moral agreement, they have reason to be drawn toward a positivistic understanding of law.

Positivists often concern themselves with describing not the best way of thinking about law, but only the minimum conditions of a legal system or with what 'law' must mean if it means anything at all. Even in its minimal manifestations, however, law is not a politically neutral phenomenon. For government under law must operate through rules that are publicized, prospective, understandable, capable of being complied with, and have some measure of generality and stability. Even in its minimal form law will promote particular virtues and values, such as self-restraint, publicity, criticism, regularity, generality, and limited power. Historically, as Judith N. Shklar points out, the commitment to legal positivism 'is an expression of the liberal desire to preserve individual autonomy, and to preserve the diversity of morals which is in constant danger of ideological and governmental interference'.[15] Law does not serve all political values and in the most unfortunate circumstances may require throwing away the rulebook. Even a liberal polity cannot live by law alone.

The most basic requirements and aims of a legal system include those highlighted by the positivists. Without widespread understanding and obedience law would fail to achieve its basic ordering and co-ordinating function. Positivists are right to insist that a morally iniquitous rule may count as valid law; legal systems are not as such necessarily moral or liberal. My concern, however, is with how law should be seen within a specifically liberal political framework, and in circumstances

---

[15] Shklar, *Legalism*, p. 42.

that permit the pursuit of legal ideals beyond mere obedience to rules. Positivism's emphasis on preserving the clear and settled quality of law could, if taken too far, lead us to drive the moralists from the temple of law, delivering a blow to public justification and the higher aims of liberal law itself.

Let us understand the aims of law as several: rule-bound order as well as moral criticism, publicity, and debate. Combining these aims within law creates certain tensions but not a forced match: government by law facilitates public discussion by respecting citizens and putting them on notice of political expectations and aims. Government by law is importantly public government. Even the minimal cases of law prefigure and promote discernibly liberal aspirations and ideals, especially once the forms and expectations of the potent ethic of legalism permeate society broadly.

We can, with liberals like Fuller and Dworkin, reject the separation of law and morality. Liberal law is composed not only of rules, but also of certain underlying aims and principles: ordered liberty, fairness, due process, reasonableness, and opposition to cruelty. Interpreting law is not only a matter of applying rules, it is also a matter of interpreting legal principles many of which have an important moral dimension.

The existence of principles within the law has a number of important implications. Moral principles underlie and help justify the law, and by extending to cover the gaps between legal rules these principles help settle hard cases, cases not settlable by reference to explicit legal rules. These moral principles exist in advance of official decisions, they help fill the gaps between rules and are binding on public officials and citizens alike.[16] For positivists, judges *make* law in hard cases. For Dworkin, there is always law to interpret and apply: 'a legal obligation might be imposed by a constellation of principles as well as by an established rule ... a legal obligation exists whenever the case supporting such an obligation, in terms of binding legal principles of different sorts, is stronger than the case against it.'[17] Because moral principles are woven

---

[16] See Dworkin, *Rights*, ch. 1.
[17] Ibid. 44.

into the fabric of law, the conscientious adjudicator is charged with weighing the principles and articulating the best interpretation of the law applying to a hard case, rather than 'creating' a rule according to his discretion.

The prior existence of legal principles and a consequent 'right to win' justifies a well-reasoned judicial decision and legitimates the creation of a new rule. Because law is a seamless web of legal rules and principles, the judge deciding a hard case need not refer to independent conceptions of policy or defer to 'more democratic' branches of government. For the positivist judge law and morality are distinct, moral principles do not fill the gaps between rules, and so hard cases arise with no right answer. Positivist judges may decide hard cases by gauging the policy preferences of legislators or their own conception of social utility or the public good. But for law as public morality, the courtroom is a moral arena, a Forum of Principle where the law is considered a seamless web of rules and principles determining the rights of parties and the duty of the judge.[18]

We should, as Dworkin puts it, 'aspire that adjudication be a matter of principle' because, even if the idealized picture is unrealizable, 'we gain even through the attempt'.[19] A morally principled judicial process helps insure that our fundamental interests depend not on mere majority will or considerations of policy, but on principled public standards. A conception of law infused with moral aspirations helps draw political practice toward the ideal of public justification.

The debate over the proper nature of legal interpretation could have wide political implications. In the constitutional context, the relevant principles will often be large and momentous: ordered liberty, equality, fairness, privacy. The virtue of law as public morality, for our purposes, is not that it is a superior analysis of the necessary meaning of 'law', but rather that it provides a way frankly of acknowledging the political value of folding the interpretation of moral principles into the task of adjudication, and thence into politics more

[18] Dworkin, 'The Forum of Principle', in Dworkin, *A Matter of Principle* (Cambridge, Mass., 1985), 33–71.
[19] Dworkin, *Rights*, p. 338.

broadly. Law as public morality endorses without embarrass-
ment a robust judicial engagement in public moral justification through law.

The interpretation of law is necessarily a political enterprise,
but it 'is not a matter of personal or partisan politics'.[20] The
public morality of law stands for a principled, publicly accessible, and even participatory process of interpretation. The
wedding of legal and moral theory predicates the authority of
official decisions on the quality of a judge's public reasoning
from principles accessible to all:

[I]t is unfair for officials to act except on the basis of a general public
theory that will constrain them to consistency, provide a public
standard for testing or debating or predicting what they will do, and
not allow appeals to unique intuitions that might mask prejudice or
self-interest in particular cases.[21]

The public morality of law creates a certain kind of moral
community, one in which political officials answer to the
public not only for following the rules but also for their
conscientious adherence to shared political principles.

One benefit of recognizing that moral principles underlie
legal rules is that those principles help settle hard cases—they
allow us to say that hard cases often have 'right answers'. But
is the publicity of legal interpretation enough to insure that
legal interpretation will not become a mere cacophony of
conflicting moral perspectives, a high-minded chaos? Making
too much of legal principles might elevate the spirit at the
expense of the letter of law. Making too much of the morally
principled character of law might lead to a flourishing of
exceptions and defeat the goal of living by clear and general
rules. Adam Smith emphasized that,

In the practice of other virtues, our conduct should rather be directed
by a certain idea of propriety, by a certain taste for a particular tenor
of conduct, than by any regard to a precise maxim or rule; and we
should consider the end and foundation of the rule, more than the
rule itself. But it is otherwise with regard to justice: the man who in

---

[20] Dworkin, 'How Law is Like Literature', *Principle*, p. 146.
[21] Dworkin, *Rights*, pp. 162–3.

that refines the least, and adheres with the most obstinate steadfast-
ness to the general rules themselves, is the most commendable, and
the most to be depended upon.[22]

Should liberal moralists worry that the acceptance of their
view of law would substitute an endless moral debate for the
order, regularity, and predictability of law? Does the principled thrust of liberal legalism risk transforming the framework of rule-governed order into a forum of principled
conflict?

We need to specify and limit the moral principles that
underlie the law. The imperatives of *public* justification, properly understood, help impose the necessary filter: in thinking
about authoritative legal principles we will favour ones that
can be widely seen to be reasonable. When we move from
public justification in the abstract to particular legal institutions, we can further refine and specify the kinds of principles
that are operative.

One way to tame the potentially divisive moralism of
principled interpretation while admitting that law cannot do
without principles would be to accept that principles underlie
rules at various points while denying that the interpretation of
these principles is a moral task. A subtle version of positivism
could admit that principles often underlie legal rules, but insist
that interpreting these principles is a historical art. We would
look to our constitution and inherited legal materials to
discern the principles and ideals 'immanent' in our legal and
political tradition, distinguishing those immanent sources
from the transcendent ideals spawned by abstract theorizing.
The question in hard cases would not be which account of the
rules, precedents, and principles makes for the morally best
outcome in this case, but which account best fits the received
legal materials: which account of the legal rules and principles
implies the fewest and smallest mistakes in the received legal
record.

Principled positivism is a coherent view of the judge's task.
Liberalism stands, however, for a certain kind of respect for
persons: respect for our shared capacity for public reasonableness. As liberals, we want to incorporate the project of critical

---

[22] Smith, *Sentiments*, p. 175.

moral justification into our political practices, crafting institutions that invite criticism and promote moral improvement. We want, in other words, public justification and not only history to infuse the spirit of legal interpretation.

Even on the moralized view of law, a grain of truth lies behind the attempt to make legal interpretation historical: authoritative legal interpretation will be less constructive than straight moral theory. The judicial office has specific functions within the scheme of liberal politics as a whole: to maintain a going system of public, prospective, and justifiable general rules. We want legal institutions to be open to better interpretations of old principles, but we also want those interpretations to be disciplined and structured by fidelity to the forms and received mass of law (including the constitution, past judicial decisions, legislative acts, and so on). The peculiar authority of the judge, and the character of law, depend on the notion that adjudication turns on the interpretation of materials that are already, in some sense, given. Received sources of law are, after all, what put people on notice as to what their legal obligations are.

We do not want judges who simply ask themselves in each instance what justice requires. The judge, as Cardozo puts it,

is not a knight-errant roaming at will in pursuit of his own ideal of beauty or goodness. . . . He is to exercise a discretion informed by tradition, methodized by analogy, disciplined by system, and subordinated to 'the primordial necessity of order in social life'. Wide enough in all conscience is the field of discretion that remains.[23]

Being a judge is not a warrant for unstructured philosophizing. Occupying the judicial office imposes a special duty of fidelity to received legal materials. Fidelity to law requires that a lawyer or judge or other public official start with provisional acceptance of a given body of law: the constitution, statutes of various kinds, precedents at different levels, implicit principles, traditions, practices. All of these help to establish the basis for a judge's theory of law, and do not merely set the outer limits of it.

[23] Cardozo, *Process*, p. 141.

Dworkin usefully distinguishes 'background' from 'institutional' rights, as a way of limiting the range and kind of moral arguments relevant for deciding hard cases: 'background rights . . . provide a justification for political decisions by society in the abstract, and institutional rights . . . provide a justification for a decision by some particular and specified political institution.'[24] The rights invoked by judges must be 'institutional rather than background rights, and they must be legal rather than some other form of institutional rights'.[25] But the force of this requirement depends upon a second metric, the degree of 'autonomy' that characterizes legal institutions: 'institutional autonomy insulates an official's institutional duty from the greater part of background political morality.'[26] So, one might believe that Rawls's distributive argument furnishes the moral basis for a right to basic welfare benefits without believing that the US Constitution provides the legal grounds for such a right. Or a public official might believe that abortion is morally wrong, but regard the grounds for that belief to be private in a way that would make it inappropriate to seek to impose it on other people through politics.

Law and the judicial office are like other institutions and offices in having a certain autonomy from morality pure and simple. Even if a chess referee is, when 'off-duty', an egalitarian, institutional constraints prevent him from awarding the prize money in a tournament to the poorest player rather than the one with the most points.[27] His duty as a referee is not only to enforce the rules but to exercise his judgment in such a way as to 'protect the character of the game'.[28] The referee, according to Dworkin, should regard his personal 'background morality' as irrelevant: the character of the game and his role are mutually defining and determinate.[29] Consider Justice Felix Frankfurter's agonized deliberations over the school desegregation case:

However passionately any of us may hold egalitarian views, however fiercely any of us may believe that such a policy of segregation as undoubtedly expresses the tenacious conviction of Southern States [is] both unjust and short-sighted, he travels outside

---

[24] Dworkin, *Rights*, p. 93.   [25] Ibid. 101.   [26] Ibid.
[27] Ibid. 101.   [28] Ibid. 102.   [29] Ibid. 101–2.

his judicial authority if for this private reason alone he declares unconstitutional the policy of segregation.[30]

Immorality alone does not establish unconstitutionality or legal nullity.

In chess as in law the referee or judge has no discretion in any strong sense; the participants have 'rights', and the officials a duty to uphold the rules and the 'character' of the game, preserving the integrity of the enterprise in which they are engaged. The integrity of the enterprise is protected from subversions (such as an egalitarian referee or participants willing to resort to bribery, or a judge committed to Marxism rather than the US Constitution's liberalism) by institutionalized enforcement mechanisms and sanctions animated by the shared understandings of players and officials who mutually acknowledge the value of the game and who accept a duty to protect its character. This duty, to be effective must regulate and subordinate the desire to take the prize or any other desire that might lead an official to favour poor players, or a player to cheat, or anyone to otherwise subvert the norms that define 'a good play of the game'.

Law has a certain measure of moral autonomy. Holding an office within a valuable institution such as law gives one special obligations and responsibilities to that institution. Every office, from that of judge to legislator to executive to citizen, is a moral filter of particular quality and strength: the rights and privileges that we should have, from the point of view of public justification, are not necessarily the ones that we do have or should have within any particular institution. Institutions have, and are suited to, particular purposes; their proper working depends upon the co-operation of participants who roughly agree on aims and purposes. Participants must realize that using an institution for purposes at odds with its intrinsic point or character risks corrupting and destroying the institution. Using a chess match to promote the redistribution of income undermines the integrity of the competition and so the institution of competitive chess. Using legal interpretation to promote moral values that have no proper

---

[30] Quoted in Richard Kluger, *Simple Justice* (New York, 1976), 684. The case, of course, was *Brown v. Board of Education* 347 US 483 (1954).

standing within the law could undermine respect for the rules and the forms of law.

Of course, if a terrible earthquake or other disaster strikes the locale of a chess competition, the referee would properly close down the match, give the prize money to the Red Cross, and pitch in to the relief effort. No office is or should be totally impervious to all moral concerns: the most basic moral claims can never be evaded because institutional imperatives cannot override them. Being subject to the orders of a superior or to the imperatives of an institution could not excuse participation in gross immorality. Referee, judge, soldier, and citizen ought all to make sure that the actions required by their roles, and the character of the institutions in which they participate, pass the test of critical moral reflection. Neither law, chess, nor any other human enterprise is entirely autonomous of morality. A judge, for example, should not blindly follow precedent, the expectations of his profession, or those of the public, any more than a soldier should blindly follow orders.

Official norms and institutional expectations always contain a certain flexibility and room for personal style, improvement, and innovation. Legal, commercial, medical, and other institutions will be open to and shaped by the participants broadest understandings of fairness, reasonable conduct, and so on. When an institution serves basic moral aims (such as the pursuit of justice and the preservation of liberty) innovation should in part be guided, and improvement measured, by public moral standards which officials must determine as best they can. Office-holders and role players must negotiate some working compatibility between official and broader personal morality.

The partial openness of offices and institutions to wider moral considerations gives rise to tensions that provoke criticism and debate. As moral beings we must often negotiate the tensions among our different institutional commitments (professional, personal, patriotic, religious) and our most comprehensive understanding of morality. The moral life of reflective individuals is animated by conflicts caused by multiple allegiances, commitments, and memberships, conflicts that are the predictable consequence of life in vast, open, and diverse liberal societies.

Just as public moral principles affirmed as such cannot be isolated and relegated to a certain sphere of our lives, so too a judge's official view of a constitution's morality is not entirely insulated from his or her 'background' or comprehensive personal moral views (the same might be said of public officials and citizens more broadly). And some laws, such as the American Constitution, explicitly pose moral questions for interpreters.

What is special about the judge's role? The judge's aim is to pursue two distinct basic values: fidelity to received law and critical public justification. Liberal legalism, as Dworkin puts it,

> does not aim to recapture, even for present law, the ideals or practical purposes of the politicians who first created it. It aims rather to justify what they did . . . in an overall story worth telling now, a story with a complex claim: that present practice can be organized by and justified in principles sufficiently attractive to provide an honourable future.[31]

Legal interpretation has complex aims: to take public justification seriously but in the context of carrying forward the valuable enterprise of law, 'A successful interpretation must not only fit but also justify the practice it interprets.'[32] Because justification is public, the reasons and arguments should be widely acceptable in the right way. Because justification as practised by the judge is legal it is interpretive: it seeks to respect the forms of law (generality, prospectivity, and so on) and received legal materials. The kind of respect for law that liberals want is informed by the morally critical spirit of public justification.

For an argument to count as an interpretation it *must* pass certain threshold tests of fit with received legal materials: it may show some but not all of those materials to be mistaken. Legal history limits the kinds of arguments that can count as interpretations. Hard cases arise when different interpretations of a statute or line of cases or constitutional provision all pass the threshold tests of fit. Then a judge's political morality

---

[31] Dworkin, *Empire*, pp. 227–8.
[32] Ibid. 285.

may be directly engaged, because then the question is which interpretation of for example the equal protection clause places the law of the political community in its best light.

The landmark case of *Brown* v. *Board of Education* presented the question of whether state-mandated segregation in public schools violated the equal protection clause of the US Constitution. The Supreme Court could, in *Brown*, look over the legal terrain and find competing intimations. The dominant precedent was *Plessy* v. *Ferguson*, which held that public facilities that were 'separate but equal' were consistent with constitutional equality.[33] While *Plessy* dominated the field, certain chinks were visible in Jim Crow's armour.

In 1938, the Supreme Court had ruled that the refusal of a state university to admit blacks to its law school constituted a violation of the equal protection clause when no comparable facility was provided for blacks.[34] Privileges created for whites must be created for blacks. The court here refused to accept the practice of allowing Southern states to pay the prospective student's expenses at an unsegregated Northern law school.

Twelve years later, the Supreme Court had overturned a Texas attempt to satisfy the equal protection requirement by setting up a separate law school overnight.[35] The Court ordered that the black plaintiff be admitted to an established 'white' law school on the grounds that the hastily fabricated black law school could not possibly be substantially equal.[36]

Despite these and other hints of greater judicial sensitivity on the race question, *Plessy* was intact. The Court needed, and quite properly, substantial reasons to justify overturning a long-standing precedent. The constitutional pretensions of separate but equal rested on the claim that laws 'permitting, and even requiring' the separation of blacks and whites 'do not necessarily imply the inferiority of either race to the other'.[37] Justice Harlan pointed out in his *Plessy* dissent that segregation is a cruel affront to black school children. The root evil of separate but equal is that it ignores the obvious purpose behind

---

[33] 163 US 537 (1896).
[34] *Missouri ex rel. Gaines* v. *Canada* 305 US 337 (1938).
[35] *Sweatt* v. *Painter* 339 US 629 (1950).
[36] See also *McLaurin* v. *Oklahoma Regents* 339 US 633 (1950).
[37] *Brown*, p. 544.

the 'thin disguise' of formal equality: the rule of separation applied 'equally' to whites and blacks, but its all too obvious purpose (given common knowledge of social facts and history) was to keep blacks away from whites and not vice versa.[38]

Brown constituted a justified departure from precedent and much political practice of the time. The decision turned on the centrality of public education to contemporary life, and the inevitable stigma to blacks of being segregated from white schools: what could such prohibitions signify but the inferiority of the once-enslaved and now barred minority? Since it brands and stigmatizes, separate is inherently unequal. The opinion might be read as grounded in social science rather than critical legal reasoning, but the stigma implied by racial segregation in America could hardly be more plain to common sense.

The range of interpretations open to the Supreme Court in *Brown* was not unlimited. Precedents, legal forms, and other constitutional practices had to be taken account of, and persuasive arguments had to be mustered where received materials were to be branded as mistaken. As usual, some holding had to be found which would satisfy at least a majority of the justices. The reactions of other courts and political actors had to be taken into account. Chief Justice Warren made it clear in conference with his brethren that *Plessy* and its progeny could not be sustained except on the grounds of the inferiority of the black race. A landmark holding of the sort he wanted required, Warren recognized, the weight of a united Supreme Court. Prudence was not cast aside: the potentially inflammatory consequences of the ruling were considered, and a manner of decisions sought that would produce 'a minimum of emotion and strife'.[39] Justices may be independent but they do not operate in a political vacuum, they often grasp the need for both principled and prudential moderation.[40]

[38] Justice Harlan's phrase, *Plessey* v. *Ferguson* 163 US 537 (1896), p. 562.

[39] In Warren's words, according to notes from the Justices' conference on *Brown*, see Kluger, *Simple Justice*, p. 679.

[40] See the excellent account of the strategies available to, and checks operative on, policy-orientated judges in Walter F. Murphy, *The Elements of Judicial Strategy* (Chicago, Ill., 1973).

In what sense did *Brown* represent an interpretation of the law superior to that of *Plessy*? In what sense does it represent legal or constitutional progress? The language of the US Constitution is broad and general: 'No state shall make or enforce any law which shall . . . deny to any person within its jurisdiction the equal protection of the laws.' The history of the passage of the Fourteenth Amendment was found by the Court to be ambiguous, but *Brown* clearly flew in the face of much precedent and practice. The superiority of *Brown* is hard to make sense of except on the grounds that separate but equal could no longer be regarded (if it ever could have been) as a reasonable authoritative standard of equality. *Brown*'s insistence on genuine equality is superior to *Plessy* because, given common sense knowledge of the grounds and consequences of segregation, anything less would render constitutional equality a fraud. Given the preamble's declaration that the Constitution aims to secure justice, liberty, welfare, and other important moral goals, the Fourteenth Amendment makes sense only when read as proscribing legally mandated separation by race.

The institutional morality of law is not entirely distinct from the 'background' morality of judges, officials, and citizens: judges and public officials in particular, but citizens as well, must find a place for the conscientious fulfilment of their official duties within the scheme of their values as a whole. Legal interpretation will, moreover, be influenced by judges' comprehensive moral views and their interpretations of the polity's public morality. We count on a reasonable convergence of moral views among judges, other public officials, and citizens broadly. The point is not to eliminate disagreement, but to structure and discipline it through the forms of law, building procedures into the system that work for constant reform and incremental improvement rather than revolution.

The forms of law and the norms of the judicial office are important public resources, but these resources do not exist in a political vacuum. As liberals committed to realizing the aims of public justification we want participants in the legal process to take critical moral reflection seriously. Officials within liberal legal institutions should be committed to preserving law, but committed to preserving law within the larger context of liberal political life, and to improving law in light of liberal political values.

There are, as I have indicated, a variety of factors (institutional, historical, political) at work to help discipline and regularize the role of moral justification in legal institutions. Those still worried that the emphasis on principle could radically unsettle the law should consider that while the moral dimension will always be relevant in legal interpretation, its urgency will be greatest in those areas of law where the most basic liberal values are at stake. When interpreting the traffic code, the rules of corporate organization, or much of private law, moral criticism will not often be among the dominant concerns. Even where issues of liberal principle are at stake, we can expect significant interpretive roles to be played by reasoning by analogy, respect for precedent, statute, local practice, generality, and continuity. As Charles Fried argues, broad moral principles cannot 'tell us whether there should be a right to privacy in a public telephone booth or in a department store dressing room, or whether the imperative that property rights be respected includes the right of ancient lights or the use of percolating waters'.[41] And of course, most cases that judges hear are easy cases not hard ones. Indeed, given the press of judicial business, the vast majority of cases *must* be treated as easy.

In much of this book I focus on legal questions on which moral criticism is urgent, not because these are representative of the law as a whole, but because these are most interesting for the argument I am trying to advance. That argument is that liberal ideals of virtue and community are rooted in the commitment to public justification at work in the institutions of liberal law and politics. It should be borne in mind, however, that we can tolerate moral controversy in some areas of the law because so much of the rest is not in a state of upheaval.

---

[41] Charles Fried, 'The Artificial Reason of Law or: What Lawyers Know', *Texas Law Review*, 60 (1981), 54.

LIBERAL CITIZENSHIP

It is certainly possible to imagine a political scheme in which the populace at large takes no part in the exercise of political power, and those with political power are excluded entirely from participation in 'private' life. Plato thought it best to entrust public power to a ruling élite with no private life at all: no possessions, family, or private property. Plato hoped that through a rigorous education and the eradication of conflicts generated by private interests, the political 'guardians' would acquire the virtues needed to govern on the basis of the public good alone.[42] Non-guardians, on the other hand, would share not at all in politics but have only private lives because, for Plato, the same persons should not fill both public and private roles and functions.

The law, as a particular sphere of politics, is sometimes treated as the preserve of legal élite, the 'professional mystery' of bench and bar.[43] Lord Coke regarded the judiciary as a kind of legal guardian class with specialized knowledge and training necessary to participate in an 'artificial reason' of law sharply distinct from the logic of natural reason.[44] While it is true that some legal questions (e.g. the law of corporations) do require arcane knowledge, we have strong reasons of political morality to resist relegating questions of basic political morality to the sphere of esoteric legal craft. A liberal polity makes deliberation on basic liberal rights and principles a matter of public concern and participation, legal arenas are especially apt to take seriously the imperatives of public justification.

Proponents of robust conceptions of citizenship often seek models among the ancients and in Aristotle in particular, who defined 'citizen in an unqualified sense' as 'sharing in decision and office'.[45] The contrast between classical citizenship as conceived by Aristotle and that in liberal theory is striking. Fearing the impassioned instability of direct democracy

---

[42] Plato, *Republic*, Book 5, esp. 456–70.
[43] The phrase is Edward S. Corwin's, *The 'Higher Law' Background of American Constitutional Law* (Ithaca, NY, 1979), 37.
[44] See Fried, 'Artificial'.
[45] Aristotle, *Politics*, Bk. 3, ch. 1, p. 87.

(amply demonstrated by the experience of classical democracy), liberals opt for representative government: citizens do not generally decide directly on policies but vote on those who will. The scale of liberal polities is vast, modern citizens cannot be personally acquainted with each other or familiar with the broad range of issues on the political agenda. And liberalism stands for freedom, diversity, and openness. Liberals reject the intrusive tutelary apparatus and rigid controls necessary to inculcate virtue and achieve the manageable homogeneity required by the demands of ancient citizenship.

The virtues of classical citizenship cannot be had on the cheap: for Plato, the serious, pursuit of political virtue required the elimination of private life. Even the moderate Aristotle insisted on common religious observances, citizen messes, and military service, as well as a pervasive regulation of private life and personal morals (including regulation of permissible ages for marriage, guidelines for childrearing, and the mandatory exposure of deformed children).[46] All this and more because for Aristotle, 'one ought not even consider that a citizen belongs to himself, but rather that all belong to the city'.[47] Classical citizenship required a small population as well: small enough for citizens to know one another and gather together to deliberate in one place.

Whoever would reclaim the glories of ancient citizenship had better be prepared to embrace the rigours of a tutelary state. Rousseau identified liberty with an austere and self-denying Spartan virtue, and called for the complete subordination of personal interests to the good of the political whole:

Liberty is a food that is good to taste but hard to digest: it sets well on a good strong stomach. . . . Proud, sacred liberty! If they but knew her, those wretched men; if they but understood the price at which she is won and held; if they but realized that her laws are as stern as the tyrant's yoke is never hard, their sickly souls, the slaves of passions that would have to be hauled out by the roots, would fear liberty a hundred times as much as they fear servitude. They would flee her in terror as they would a burden about to crush them.[48]

[46] Aristotle, *Politics*, Bks. 7 and 8.
[47] Ibid. 229.
[48] Jean-Jacques Rousseau, *The Government of Poland*, trans. Willmoore Kendall (Indianapolis, Ind., 1985), 29–30.

Rousseau's 'liberty' is that of the monastic Spartan barracks; it is not what liberals have in mind.

The liberal founders of the American polity rejected political visions with similarities to classical citizenship. The Anti-Federalist Agrippa wrote on behalf of small, closed states, determined 'to keep their blood pure' and preserve 'their religion and morals', all in order to promote 'that manly virtue which is equally fitted for rendering them respectable in war, and industrious in peace'.[49]

Liberal political theory rejects the rigours of classical citizenship. Constitutional regimes, nevertheless, typically provide an important political role for citizens, making them sharers in political power, not mere subjects of authority. Liberal polities expect and require a certain level of participation and quality of virtue in citizens; interpreting the law and reviewing the decisions of other interpreters is everyone's business. Liberalism even takes account of the need for educative measures, but its ends are not nearly so demanding and the means far gentler than Rousseau's republican nightmare.

Liberal social contract theories dramatize the responsibilities of citizens by making them both parties to an original contract and the ultimate judges of the compliance of the other parties and of the state.[50] This is true even of Hobbes, who so feared instability and chaos that he attempted to exclude the exercise of 'private judgment' in politics. He so wished to disallow anything approaching popular political participation that he conceived the parties to the social contract as simply renouncing their wills to the sovereign. Hobbes's sovereign, in turn, is only a beneficiary and not a party to the original contract. Nevertheless, even Hobbes acknowledged limits to the obligations of citizens, limits that citizens themselves were to judge. He allowed that since persons contracted to have their lives saved from violent death, their obligations were at an end if the sovereign became incapable of protecting them or put them in danger of death.[51] Even Hobbes could not completely banish the dependence of politics on popular

---

[49] Letters of Agrippa, IX, *The Anti-Federalist*, ed. Storing, p. 245.
[50] This is especially clear in Locke's *Second Treatise*, para. 240–2, in *Two Treatises of Government* (New York, 1965), ed. Laslett, pp. 476–7.
[51] Hobbes, *Leviathan*, Part 2, ch. 21, pp. 269–70.

judgment; he could only limit popular judgment and participation to the fringes of politics and the most extreme
circumstances.

Liberals are generally more fearful than Hobbes of state
power and less sceptical about the prospects for a widely
affirmed public morality. In an argument that inspired the
American founders, Locke emphasized that citizens should be
prepared to stand up to tyrants not only for their lives but for
their rights. Liberals typically seek in politics not only the
goods of private citizenship (order, peace, and prosperity) but
a principled and active public life. The Millian spirit of Justice
Brandeis's concurring opinion in *Whitney* v. *California* exemplifies a liberal hope for active citizenship; the founders
believed, he argued, that in government

> the deliberative forces should prevail over the arbitrary. . . . They
> believed that freedom to think as you will and to speak as you think
> are means indispensable to the discovery and spread of political truth
> . . . that the greatest menace to freedom is an inert people; that
> public discussion is a political duty. . . .[52]

Liberals such as Rawls and Dworkin place great weight on
the capacity of citizens to act as conscientious interpreters and
enforcers of the liberal public morality. For Dworkin, judicial
decisions in hard cases are legitimated by the existence and
correct application of binding moral principles that are accessible to everyone in the community and so may be invoked by
citizens against the government. Contemporary liberal theory
assumes that liberal citizens are capable of self-restraint and
conscientious political judgment.

The politically actualized capacity for criticism answers a
real moral imperative: liberal rights and liberal public moral
reasons are not created and cannot be abrogated by fiat. As
Dworkin puts it, an incorrect judicial decision or 'even passing
a law cannot affect such rights as men do have'. To hold
otherwise would be to abandon the idea of moral rights
against the state.[53] Liberal rights and norms are no more

---

[52] 274 US 357 (1927), at 375.
[53] Dworkin, *Rights*, pp. 192, 196.

created or destroyed by popular political action than they are by legislative or judicial action.

The broad accessibility of liberal justice is a two-edged sword. Because the judge's authority depends not, or not simply, on his properly holding an office or on the 'quality of his process', but rather on the quality of his reasoning, the moral obligation to obey a judge's ruling depends on his articulation of the best available argument:[54] 'the [judicial] process, even in hard cases, can sensibly be said to be aimed at discovering, rather than inventing, the rights of the parties concerned . . . the political justification of the process depends upon the soundness of that characterization.'[55] Dworkin's 'rights thesis' furnishes a remarkably 'thin' theory of judicial authority: if a judge makes a 'mistake' and fails in the eyes of others to 'discover' the correct ruling, if he fails to arrive at the best overall justification for his decision, then his ruling may reasonably be challenged by a person believing his rights have been violated. Civil disobedience may be justified when the judge's reasoning is faulty, or when one can formulate a better 'overall' justification for another decision. Dworkin provides no basis for judicial authority other than the articulation of good arguments drawing on the rules, precedents, and moral principles inherent in law:

There are no shortcuts to meeting a citizen's claim to a right. If a citizen argues that he has a moral right not to serve in the Army, or to protest in a way he finds effective, then an official who wants to answer him, and not simply to bludgeon him into obedience, must respond to the particular point he makes, and cannot point to the draft law or a Supreme Court decision as having even special, let alone decisive, weight.[56]

The judge *qua* judge has no special status, no authority inheres in his office, he is on a level plain with everyone else who chooses to reason about the law.

And this, indeed, is one of the most striking features of the public morality of law: all citizens are made interpreters of the law, thus embracing what Lon Fuller called a 'horizontal', and

---

[54] Ibid. 5.
[55] Ibid. 280.
[56] Ibid. 196.

Sanford Levinson a 'protestant', theory of law.[57] Rulings are not simply handed down from a sovereign, or peculiarly qualified authorities, or a judicial 'priesthood'. Rather, all citizens are called upon to interpret, reason about, and apply the morality of law in their own conduct and in challenging and perhaps disobeying official decisions. By denying the judiciary (and public officials generally) special authority from either inherent institutional qualities, or from access to a supposed 'artificial reason' of law, liberal legalists invite challenges to official decisions from any private, amateur Hercules: 'Our legal system . . . [invites] citizens to decide the strengths and weaknesses of legal arguments for themselves, or through their own counsel, and to act on these judgments, although this permission is qualified by the limited threat that they must suffer if the courts do not agree.'[58]

Liberal norms are not imposed from above, the products of a superior or sovereign will. The public morality of law levels interpretive authority and disperses it to all citizens. Judges are not simply brought 'down', citizenship itself becomes a genuinely moral enterprise, and is thereby elevated in the way Rousseau hoped to accomplish by democratic participation in lawmaking. Liberal citizens are called upon to take up the attitude of the ideal judge, Hercules, and to act in politics as critical interpreters of public moral principles. Liberal citizens participate in the ongoing moral self-constitution of political life.

In the ideal liberal community liberal justice is affirmed and maintained as a public morality by citizens self-critically giving and receiving reasons. Power lies in political institutions, but ultimate rightful authority resides in what can be publicly defended as the best reasons of political morality.

It must be admitted, however, that the fears of positivists and sceptics are not groundless. If liberals mean to predicate legal validity, and hence the obligation to obey the law, on the personal appeal of 'fresh moral insights' of the sort provided by Rawls, then we might expect the populace as a whole to

---

[57] Fuller, *Morality of Law*, passim, and Sanford Levinson, '"The Constitution" in American Civil Religion', *The Supreme Court Review, 1979*, ed. Philip Kurland and Gerhard Caspar (Chicago, Ill., 1980), 123–51.

[58] Dworkin, *Rights*, p. 217.

achieve no greater consensus than have professional philo-sophers.[59] Thus, John Hart Ely wonders how Supreme Court decisions would avoid the arbitrariness of, 'We like Rawls. You like Nozick. We win 6–3.'[60] The project of fusing law and ordinary morality, with its levelling of authority and its call for the 'lawyerhood of all citizens' (or perhaps better, philosopherhood of all citizens), is enormously attractive, but can it avoid degenerating into a chaos of conflicting private judgments reconcilable only by the power of a powerful sovereign?

Ely overstates his point by ignoring the fact that liberals require a certain form and quality of reasoning for an opinion to have any public force. 'Liking' Rawls or Nozick (or Ely for that matter) counts for nothing. At the very least 'Herculean' judges, public officials, or citizens must have public reasons and arguments to support their political actions. These public reasons should be further disciplined by contact with the reasonable and defensible aspects of our constitution and legal tradition. Even when no one view gains the assent of all, the gaps among views may be narrowed and unreasonable views ruled out. Liberal moderation helps make adequate con-vergence a reasonable expectation. Ely undercuts the force of his own case for democracy by implying that arguments turn on likes and dislikes. By his own example (excepting the above quotation), Ely shows that he recognizes that the appropriate way to participate in politics is by reasoned arguments rather than blunt assertions of arbitrary preference.

In order to justify our political arrangements with good reasons we assume we can be true to something beyond mere 'likes and dislikes', personal will, and arbitrary preference: to reasons that count as reasons for others and not only for ourselves, to reasons that can be publicly stated and knit into a critically defensible and widely accessible moral framework. The only alternative to the search for good reasons and public justification is the mere assertion of preference or power, which others may acquiesce in, but which can never be the basis of a moral community.

---

[59] Ibid. 149.
[60] Ely, *Democracy*, p. 58.

If the authority of official decisions is to depend ultimately on the judgments of individual citizens about the rightness of those decisions (or at least on the judgment that these decisions fall within acceptable bounds), Dworkin's defence of civil disobedience raises a possible problem. He argues that a man may have a 'right to do as his conscience tells him' and sometimes seems to admit the political decisiveness of merely private moral visions: 'In the United States, at least, almost any law which a significant number of people would be tempted to disobey on moral grounds would be doubtful—if not clearly invalid—on Constitutional grounds as well.'[61] To argue for the political decisiveness of private 'conscience' would undermine the symmetry of the duties the law imposes, the complementarity in the relationship of citizen and lawgiver that Fuller calls the 'reciprocity' of the morality of law.[62] Dworkin provides no warrant for excusing citizens from the duty of justifying their conduct in public moral terms and by reference to the same public standards that bind officials. With the privilege of participating in public debate over basic political principles must come the responsibility to acquire at least a modicum of the relevant information and to act, like public officials, as conscientious interpreters of public moral standards.

Rawls's defence of civil disobedience properly holds citizens to the same public standards of justice which bind officials. Justified civil disobedience 'does not appeal to principles of personal morality or to religious doctrines . . . [and] civil disobedience cannot be grounded solely on group or self-interest. Instead one invokes the commonly shared conception of justice that underlies the political order.'[63] Civil disobedience should be thought of as the breaking of a law in the name of 'fidelity to the law' in some higher sense, in the name of the reasons of public morality that underlie and justify the legal order. Where a basic sense of justice is shared, and where received legal materials are reasonably just, civil disobedience is not chaotic or revolutionary, but a stabilizing device

---

[61] Dworkin, *Rights*, p. 208.
[62] Fuller, *Morality of Law*, pp. 19–27.
[63] Rawls, *Theory*, p. 365.

designed to 'inhibit departures from justice and to correct them when they occur'.[64]

Liberal legalists argue that each citizen must decide for himself whether public officials have reasonably interpreted what the law requires. Citizens are both autonomous and responsible: autonomous because they have a right to reflect critically on the reasons of public morality for themselves, and responsible in having a duty to go beyond 'personal interests', 'political allegiance narrowly construed', and even 'personal morality', to grapple with the reasons composing the public morality of a reasonably just political order.[65] Citizens should participate in the spirit of public justification: not simply asserting their own positions, but considering and addressing the reasonable arguments of others, including those of public officials.

There is nothing incompatible between liberalism and a robust conception of responsible citizenship. Indeed, to the extent that liberals draw citizens into the political process, into a political process importantly conceived in terms of reason-giving, it is with the hope and the expectation that citizens so engaged will be prepared to act as conscientious interpreters and enforcers of liberal public values.

Some would dissent from the liberal defence of civil disobedience. Discerning what justice requires is extremely difficult, and the violation of even unjust laws may undermine respect for law in general and defeat law's ordering function. Citizens of a basically just regime, according to Herbert Storing, owe respect to 'law as law': 'Do we not, as beneficiaries of the law, have an interest in having the law obeyed even where there is disagreement about its justice? Do we not benefit from a community of law–abiding men?'[66] Civil disobedience tends inexorably, on Storing's view, to become revolutionary action because it rejects the means of reform, namely, the channels of normal politics.

---

[64] Ibid. 383.
[65] Ibid. 389–90.
[66] Herbert Storing, 'The Case Against Civil Disobedience', in Robert A. Goldwin ed., *On Civil Disobedience* (Gambier, Ohio, 1968), 103. This discussion is indebted to conversations with John Harper.

Part of the problem with Storing's analysis is that he identifies 'law as law' with law as rules (or even, law as 'command, enforcement, and habituation') when, as we have seen, that is only one, and by no means the most appealing, view of law.[67] And, puzzlingly, Storing holds that civil disobedience is the 'subject's' alternative to citizenship because the question of whether or not to obey suggests a certain responsiveness and dependency, while,

the decent pursuit of self-interest through politics is, in the American system of ruling and being ruled, the beginning from which the subject of the law is stimulated and guided, through alliances and bargaining and compromises, to something like the comprehensive view of the true citizen. In such citizenship . . . lies not only a power but a dignity surpassing anything accessible through the mere subject's tactics of civil disobedience.[68]

Bargaining and compromise are necessary parts of political life, and one contemplating civil disobedience should first weigh the deference that is due to reasonable public rules. But the dignity of the citizen who bargains while respecting the 'law as law' does not seem to me especially fine, and the essentially private citizen Storing describes has no obvious concern with justice or a 'comprehensive view' of the political good.

Underlying the conservative critique of civil disobedience is an exaggerated sense of the fragility of the political order, and the suspicion that passion rather than reason underlies the disobedient's actions. In some circumstances, certainly, civil disobedience would be very hard to justify: where conflict manifests itself more in violence than argument and where society is held together by a fragile *modus vivendi* among opposed groups. But it is by no means clear that the conservative prescription (a reaction in the USA to the tumult of the 1960s) rests on an accurate diagnosis of social conditions. Even when the terrible conflict over race was piled on top of a horrible and horribly unpopular war, plus the assassination of popular political leaders, and the scandal of Watergate, the

---

[67] Storing, 'The Case Against Civil Disobedience', p. 116.
[68] Ibid. 119.

scales never tipped toward revolution in America. Far from being a prologue to revolution, civil disobedience may provide an outlet for frustrations that might otherwise become far more explosive.

One might survey political life in liberal commercial republics and be struck not by the fragility of political order but the tendency toward apathy and political inertness. Tocqueville, for one, most feared the hardening cement of conformity and narrow self-interest:

If the citizens continue to shut themselves up more and more narrowly in the little circle of petty domestic interests and keep themselves constantly busy therein, there is a danger that they may in the end become practically out of reach of those great and powerful public emotions which do indeed perturb peoples but which also make them grow and refresh them.[69]

Liberalism seeks to draw citizens into the process of critically interpreting the law. If we take that goal seriously, and also accept in some measure the warning implicit in Tocqueville's diagnosis, we have reason to encourage citizens to formulate and act on their own critical judgments about what the law means.

Providing space for justified civil disobedience not only encourages citizens to think critically about the principles of political morality that underlie the law, it permits them to act directly in the name of and on behalf of those principles. Civil disobedience is not an alternative to citizenship because it is action on behalf of the public principles of the political order. It rejects the usual forms of citizenship; it is distinguished by the directness of the connection between citizen and public principle. In civil disobedience the citizen seeks to mediate between public rules and principles of political morality. In civil disobedience properly undertaken, then, citizens approach the same status of principled interpreter which we associate with adjudication (Storing aptly characterizes judicial review as 'a kind of tamed or civilized "civil disobedience"').[70]

The aims of the political order are complex, including not

---

[69] Tocqueville, *Democracy in America*, ed. J. P. Mayer, trans. George Lawrence (New York, 1969) p. 645.
[70] Storing, 'Case', p. 97.

only public justification and liberal freedom but also order and fairness. The decision to disobey, when undertaken properly, reflects more than the injustice of a particular law or government action. To be governed by law is, in a sense, to accept a certain degree of injustice: general, prospective rules imperfectly embody justice, and principled adjudication engages in critical interpretation not pure justification. The appropriate question for the potential civil disobedient is whether a government act or policy (or more likely a series of government acts or policies), given the inherent difficulties of governing, falls outside of acceptable bounds. The law to be disobeyed must not simply be unjust but pass a certain threshold level of injustice.

The appropriate threshold must be sensitive to a variety of circumstantial considerations: the seriousness of the injustice itself, of course, but also politically environmental factors such as the robustness of respect for law within the political community, the vulnerability of the political order (is a war near?), the existence of other and more urgent injustices (impinging, perhaps, on other groups). To justify civil disobedience requires, then, not simply a moral judgment but a complex political judgment.

Interpreting the law in hard cases will be difficult, and making proper judgments about civil disobedience will be more difficult still. And yet we want citizens to form and act on their own conscientious convictions about what the law requires; we want citizens to participate in the process of public justification by testing their interpretations or hypotheses about what the law is.[71] We do this by allowing that a citizen may sometimes be justified in refusing to accept a court's decision. No citizen should simply ignore a court's pronouncement; the responsible citizen will consider and address the reasons and arguments of judges and other public officials.

Public officials may on reflection have to punish those who disobey the official view of what the law is but, Dworkin argues, they should not do so automatically; they too should make a more complex political judgment: 'When the law is

---

[71] See Dworkin, *Rights*, p. 212.

uncertain, in the sense that a plausible case can be made on both sides, then a citizen who follows his own judgment is not behaving unfairly.'[72] The best thing for a public official to do when the law is unclear might be to treat the conscientious but perhaps erroneous citizen with leniency, at least when there is no imminent danger of widespread lawlessness.

Leniency toward a citizen who has followed his own best lights in a hard case recalls the liberal virtue of moderation. Leniency toward conscientious disobedience offers a way of respecting not only the force of the best argument but also the force of the good argument, and those citizens who conscientiously participate in the process of public deliberation.

Leniency in the face of disobedience might appear to flaunt the value of adherence to a common standard of permissible conduct. The danger of lawlessness is, indeed, something that public officials would have to consider, but that danger may often be small. A polity that tends toward placidity and apathy, a regime amply ballasted by commercial self-interest, may well benefit from the encouragement of conscientious, public, direct engagement with principle.

If civil disobedience helps facilitate citizen participation in public justification, permitting conscientious objection recognizes the limits of public justification. Conscientious objector status is an exemption for those who object, on non-public grounds, to being forced to carry out publicly justified policies.

A liberal public order cannot be founded on the basis of principles that are essentially private, such as religious convictions or other beliefs the grounds of which are not presentable to others and so are not publicly accessible in the right way.[73] But an order founded on public principles can recognize the reasonableness of certain doubts about its own soundness. It can, as it were, recognize that not all sources of value and meaning in human life are easily captured in public terms.

The validity of Quaker religious beliefs (as religious beliefs) is not readily testable in public arguments. Quakers could not claim a *right* to be exempted from a draft requirement when the

---

[72] Ibid. 215.

[73] An instructive discussion of the distinction between public and private reasons can be found in Nagel, 'Moral Conflict'.

grounds for the claim are private. Rights-claims, as part of our public morality, must be supported by reasons and evidence consistent with the model of public justification. But Quakers could appeal to claims about the limits of public justification itself, claims which we can acknowledge have some force, even if we cannot easily define the limits of public reasons.

Quakers claim allegiance to a source of meaning which is higher for them than the claims of public morality. The problem is that this source of meaning, though shared by the Quakers, is private from the point of view of public justification. The duty not to kill overrides, Quakers believe, the imperatives of defending the liberal order. Liberals must suppose that Quakers are wrong, just as it must be supposed that intolerant religions are wrong, for otherwise the policy of using force to defend the polity could not be justified. (Some, admittedly, assert a special and *personal* renunciation of war-making analogous, as Walzer points out, to a monk's attitude toward sex.)[74] How can we justify accommodating Quaker pacifism but not Islamic fundamentalism when each is founded on grounds that liberalism rejects and that are not readily testable or criticizable in the right public way?

There is a great difference between exemptions for those opposed to war and those opposed to toleration. Quaker pacifism can be accommodated without violating basic liberal rights, whereas Islamic fundamentalism cannot be. Pacifism is opposed to policies that liberal regimes require to preserve themselves given the way the world is, but pacifism is not directly opposed to the core beliefs of liberal public morality itself.[75] There is, as well, a great difference between requiring people to respect the equal rights of others and conscripting them to make them actual enforcers of a policy deeply at odds with their conscientious beliefs. The latter is a deeper and more direct assault on the integrity of people's religious beliefs.

The principle of fairness might seem to be opposed to conscientious objection: if others are required to make great

---

[74] Walzer, *Obligations: Essays on Disobedience, War, and Citizenship* (Cambridge, Mass., 1970), 127. My discussion here is much indebted to Walzer's insightful book.

[75] We could say that pacifism is contingently, but not inherently, opposed to the liberal political order.

sacrifices how can we exempt a few on private or any other grounds? The fair distribution of burdens is important, but forms of alternative service should be required of pacifists, and some of them (ambulance service at the front) may be more dangerous than combat. Given the availability of alternative service imposing a comparable burden on objectors, pacifism can often be accommodated without causing a 'bandwagon effect' that would make it impossible to defend the political order.

The encouragement often owed to civil disobedience and the forbearance sometimes merited by conscientious objection should be denied to other acts (such as zealous intolerance or the disruption of speakers representing unpopular causes) that do not facilitate or transcend, but rather cut off public debate and short-circuit deliberation. Liberals must hope that those charged with enforcing liberal norms are capable of making the relevant distinctions, mindful that the point is to promote a legal order compatible with the demands of public reasonableness and moral criticism. Wise decisions on these matters of principle require judgments that go beyond principle, engaging a more comprehensive and political perspective. We never escape the jurisdiction of the moral court, but in politics we rarely answer only to that court.

LAW AND POLITICS

Civil disobedience reveals certain features of liberal law and the duties of citizens. Its dramatic possibilities for liberal citizenship are grasped by at least a few on a fairly regular basis: pro- and anti-abortion groups, gay rights activists, anti-nuclear groups, and protesters of all sorts use civil disobedience as a dramatic form of public expression. But civil disobedience remains at the fringes of normal politics: not as far from normal politics as revolutionary activity, but still a mode of political activity that most citizens will observe but not undertake.

What do we say about 'normal' politics? How great is the overlap between the politics of principle (undertaken by judge or citizen) and the politics of legislation and policymaking? It would be nice if all politics were as principled and high-minded as adjudication aspires to be, but we should avoid unrealistic expectations, ones the striving for which would distort valuable practices and entail high costs. We should, at the same time, resist throwing in the moral towel: we do better than a cynical view of politics suggests, our perform-ance is gradually improving, and we have good reasons for trying to do better.

One way of rendering an unrealistically low portrait of normal politics is by drawing a too sharp distinction between law and politics. Law is a way of organizing *political* life, and non-legal institutions are sustained by many of the same values and aims that inform law. Like many other contempor-ary liberal democrats, Dworkin distinguishes policy from principle and contrasts too sharply the moral character of adjudication and legislation. As Dworkin puts it,

I call a 'policy' that kind of standard that sets out a goal to be reached, generally an improvement in some economic, political, or social feature of the community. . . . I call a 'principle' a standard that is to be observed, not because it will advance or secure an economic, political, or social situation deemed desirable, but because it is a requirement of justice or fairness, or some other dimension of morality.[76]

To separate principle and policy too completely is to flirt with the prevailing 'interest group' model of democracy, in which groups seek to advance their narrow goals at the expense of others. Legislators, on this model, simply curry the favour of self-interested groups in order to secure electoral support. Hovering above interest group politics are judges, ready to intervene and infuse a modicum of principle, a minimal degree of majority respect for the rights of minorities.

The 'low' view of legislative politics, which serves as a foil to the workings of principle in the courtroom, furnishes neither an accurate model of our actual practices nor an acceptable moral standard for lawmaking. Politics is not a

---

[76] Dworkin, *Rights*, p. 22; and elsewhere, 'Judicial review insures that the most fundamental isues of political morality will finally be set out and debated as issues of principle and not simply as issues of political power, a transformation that cannot succeed, in any case not fully, within the legislature itself': Dworkin, *Matter*, p. 70.

kind of game in which players compete to advance their interests. When the gentler political mechanisms fail politics becomes coercive and sometimes brutal. Proudhon's memorable depiction of what governing comes to is one-sided but not entirely wrong:

> To be GOVERNED is to be watched, inspected, spied upon, directed, law-driven, numbered, regulated, enrolled, indoctrinated, preached at, controlled, checked, estimated, valued, censured, commanded, by creatures who have neither the right nor the wisdom nor the virtue to do so. To be GOVERNED is to be at every operation, at every transaction noted, registered, counted, taxed, stamped, measured, numbered, assessed, licensed, authorized, admonished, prevented, forbidden, reformed, corrected, punished. It is, under pretext of public utility, and in the name of the general interest, to be placed under contribution, drilled, fleeced, exploited, monopolized, extorted from, squeezed, hoaxed, robbed; then, at the slightest resistance, the first word of complaint, to be repressed, fined, vilified, harassed, hunted down, abused, clubbed, disarmed, bound, choked, imprisoned, judged, condemned, shot, deported, sacrificed, sold, betrayed; and to crown all, mocked, ridiculed, derided, outraged, dishonoured. That is government; that is its justice; that is its morality.[77]

Politics is serious business; its harsher aspects provide a problem of justification not easily disposed of. That each dog is free to try and eat the others before being eaten cannot justify the process to those who neither wished nor consented to play in the first place and who believe they have a right to be let alone.

People play games by choice but they have politics thrust upon them. While liberal democratic political institutions help generate moral capital by providing opportunities for participation and consent, we should not be fooled by the pleasing myth that an initial act of consent supplies the legitimacy that a liberal regime requires.

Apart from those who have sworn allegiance in loyalty and naturalization oaths, most Americans have not explicitly consented

---

[77] P. J. Proudhon, *General Idea of the Revolution in the Nineteenth Century*, trans. John Beverly Robinson (London, 1923), 293–4, with some alterations from Benjamin Tucker's translation in *Instead of a Book* (New York, 1893), 26; quoted in Robert Nozick, *Anarchy, State, and Utopia* (Oxford, 1980), 11.

to the Constitution and the institutions it establishes.[78] That much of the founding generation actually consented no more binds the present population to the Constitution than Washington's marriage oath weds them to Martha. Conceptions of tacit consent attribute to the enjoyment of political benefits or to voting a meaning that they need not have: using public roads or voting does not necessarily constitute consent to the political system or the electoral process (one could use the roads to drive a truckful of bombs to Washington or cast a ballot for a Stalinist). We must not think that people actively accept or affirm the value of a country's political arrangements simply by remaining there; the price of exit is high.

Being the beneficiary of a collective scheme might impose an obligation of fairness to do one's part to support that scheme; as H. L. A. Hart argues, '[W]hen a number of persons conduct any joint enterprise according to rules and thus restrict their liberty, those who have submitted to these restrictions when required have a right to a similar submission from those who have benefited by their submission.'[79] This argument will work sometimes but not always. What constitutes a benefit will often be controversial (a free, public, and secular education may seem a disability to many religious parents). There is, moreover, something irreducibly troubling about imposing even the most reasonable benefits on nonconsenting responsible adults: it is hard to be a beneficiary against your will.

There are, then, reasonable reservations about the legitimacy of liberal politics, doubts we should try to allay as best we can by conducting our politics in a reasonable and principled manner. Even putting aside the question of fundamental legitimacy, other serious problems of justification arise in politics all the time. A multitude of more-or-less reasonable demands press forward, many of which invoke moral principles and claim to be a matter of right, but not all of which can be satisfied. Political values and not unreasonable claims conflict with one another, we must reconcile ourselves

[78] For an important discussion of loyalty oaths and the problems they raise, see Sanford Levinson, *Constitutional Faith* (Princeton, NJ, 1988).

[79] H. L. A. Hart, 'Are There Any Natural Rights', *Philosophical Review*, 64 (1955), 185.

to that but also try to conduct the political process in a way that is appropriate given the seriousness of the claims at stake.

My point is not that liberal societies face an urgent crisis of legitimacy: the problem seems to me intractable but not overwhelming. Shortfalls of legitimacy and moral justification nag our politics; these are moral deficits that we should make payments on as best we can. We should prize institutions that participate in the process of public justification because they help generate moral capital.

The moral deficit of liberal politics is not simply a liability against society as a whole, it is apportioned to all those whose actions or inactions support the political arrangements in question. Voting, paying taxes, abiding by laws—all of these implicate us to some degree in the political scheme we thus help sustain. Each of us acquires some measure of responsibility to reflect on and improve the moral quality of the political order. All of political life takes place against the background of the moral deficit of politics. To employ political power (and so other people) simply as a means to promote one's narrow self-interest, whether as judge, legislator, or citizen, irresponsibly contributes to the problem of legitimacy.[80]

Judges do not invent the reasons of public morality that justify people's rights. At most they articulate reasons and arguments not previously announced in political forums, and litigants and other participants often articulate reasons of political morality to support their claims well before the stage of adjudication. If their reasons are good then they ought to be recognized and acknowledged as such by other citizens and legislators without waiting for a court case. No one may rightly pursue his interests in politics or elsewhere in a way that violates the rights of others or to the detriment of some other requirement of justice or procedural fairness. Valid rights claims properly override and pre-empt the majority's pursuit of its interests at all stages of the political process and for all political actors. Principled adjudication merely solemnizes and makes official a process of argument and reflection that could, and should, go on in politics all the time.

---

[80] Rawls speaks of a natural duty to be just, *Theory*, pp. 108–17, which may lie behind these reflections.

It is wrong for unjust verdicts to be handed down but also for unjust laws to be passed and for citizens to work for the passing of unjust laws. Moral responsibility is not confined to the courtroom, because moral reasons are advanced outside the courtroom. Moral reasons and liberal rights are not created by courts late in the political day. Segregated public schools did not become wrong when the US Supreme Court announced its decision in *Brown* v. *Board of Education*. Segregated public schools should have been abolished when good reasons, arguments, and evidence became available showing that 'separate but equal' was self-contradictory, and so could not be justified.

In spite of the moral seriousness of legislative politics it is in practice not quite the Forum of Principle which the courtroom, at its best, aspires to be. We might be tempted to respond to this divergence of moral demand and performance in either of two extreme ways: by falling back on cynicism or by deploying unrealistically high and austere moral standards.

Much contemporary political science reflects a morally cynical view of politics. 'Interest-group liberalism', Theodore Lowi has said, 'possesses the mentality of a world of universalized ticket-fixing.'[81] 'In a rough sense', Robert Dahl asserts, 'the essence of all competitive politics is bribery of the electorate by politicians.'[82] There is no real difference, Dahl implies, between the 'bribed stumble-bum' and the farmer promised higher price supports for his crops. But we insist on making such a distinction because otherwise 'politics as we know it' could not serve as a model for political science.

Our moral expectations of citizens are often very low. They are not allowed to sell their votes directly for cash but we apparently countenance the pursuit of personal gain by citizens all the time. Farmers support increased farm subsidies, veterans want higher benefits, teachers want more money spent on schools, textile manufacturers want the tariff increased, and a presidential candidate can run on the question, 'Are you better off than you were four years ago?' Direct conflicts of interest that would raise alarms around legislators

---

[81] Theodore Lowi, *The End of Liberalism*, 2nd edn. (New York, 1979), 297.

[82] Robert A. Dahl, *A Preface to Democratic Theory* (Chicago, Ill., 1956), 68.

and provoke impeachment proceedings for judges are hardly remarked upon when the people express their will.[83]

Cynicism should not blind us to the fact that the very volume and intensity of criticism directed at special interest politics indicate that many people feel we can and should do better. Outside of academia, public defences of special interest politics are often embarrassed. The average citizen would probably identify with William Leggett's remarks:

Nothing could be more self-evident than the demoralizing influence of special legislation. It degrades politics into a mere scramble for rewards obtained by a violation of the equal rights of the people; it perverts the holy sentiment of patriotism; it induces a feverish avidity for sudden wealth; it fosters a spirit of wild and dishonest speculation. . . .[84]

At the opposite pole from the cynical view is a highly moralized conception of politics. Legitimate political activity, it may seem right to insist, should be not only constrained and shaped by principled considerations, but should aim only at impersonal moral ends, such as the protection of rights and the good of all. To charge policy with the pursuit of a moral end or purpose fills the space left by principled political side-constraints and procedural norms, precluding or displacing altogether the pursuit of narrow interests. To make this move, to define legitimate liberal politics in terms of moral purposes, is to insist on the complete fusion of policy and principle and to elevate our expectations about the virtue of participants.

Judges have no constituency but justice and the law, so why should legislators not be expected to put aside the particular interests of their constituents and the groups that form their electoral base and represent only the public good? Not mere

---

[83] Some studies do suggest that changes in personal financial well-being do not affect voting behaviour, whereas perceptions of how the economy as a whole is faring do make a difference; see Donald R. Kinder and D. Roderick Kiewiet, 'Economic Discontent and Political Behavior: The Role of Personal Grievances and Collective Economic Judgments in Congressional Voting', *American Journal of Political Science*, 23 (1979), 495–527, and Kinder, 'Presidents, Prosperity and Public Opinion', *Public Opinion Quarterly*, 45 (1981), 1–21. It is difficult to draw conclusions about voters' motives from these studies, since the rational self-interest maximizer may take aggregate economic performance as a reasonable index of his own prospects.

[84] William Leggett, 'The Morals of Politics', *Plaindealer*, New York, 3 June, 1837, reprinted in Joseph L. Blau, ed., *Social Theories of Jacksonian Democracy: Representative Writings of the Period 1825–1850* (New York, 1954), 87.

individual rights but the rights of thousands are at stake in the legislature every day. As it is, legislators are expected to put aside personal financial interests and many narrow interests (such as the financial interests of business associates and family members).

The legislator, viewed from high ground, represents not the good of his constituents or other narrow interests but the good of the whole. Edmund Burke famously argued that the legislator's duty is to eschew narrow interests. Even as candidate for Parliament, Burke assumed a detached, distinctly judicial demeanour, telling the electors of Bristol that he 'stood on the hustings . . . less like a candidate than an unconcerned spectator of a public proceeding'.[85]

Government and legislation are matters of reason and judgment, and not of inclination. . . . Parliament is not a *congress* of ambassadors from different and hostile interests, which interests each must maintain, as an agent and advocate, against other agents and advocates; but Parliament is a *deliberative* assembly of *one* nation, with *one* interest, that of the whole. . . . If the local constituent should have an interest or should form a hasty opinion evidently opposite to the real good of the rest of the community, the member for that place ought to be as far as any other from any endeavour to give it effect.[86]

For Burke the disinterested persona of the legislator served as the appropriate standard for citizens themselves, and so he praised his supporters for wishing 'that the member for Bristol should be chosen for the city, and for their country at large, and not for themselves'.[87]

Like Burke, Michael Oakeshott emphasizes that proper legislation involves the assumption of a certain demeanour or persona, one appropriate to (though Oakeshott never puts it this way) disinterested reflection. Oakeshott champions a narrow conception of the ends of politics, quite like the classical liberal idea of the 'nightwatchman' state: government should maximize individual liberty by enforcing a rule of law whose only purpose is the protection of equal freedom. The proper ends of Oakeshottian politics are limited to the main-

---

[85] Edmund Burke, Speech to the Electors of Bristol, in *Orations and Essays* (New York, 1900), 65.

[86] Ibid. 68–9.

[87] Ibid. 67.

tenance of 'the rule of law', which he conceives of in opposition to the promotion of interests. This conception of lawmaking, says Oakeshott, 'attributes a *persona* to the occupant or occupants of this [the legislative] office which reflects the engagement of enacting authentic rules: a persona without interests of its own and not representative of the interests of others'.[88] To make authentic law one must, says Oakeshott, occupy the proper office and occupy the office properly, and that means assuming the appropriate 'persona' or attitude:

A usurper and a tyrant are alike without authority, but for different reasons. A usurper may have the disinterested *persona* required of a legislator but he cannot make authentic law because he does not properly occupy the office. A tyrant may properly occupy the office but he uses his occupation to promote *interests*, chiefly his own, and therefore does not make genuine law.[89]

Like Burke, Oakeshott calls upon liberal citizens themselves to take up the attitude of legislators or judges; an impartial perspective, eschewing the politics of 'party' (understood as the politics of narrow interests) in favour of public moral standards reconciling the freedom of each with the freedom of all:

Political 'parties' have rarely escaped the character of organizations of interests, not necessarily the interests of their electoral supporters but interests of some sort which they regard themselves as committed to promote if returned to office. And, of course, this runs counter to the rule of law which is not concerned either to promote nor to obstruct the pursuit of interests. That resignation of its own character which is required of a party if it is to acquire the *persona* of a legislator is, to say the least, an unlikely occurrence.[90]

In his attack on party, Oakeshott goes even further than Burke, who had room in his elevated scheme not only for parties but for the representation of broad but still partial interests.[91] Oakeshott's strict conception of the demeanour of

---

[88] Oakeshott, 'Rule of Law', p. 138.
[89] Ibid. 139.
[90] Ibid. 154.
[91] See Hannah Fenichel Pitkin's discussion, *The Concept of Representation* (Berkeley, Calif., 1972), 174–5.

political life constitutes a radically moralistic critique of politics as we know it.

Oakeshott extends the full-blooded ethic and persona of the conscientious adjudicator from judges to legislators and citizens: utterly impartial adjudication becomes the defining moment of politics as a whole. The liberal citizen as much as the legislator and judge occupy not positions providing opportunities to advance narrow interests, but public offices in a scheme of politics concerned to articulate and enforce the best reasons of public morality. By extending a strict conception of moral purpose from law to politics as a whole, all political roles and all proper participation in politics come to entail the renunciation of narrow interests.[92] Reasons of public morality provide the ends for, and not simply side-constraints upon, political action.

Taking the highly moralized view too much to heart could, in any event, endanger our commitments to liberty and equality. Democratic liberalism stands for individual liberty and a broad political franchise, and these are inconsistent with a politics that cannot accommodate self-interest. Liberalism rejects the kind of intrusive tutelary state that would be required to prepare citizens for the rigid self-control demanded by the politics of strict virtue. Liberals are not Spartans, but they would need to become so before we could treat politics as a radically disinterested arena.

The cynical, interest group model imperfectly captures our actual practices and stands sharply at odds with the more principled aspects of liberal politics. The moralized ideal complements the role of principle in courts, but it is too far from the realities of liberal politics to serve as an approachable ideal. Both of these extreme views should be rejected in favour of a vision of political life that provides an active political place for principle and the public good while accepting the inevitable play of narrower interests in a free society.

[92] Dworkin never articulates this point clearly; he does not think of policy, as opposed to law, purposively. Likewise, Oakeshott is too much of a moral sceptic to use the language of rights and justice or to think of law in terms of moral purpose. He insists, confusingly, on referring to proper law as 'non-instrumental' when what he really means, I believe, is that it should pursue only the liberal purpose of reconciling the freedom of each with the freedom of all.

Policy and principle do not characterize distinct political spheres, even in actual practice. Principles, at the very least, enter into and define the policy process and legitimate policies in several widely accepted ways. First, principles help define and constrain the process of legislative policymaking. We expect political deliberations to be open and 'above board' rather than conducted via secret deals. Lawmakers' public acts of deliberation and justification—committee hearings and deliberations, floor debates, speeches back home in the district —are supposed to count for something: they are, indeed, expected to be the basis upon which decisions are made and votes are taken.

Principled constraints operate on the means of exerting influence over legislators. While legislators may court certain powerful interest groups in the quest for re-election, we all expect legislators to refrain from accepting bribes and interest groups to resist offering them. Some would say that campaign contributions from special interests are a form of bribery, and certainly, such contributions are subject to critical scrutiny.[93] The intense concern in America about influence-peddling and conflicts of interest is a hopeful sign of rising ethical expectations.

Rights and principles of justice also establish the boundaries of policy discretion. Interests and preferences that violate liberal principles of justice, Rawls says,

> are indeed mere preferences without any foundation in the principles of justice antecedently established, [they] have no weight. . . . [T]he satisfaction of these feelings has no value that can be put in the scales against the claims of equal liberty. . . . Against these principles [of liberal justice] neither the intensity of the feeling nor its being shared by the majority counts for anything. . . . Indeed, we may think of the principles of justice as an agreement not to take into account certain feelings when assessing the conduct of others.[94]

Even die-hard democrats like John Hart Ely and Michael Walzer place certain participatory rights beyond the control of any majority: rights like freedom of speech, the press, and of political association protect the openness of the political

---

[93] It may be that public financing of campaigns would help elevate the political process.

[94] Rawls, *Theory*, p. 450.

process. Legislators themselves often acknowledge and enforce such boundaries.[95]

Another principled constraint often thought to enter into policy choices is the Rousseauian requirement of legislative generality or inclusiveness.[96] Legitimate policies should not only reflect the fair and open procedures already specified, but also take account of or represent a conscientious vision of the good of all. If the interests of a 'discrete and insular' minority are consistently left out of account in the making of policy, that minority has a serious complaint and the lawmaking process a serious flaw.[97] Where a minority's good (or a majority's good) and its view of its own good are simply left out of account in policymaking, there can be no public justification for the resulting policy: no justification that all ought to be able to accept. Those who have not been accorded 'equal concern and respect' will rightly feel they have no reason to recognize the legitimacy of the lawmaking process.[98] The courts can and do help insure that laws are based on reasonable interpretations of the public good rather than the 'naked preferences' of the politically powerful.[99]

A number of moral requirements are built into the very notion of legitimate policy and are widely held to be binding on legislators. Those who have carried the political day should be, and often are, required to present the rest not simply with the fact of raw power but with good reasons to justify the policies that have been chosen. Public justification and moral principles are not confined to a special category and assigned to judges.

We cannot hold citizens and legislators to the same thickly textured set of constraints as judges. Judges must interpret, but others may change statutes. And a well-informed policy-

[95] See Ely, *Democracy*, chs. 4 and 5, and Walzer, 'Philosophy and Democracy', p. 391 n. 21.

[96] Jean-Jacques Rousseau, *The Social Contract*, Bk. 2, ch. 1 and 3. For an important defence of the role that the common good plays in the workings of Congress, see Arthur Maass, *Congress and the Common Good* (New York, 1983).

[97] The phrase 'discrete and insular minority' is, of course, from *US* v. *Carolene Products* 304 US 144 (1938).

[98] See Dworkin, 'Do We Have a Right to Pornography', *Principle*, esp. pp. 353–5.

[99] See Ely, *Distrust*, ch. 6, and Cass Sunstein's excellent work, 'Naked Preferences', *Columbia Law Review*, 84 (1984), 1689–732, and 'Interest Groups in American Public Law', *Stanford Law Review*, 38 (1985), 29–87.

making process may require that narrow interests come into play at some points.[100] Nevertheless, even when legislators and citizens are changing rather than interpreting the law, and even when interests are acceptably engaged, public principles often constrain, broaden, and elevate the pursuit of interests.

Not every piece of legislation is the moral equivalent of a 'water project'. Civil rights legislation, defence policy, foreign aid, medical and scientific research, and broad questions of social policy often involve the serious consideration of broad national concerns. Most congressmen at least profess a belief that their broader lawmaking responsibilities take priority over constituent services and the representation of local interests.[101] Many incumbent congressmen have safe seats, and those with seniority often feel secure and act with a degree of independence.[102]

Lawmakers are often motivated at least in part by general ideas about the public good, liberal rights impose side-constraints on the policy goals pursued by legislators and citizens, procedural norms of fairness and openness help structure and broaden public deliberation, and constitutional requirements of reasonableness place a moral floor below acceptable government acts.[103] At least some political scientists argue that American citizens have an active sense of justice that influences their judgments of political candidates more than perceived self-interest.[104]

---

[100] See Aaron Wildavsky, *The Politics of the Budgetary Process*, 4th edn. (Boston, Mass., 1984).

[101] '[M]embers generally believe that the lawmaking role (such as studying and developing legislation, engaging in floor activities, working in committees and subcommittees) should hold higher priority than certain constituency and representative activities (meeting with constituents . . . making sure their districts secure government projects . . .)': William J. Keefe, *Congress and the American People* (Englewood Cliffs, NJ, 1980), 26–9.

[102] See John Kingdon, *Congressmen's Voting Decisions*, 2nd edn. (New York, 1981), 60–8.

[103] Disaggregating the influence of political ideas and constituent interests on the decisions of lawmakers is difficult, but some studies suggest that ideology plays a significant role, especially on issues of national significance: see Joseph P. Kalt and M. Zupan, 'Capture and Ideology in the Economic Theory of Politics', *American Economic Review*, 74 (1984), 279–300.

[104] As Robert Lane argues: 'The public is endowed with an active sense of justice, a sense that has been said to be "the basic template for organizing one's view of the world." The sense of justice seems to influence judgments of candidates more than

The low, cynical view of politics represents citizens only as seekers of narrow self-interest, and legislators as single-minded pursuers of re-election. This view is both too narrow to capture the full range of political activity in the American polity and too venal to be acceptable, given the real problem of political justification. The high moralistic view, on the other hand, is too demanding: it represents citizens and legislators as impassively disinterested seekers after the public good. Such a view is unrealizable in conjunction with the latitudinarian spirit of liberalism.

What we need is a view that in effect allows for complexity in the way the political process represents us. Our account of public justification prepares the way for complex representation: it acknowledges both our shared capacity for reasonableness but also the limits of reason in citizens as we know them. The American constitutional scheme adds further complexity, reflecting both our tendency to fall back on particular interests but filtering out manifestly unreasonable interests and encouraging our capacity for a sense of the good of the whole.

The Burkian trustee represents the kinds of judicious virtues that, in a different world, participants in the serious business of politics would cultivate and exemplify. But quite apart from the excessively high demands it entails, the trusteeship model is inadequate to the basic goals of political life. The disinterested display of enlightened policy by a distant national government may not provide all the prerequisites for political trust, allegiance, and stability. A less impersonal and more local element in representation may be a necessary prop for the politics of good government.

In a most revealing exchange at the New York State ratifying convention, the Anti-Federalist Melancton Smith worried that House districts would be so large that the 'middling classes' and sturdy yeomanry would fail to win seats. Their peculiar qualities of temperance and moderation would be lost to national politics and, perhaps more importantly, those classes would feel alienated from a government

does perceived self-interest; it is employed in interpersonal relations, and in appraising the police, the courts, and not least, market processes.' See 'Market Justice, Political Justice', *American Political Science Review*, 80 (1986), 397, 398.

composed of lawyers, professionals, and other high-brow and virtuous types.[105] Federalist Chancellor Robert Livingston countered by arguing, in effect, that all Americans aspire to the same virtues:

We are told that, in every country, there is a natural aristocracy, and that this aristocracy consists of the rich and the great: nay, the gentleman goes further, and ranks in this class of men the wise, the learned, and those eminent for their talents and great virtues. . . . As the gentleman has thus settled the definition of aristocracy, I trust that no man will think it a term of reproach; for who among us would not be wise? Who would not be virtuous? Who would not be above want? . . . We are all equally aristocrats.[106]

The Anti-Federalist Smith believed, in effect, that good government defined in impersonal terms would not readily attract the loyalties and the trust of mechanics and labourers (everyday folk). Trust in government is facilitated when people can see people like themselves in representative bodies standing up for their particular interests.[107] Federalists like Livingston and Alexander Hamilton, on the other hand, argued that 'popular confidence' would be attracted by 'good administration' and 'a train of prosperous events, which are the result of wise deliberation and vigorous execution'.[108]

Smith recalls (in milder form perhaps) Aristotle's claim that representation on the basis of virtue is politically inadequate: it will fail to attract the allegiance of the many whose claim to power is based on their freedom to choose and not on their special virtue.[109] The best regime in practice is, for Aristotle, a 'mixed' regime within which virtue and several other principles provide grounds for political representation. Both Smith and Aristotle seek to respect and, as it were, to some degree represent intact the differences among classes and groups. They must do so because no single basic standard captures the felt interests of all. Not everyone will easily identify with the efficient pursuit of the great objects of the

---

[105] *The Anti-Federalist*, ed. Storing and Dry, pp. 340–3.
[106] Ibid. 358 n. 23.
[107] See the 'Letters of the Federal Farmer', esp no. 7, and the speeches of Melancton Smith in the New York State ratification debates, ibid. 23–101, 331–59.
[108] Ibid. 357 n. 13.
[109] In Book 3 of the *Politics*.

national government (security, liberty, justice, and commercial prosperity). People with relatively narrow minds and local views will feel suspicious unless they see that some 'everyday folk' like themselves are present in the councils of government.

The US Constitution's scheme of representation is not a choice of trusteeship over mirroring but a mix or combination of the two. Publius did not expect that partial interests would be put aside: the argument of the *Federalist*, no. 10, is precisely that since liberty makes factions inevitable their effects should be controlled by embracing a vast number of them in an extended commercial republic. Partiality and particularity are accepted, but also elevated and enlightened in various ways through the forms and processes of representation and deliberation. Groups representing narrow interests will continue to exist, but will find it necessary to combine with one another in coalitions representing broader views.[110]

The states were not totally swallowed up: the means of apportioning Senators (among other things) guarantees their continued significance. More importantly, although smaller House districts might promote closer correspondence between representative and constituents, the choice of fairly small single-member districts signifies that local interests will weigh more heavily than they would in larger multi-member districts or in a system of at-large representation.

Congressmen in the American system engage in a host of activities in their districts that have little direct relation to principled deliberation on public policy but much to do with the cultivation of personal trust and sympathy between representative and local constituents. Richard F. Fenno's *Homestyle* chronicles the pattern of activities that Congressmen deploy to cultivate the trust of their various constituencies: making frequent trips home, maintaining contact with supporters, speaking widely, helping constituents cope with government bureaucracy, and explaining what goes on back in Washington. For Fenno's House members at home, substantive 'issues are vehicles that some House members choose to convey their qualifications, their sense of identifica-

110 See no. 35, pp. 214–55.

tion, and their sense of empathy'.[111] All this might seem a terrible distraction from the 'real' business of governing: studying policies, deliberating, building coalitions in Congress, and so on. But governing is a complex business, and widespread trust and allegiance should be among its primary goals. For all the opportunism of individual congressmen polishing their own images at the expense of the institution, and for all the institution's dilatoriness, the House of Representatives does provide impressive opportunities for citizen access:

Although Congress is in no sense that 'exact transcript' of American society which some of the founders sought, nonetheless its members remain accessible to, in contact with, in communication with, and understanding of a vast variety of constituencies. Congress, not the president, best represents the diversity of the country; and members of Congress, not the president, are in closest touch with the people who live in the country.[112]

American constitutionalism has room for the pursuit of both impersonal principle and narrower interests: the former dominates in certain settings such as courts but is never wholly absent, the latter enters fairly freely into legislatures but is elevated and shaped in a variety of ways. By aiming lower than the ideal of pure trusteeship and allowing the pursuit of certain narrow interests the USA may well come closer to a stable, orderly, and just society in practice. There can be no doubt, however, that this mixed conception of representation in legislative politics tempers the pursuit of principle on prudential and pragmatic grounds.

CONCLUSION

The liberal invitation to 'citizen review' of official acts implies that citizens have a duty conscientiously to interpret and support the public morality of law. But as Madison noted in *Federalist*, no. 10:

---

[111] Richard F. Fenno, *Homestyle: House Members in Their Districts* (Boston, Mass., 1978), 134.
[112] Ibid. 244.

No man is allowed to be judge in his own cause, because his interest would certainly bias his judgment, and, not improbably, corrupt his integrity. With equal, nay with greater reason, a body of men are unfit to be both judges and parties at the same time; yet what are many of the most important acts of legislation but so many judicial determinations, not indeed concerning the rights of single persons, but concerning the rights of large bodies of citizens? And what are the different classes of legislators but advocates and parties to the causes they determine? . . . Justice ought to hold the balance between them. Yet the parties are, and must be, themselves the judges. . . .[113]

Liberal justice does not depend upon an esoteric level of reason accessible only to a specially trained élite (such as Plato's philosopher kings, or Lord Coke's lawyerly priesthood). Liberalism stands for 'self-government' in a radical sense of that term. Citizens are both parties to and the ultimate judges of political controversies. The reasons of liberal justice are sought, offered, criticized, debated, and revised in public, in an ongoing, self-critical debate over the best ways to live.

There is no final court of appeal on the issue of whether an act of civil disobedience is justified. Controversies are channelled into, structured, and practically resolved by political institutions. The fact that many difficult issues at some point make it into court will help to shape and elevate political debates. The moral sense of the community can be expected eventually to make itself felt via democratic institutions, providing at least a tentative political resolution for any given controversy. Ultimate authority for a community of interpreters lies not in any institution or the will of any sovereign, but in the practice of public justification and the principles of liberal public morality.

Liberal justice calls for critical reflectiveness on public principles, a demeanour that complements the reflective attitude of autonomous liberal agents, shaping, criticizing, revising, and pursuing their personal commitments and projects within the limits and conditions of liberal justice. The liberal public morality, as we will see, nurtures and draws upon the same capacities needed by persons to flourish in a

---

[113] And see Locke, *Second Treatise*, para. 242, 'the injured party must judge for himself', ed. Laslett, p. 497.

pluralistic liberal society. These traits of character, or liberal virtues, include a reflective, self-critical attitude, tolerance, openness to change, self-control, a willingness to engage in dialogue with others, and a willingness to revise and shape projects in order to respect the rights of others or in response to fresh insight into one's own character and ideals.

In public justification, philosophy comes to terms with the limitations of liberal political life: critical justification is melded with equal respect. Liberal justification makes room for moderation and that helps prepare the way for the temperate pursuit of a politics of principle. The strongest *principled* case for moderation arises when we face opposing positions supported by arguments whose level of reasonableness is quite high. In legislative and electoral politics we accept the play of not unreasonable (but, often, not especially reasonable) interests on grounds less closely related to the imperatives of public justification. We moderate our insistence on the pervasive operation of principle out of our attachment to liberty: making everyone an upstanding Burkian trustee would transform the Great Society into an oppressively intrusive school of citizenship. And we moderate our insistence on principle on pragmatic grounds: to engage through local and interested appeals allegiances not so easily attracted by the rule of impersonal reasonableness. Compromises on principle are made to preserve liberty, engage popular allegiance and trust, and also to draw people into a political process that holds out some hope of gradual refinement and elevation.

Political goods are many, and the workings of authoritative institutions must engage the allegiances of citizens with a limited capacity to rise above narrow interests. Liberal politics provides room and encouragement for principled citizenship, making payments against its moral deficit but without spending its operating capital. In politics, even virtue must be kept in its place. As Montaigne remarked:

We can grasp virtue in such a way that it will become vicious, if we embrace it with too sharp and violent a desire. Those who say that there is never any excess in virtue, inasmuch as it is no longer virtue if there is excess in it, are playing with words:

The fair man should be termed unfair, the wise unsound,
If he seeks even virtue beyond the proper bound.

Horace

This is a subtle consideration of philosophy. A man may both love virtue too much, and perform excessively in a just action. The Holy Writ fits this bias: 'Be not wiser than you should, but be soberly wise.'[114]

[114] Michel de Montaigne, 'Of Moderation', in *The Complete Essays of Montaigne*, trans. Donald M. Frame (Stanford, Calif., 1985), 146. (The biblical passage is Romans 12: 3).

4

The Institutions of Justification

Communitarians often charge that liberal political theory is too abstract and universalistic to capture the distinctive traditions and common understandings of particular polities. Others contend that liberal individualism all too accurately captures the essence of American politics. John P. Diggins argues that the United States has lost the Calvinist soul that once ennobled our liberal or Lockian politics. Lacking a public morality, says Diggins, Americans have sunk in a morass of materialism: 'The liberal legacy has troubled generations of American intellectuals. Individualism seemed to leave America without a sense of moral community and pluralism without a sense of national purpose.'[1] George F. Will argues that self-interest has been the basis of American politics since the founding. The founders' attempt to control political conflict by harnessing 'opposite and rival interests' leads, says Will, to a nation of individuals and interest groups given over to self-indulgence and acquisition. And so Will is, like MacIntyre, 'concerned about the slow-motion barbarization from within' of the American polity.[2]

For communitarians, liberalism is insufficiently rooted in particular traditions and political practices. According to Diggins, Will, and others, liberal individualism is morally bankrupt and unable to supply the ideals that would unify and elevate our politics. To defend the rootedness of liberal ideals in America and liberal constitutionalism against charges of moral vacuity, this chapter sketches an ideal of liberal constitutional

---

[1] John P. Diggins, *The Lost Soul of American Politics: Virtue, Self-Interest, and the Foundations of Liberalism* (New York, 1984), 5.

[2] George F. Will, *Statecraft as Soulcraft* (New York, 1983), 15.

community. America's founding document commits her political institutions to the project of public justification. It announces a liberal morality and empowers a variety of institutional interpreters: the judiciary, Congress, the President, state officials, and the citizens themselves. The interactions of these competing interpreters constitute the complex institutional setting of public justification.

'Separation of powers, bicameralism, judicial review, the Bill of Rights, federalism. How splendid, how familiar, how dull! Let us acknowledge the secret ennui that greats these words.'[3] It is no accident that the separation of powers heads this list of constitutional sedatives. The soporific effect results, I think (and hope), from America's poor understanding of the proper role of separated powers in constitutional interpretation and public justification. Liberal public justification is provoked, channelled, and tempered by the interbranch scrutiny and competition set in motion by the separation of powers. The differing perspectives of the three branches guarantees conflict, conflict that translates into disagreements about the meaning of the Constitution. Liberal citizens help resolve these conflicts by supporting one branch or another.

Constitutional commentators often lop off constitutional law from politics more broadly; the former becomes a special judicial preserve far above politics, and the latter a barely constrained brawl among political candidates and interest groups. Judicial boundary drawing, limit setting, and rights enforcement are, on this popular view, essentially distinct from the practice of politics. This constitutional double vision makes adjudication appear more pristinely extra-political than it is, while the rest of politics languishes in the moral gutter.

Constitutional law and politics are aspects of a common enterprise which could be improved by recognizing how closely they intertwine. Supreme Court justices, legislators, executives, and citizens all participate in conscientious constitutional interpretation—a dialogue in which neither the Supreme Court nor anyone else has the final word. The politics of interpretation is a fine mess which we should accept, even promote, and be proud of.

---

[3] Martin Diamond *et al.*, *The Democratic Republic* (Chicago, Ill., 1966), 67.

INTERESTS AND VIRTUES

It is not only the prominence of liberal law and rights that makes American constitutional practice vulnerable to communitarian criticisms. Certain widely shared understandings of politics, including the Madisonian (as usually interpreted) and the contemporary interest-group models of democratic theory, take narrow interests to be the motive force of US politics. According to these popular understandings, the framers believed that republican government could work like an engine powered only by the fuel of 'motives of a more selfish nature'.[4] And indeed, in order to check the 'gradual concentration' of governmental powers in the hands of one of the branches of the federal government, the Constitution, according to the *Federalist*, no. 51, seeks to provide,

> to those who administer each department the necessary constitutional means and personal motives to resist encroachments of the others. . . . Ambition must be made to counteract ambition. The interest of the man must be connected with the constitutional rights of the place. It may be a reflection on human nature that such devices should be necessary to control the abuses of government. But what is government itself but the greatest of all reflections on human nature? . . . [T]he constant aim is to divide and arrange the several offices in such a manner as that each may be a check on the other—that the private interest of every individual may be a sentinel over the public rights.

It is true, as I have already argued, that liberal politics accepts the inevitability of less than fully principled motives. In the American constitutional scheme, interests are engaged in support of constitutional norms both within the government (in the scheme of checks and balances) and in the polity as a whole. *Federalist* no. 10's cure for the 'mischiefs of faction' is the extension of the political sphere over a vast heterogeneous nation, so as to 'take in a greater variety of parties and interests . . . [and thereby] make it less probable that a majority of the whole will have a common motive to invade the rights of other citizens'. In a polity of many diverse interests no one faction will always have the upper hand, coalitions will need to

---

[4] *Federalist*, no. 57.

be built, and these will be fluid and open. The politics of interest, especially commercial interests, would, it was hoped, promote political compromise and stability.[5]

In its reliance upon narrow interests as a means of promoting the public good, the constitutional system reflects Humean concerns and assumptions:

in contriving any system of government, and fixing the several checks and controuls of the constitution, every man ought to be supposed a *knave*, and to have no other end, in all his actions, than private interest. By this interest we must govern him, and, by means of it, make him, notwithstanding his insatiable avarice and ambition, co-operate to public good. . . . It is, therefore, a just *political* maxim, *that every man must be supposed a knave*: Though at the same time, it appears somewhat strange, that a maxim should be true in *politics*, which is false in *fact*.[6]

Thus, Hume defended the crown's ability to influence political actors by distributing offices, a practice that may be called 'corruption and dependency' by some, but one that he accepted as necessary to the stability of the English Constitution and the preservation of mixed government.[7]

Hume went beyond defending the usefulness of interests and took a further step which would, if accepted as necessary to the stable working of American constitutionalism, impugn the viability of the morally self-conscious politics of liberal community. He distinguished parties of interest from parties of principle, and argued that the latter are positively dangerous to political stability. As Hume put it, '*Real* factions may be divided into those from *interest*, from *principle*, and from *affection*. Of all factions, the first are the most reasonable, and the most excusable.'[8] 'Parties from *principle*,' on the other hand, 'especially abstract speculative principles, are known

[5] See *Federalist*, no. 11, and Albert O. Hirschmann's discussion of the eighteenth-century belief that commerce helped soften manners and promote political stability, in *The Passions and the Interests: Political Arguments for Capitalism before Its Triumph* (Princeton, NJ, 1977).

[6] David Hume, 'Of the Independency of Parliament', in *Essays: Moral, Political, and Literary*, ed. Eugene F. Miller (Indianapolis, Ind., 1985), 42–3, emphasis in original.

[7] Ibid. 45. Like Hume, and indeed Hobbes, the American founders feared that men were apt to be more vicious in their public dealings than in their private ones, as Madison observed in *Federalist*, no. 55: 'Had every Athenian citizen been a Socrates, every Athenian assembly would still have been a mob'.

[8] Hume, 'Of Parties in General', in *Essays*, p. 59, emphasis in original.

only to modern times, and are, perhaps, the most extraordinary and unaccountable *phenomenon*, that has appeared in
human affairs.'[9] Parties of principle are dangerous, said
Hume, and those based on principles of religion 'are more
furious and enraged than the most cruel factions that ever
arose from interest and ambition'.[10] Though 'Sects of philosophy, in the ancient world, were more zealous than parties of
religion . . .'.[11]

Hume's remarks suggest that a morally principled concern
with justice could itself generate political passions dangerous
to the stability of the polity: 'whatever disadvantageous sentiments we may entertain of mankind, they are always found to
be prodigal both of blood and treasure in the maintenance of
public justice.'[12] It was partly out of fear of the unpredict-
ability of popular political 'enthusiasms' that the founders
made amending the American Constitution difficult and discouraged frequent resort to the amending process. The
'enthusiastic confidence of the people in their patriotic leaders,
which stifled the ordinary diversity of opinion on great
national questions' was not, according to the *Federalist* no. 49
at least, to be counted upon in more tranquil times; a 'nation of
philosophers is as little to be expected as the philosophical race
of Kings wished for by Plato'.

Certainly, political stability and social peace are prerequisites of all other social goods. A weak government can lead, as
the founders feared, to instability, bloody turmoil, and,
eventually, to the abandonment of republicanism.[13] Governments ought to be strong enough to resist a populace swayed
by breezes of passion and transient impulses that are contrary
to justice and the public good. The mechanisms of representation and governance ought to be complex enough, furthermore, to refine, elevate, and broaden narrow interests,

[9] Ibid. 60, emphasis in original.
[10] Ibid. 63.
[11] Ibid.
[12] Hume, 'Of the First Principles of Government', in *Essays*, p. 33. John Marshall,
like Hume, regarded the principles of ancient politics as 'too disinterested, and too
difficult to support, it is requisite to govern men by other passions, and animate them
with a spirit of avarice and industry, art and luxury': see Robert Faulkner's excellent,
The Jurisprudence of John Marshall (Princeton, NJ, 1968), 11–12, and ch. 1 generally.
[13] See *Federalist*, no. 11.

through public discussion and by giving powers to institutions with some measure of insulation from popular will.

Hume and the founders furnish a lesson in temperance for those who would aim at too high or intense a level of political virtue. And so, I have dismissed as impossibly demanding the model of pure trusteeship. I have endorsed a public conception of reasonableness and have provided room for principled moderation. We should be realistic in our expectations about virtue and acknowledge the fact that liberal freedom precludes the kind of paternalistic and intrusive apparatus that a high level of citizen virtue would require. None of this precludes, however, the formation of realistically demanding expectations about the way that people ought to behave in politics. Moral principles often have been (and are) vibrant forces in political life; liberal institutions are shaped and genuinely ennobled by moral ideals. Absent a substantial case for the imminence of serious instability or violence, we should acknowledge the force that principled considerations should have in our politics. American politics is amply ballasted by sober self-interest and the private pursuit of happiness.

The image of liberal politics as a machine powered solely by narrow interests matches a number of popular presentations, but it does not fully capture the expectations of either Hume or the founding fathers, and hardly constitutes a fair picture of our politics as a whole. The simple, self-interested picture of politics also represents a partial view of the interpretation of constitutional institutions in *The Federalist Papers*. That interpretation has yet to be rivalled, and for that reason (not because the 'intentions' of the framers are authoritative for us) Publius's account of constitutional government deserves close examination.

Liberal constitutionalism, as presented in the *Federalist Papers*, requires and expects more than a political scramble for narrow interests. If the public is going to perform its political duty and preserve the supremacy of ultimate constitutional values like justice, liberty, and the general welfare, then citizens must be supporters of constitutional values. '[W]hat is to restrain the House of Representatives from making legal discriminations in favour of themselves and a particular class of society?' asked *Federalist* no. 57. 'I answer: the genius of the whole system; the nature of just and constitutional laws; and, above all, the vigilant and manly spirit which actuates the people of America—a spirit which nourishes freedom, and in return is nourished by it.' Public virtue, or the willingness and capacity to support liberal constitutional norms cannot be completely supplanted by narrower, interested motives.

The authors of the *Federalist* made clear judgments about the types of character required by the three branches and by the citizenry. These qualities or virtues would not be supplanted but 'strengthened by motives of a more selfish nature'.[14] Neither the Constitution nor the *Federalist Papers* support the contention that America's scheme of government was expected to operate wholly without reliance on virtue. Indeed, as *Federalist* no. 57 puts it,

The aim of every political constitution is, or ought to be, first to obtain for rulers men who possess the most wisdom to discern, and most virtue to pursue, the common good of the society; and in the next place, to take the most effectual precautions for keeping them virtuous whilst they continue to hold their public trust.

And so, the judiciary was not expected alone to possess the requisite wisdom and virtue to preserve constitutional liberties:

What is the liberty of the press? Who can give it any definition which would not leave the utmost latitude for evasion? I hold it to be impracticable; and from this I infer that its security, whatever fine declarations may be inserted in any constitution respecting it, must altogether depend on public opinion, and on the general spirit of the people and of the government. And here, after all, . . . must we seek for the only solid basis of all our rights.[15]

All of the checks and obstacles that our complex system of indirect self-government places in path of unjust laws could act equally to obstruct just laws were not political participants often inclined, on reflection, to favour justice and the public good. Constitutional self-government requires political virtue, and the mechanisms of representation in a large republic with separated powers, staggered terms, and all the rest, are meant to elicit that virtue.

[14] *Federalist*, no. 57.
[15] Ibid., no. 84.

In a large republic, Hume argued, 'the parts are so distant and remote, that it is very difficult, either by intrigue, prejudice, or passion, to hurry them into any measures against the public interest'.[16] Building and animating large political coalitions takes time, and time allows for cooled passions and reflection. Coalitions in the Great Society are more likely to be diverse and relatively inclusive. And the very fact that political communications in a large republic will have to be public and open will itself, as Madison argued, help select out unjust measures: 'where there is a consciousness of unjust or dis-honourable purposes, communication is always checked by distrust in proportion to the number whose occurrences is necessary.'[17]

Our thinking about virtue and self-interest are likely to be skewed by the conflicting legacies of the political theorists Hobbes and Kant, which tend, respectively, to lower our ex-pectations and raise our moral standards excessively. Hobbes bequeathed to us an image of human nature as inclined irretrievably to pride and vanity, competing relentlessly for 'Riches, Honour, Command, or other power', and prone inexorably 'to Contention, Enmity and Warre'.[18] Kant, on the other hand, identified virtue with the pure motive, the good will, and striving to do the right thing for its own sake.[19] From Hobbes, economists, political scientists, and others draw an image of how man *does* behave. From Kant, moralists draw an image of how man *should* behave. The gap is immense.

We do well, I think, to resist both Hobbesian cynicism and Kantian moralism. Self-interest comes in a variety of forms, some of which are not only acceptable but good and admir-able. Elevated and enlightened self-interest may not be the noblest form of virtue, but it should not be regarded as dishonourable. At the same time, genuine forms of political virtue do not require the complete abnegation of self-interest. The pursuit of self-interest ranges from the scramble for

---

[16] Hume, 'Idea of a Perfect Commonwealth', *Essays*, p. 528, and see Douglas Adair's excellent discussion, *Fame and the Founding Fathers* (New York, 1974), 99–100 and *passim*.

[17] *Federalist*, no. 10.

[18] Hobbes, *Leviathan*, p. 161.

[19] See Kant, *Groundwork of the Metaphysic of Morals*, trans. H. J. Paton (New York, 1964), ch. 1. This point is properly emphasized by Pangle, *Spirit*, pp. 16–20.

spoils and 'get-rich-quick' schemes to the sober efforts exerted in a solid career, a striving for professional respectability, the support of one's family and friends, and the noble love of fame. While seeking to engage other motives, liberalism accepts reasonable self-interest and then tries to elevate and shape it in a variety of institutional settings. To say that free government accepts a fair measure of individual self-interest is true, but that tells us very little.

We should not regard the human personality as immovably fixed, eternally recalcitrant, or impervious to life under just liberal institutions. No doubt, certain basic tendencies are extremely widespread and more or less given, but even the basic desires for self-preservation and sexual gratification are channelled and shaped in a variety of ways. People have a variety of interests, and the self-interest at work in politics will be as much a social as a natural phenomenon.

We certainly have no good reason to conceive of human motives as rigidly fixed by the Hobbesian war of all against all—even Hobbes did not. The experience of orderly co-operation in civil society would, Hobbes thought, elevate and shape self-interest. Hobbes's laws of nature are prudential maxims that explain how rational self-interest leads men to become sociable and respectful of law and justice. Reasonable self-interest rounds off the sharp edges of natural men, generating maxims such as: reciprocate good will, accommodate yourself to others, let bygones be bygones, do not be arrogant or insulting (you are no better than anyone else), respect neutral judges, and summing up, 'Do not that to another, which thou wouldest not have done to thy selfe'.[20] Not quite the golden rule, but pretty close. The common interest in peace, the shared capacity to foresee distant effects, and the mutual recognition of interdependence combine to promote a set of moral virtues—quiet and not heroic virtues ('Justice, Gratitude, Modesty, Equity, Mercy, & the rest') but genuine virtues none the less, virtues conducive to peace, prosperity, and ordered liberty.[21]

My point is not that one can start from Hobbesian premisses

---

[20] Hobbes, *Leviathan*, p. 214, and see generally pp. 201–17.
[21] Ibid. 216.

and arrive at Mother Teresa. If, however, even a thinker as undisposed to Pollyannaism as Hobbes expected men's character to be importantly elevated and shaped by social and political life, we should not resist the idea that liberal institutions and practices will have a similar effect. Elevated self-interest itself takes us part of the way toward liberal virtues, and it is not unrealistic to assume that many people take some independent interest in acting according to principles that could be justified to others. Our concern is not with natural man but with citizens of liberal regimes and participants in liberal political institutions. Persons reared in liberal societies will be shaped from early on by liberal values. We should avoid the errors of cynicism and utopianism and instead adopt a realistic hopefulness that allows us to see what liberal citizens can be at their best.

The broadening of self-interest through rational foresight and co-operativeness should be widespread in a liberal society. Particular offices and institutions should also help shape and elevate the interests of participants. The political arena of an 'extended republic' should, as we have seen, elicit coalition-building, compromise, and broadened self-interest. Liberal political culture should help instil a love of freedom, jealousy of rights, and pride in being self-supporting citizens. Democratic representation (by election rather than, say, by lot) itself helps insure that relatively well-informed and enlightened characters will make the laws.[22] There may be something to Steven Kelman's claim that, 'People who go into public life have chosen to work in an arena where they are visible to others, and it is frequently suggested that people in public life choose to do so because the regard and esteem of others is particularly important to them.'[23]

Political actors seek the approval of particular audiences in ways that should shape and elevate their interests. New Right scholar Lino A. Graglia has written that, 'Judges are simply lawyers in robes, people skilled only in the manipulation of

---

[22] See *Federalist*, no. 35.

[23] Steven Kelman, *Making Public Policy: A Hopeful View of American Government* (New York, 1987), 33. This book provides a very helpful, though one-sided, survey of evidence showing that public-spiritedness plays an important role in American politics.

language; they are not embodiments of moral virtue.'[24] Graglia here completely neglects all that is distinctive about the judge's role, especially the political and professional expectations and review mechanisms to which they are subject. Professional responsibility is especially important to judges, but many legislators also seek the approval not only of the voters but also their colleagues and the media. Institutions create role expectations and standards of success that provide inducements to forms of behaviour that serve public aims.

Self-interest comes in many forms, the more elevated and enlightened of which conduce to political virtue. The legislator's desire to be reputed competent and clean, the statesman's love of the esteem of responsible citizens, and the founder's longing for fame—all these are elevated forms of self-interest that count among the springs of political virtue.[25] Interest broadened and elevated encompasses a concern for others, role expectations, institutional imperatives, and public principles and ideals. 'Self-interest' is too blunt a concept to be of much use, and its facile deployment can lead us to think we know more about human motives than we really do.

The purest virtue (which prefers the right action for its own sake) can be expected in a few, as even Hobbes recognized:

That which gives to humane Actions the relish of Justice, is a certain Noblenesse or Gallantnesse of courage, (rarely found,) by which a man scorns to be beholding for the contentment of his life, to fraud, or breach of promise. This Justice of the Manners, is that which is meant, where Justice is called a Vertue; and Injustice a Vice.[26]

But various enlightened forms of self-interest are well within the grasp of most, and will often be enough to elicit reasonable political behaviour.

Little by little, we do make moral progress—not by leaping for our full-fledged ideals so much as by fighting the worst examples of abuse and corruption. Even when we do not live up to ideals, they may help check the full play of our lower

---

[24] Lino A. Graglia, 'Judicial Activism: Even on the Right, it's Wrong', *The Public Interest*, no. 95 (1989), 71.

[25] This discussion is indebted to Adair, *Fame*.

[26] Hobbes, *Leviathan*, p. 207; and see his elegy to his friend Sidney Godolphin, p. 718.

tendencies and gradually improve our moral performance overall. Moral ideals, even when not attainable, furnish a sense of direction that can become especially important in times of crisis and reform.

It would be foolhardy to neglect the importance of active popular support for liberal values. While the American regime has become more popular in character many important rights and guarantees (including those of speech, the press, religious practice, and racial and sexual equality) have become more secure than they were at the founding. Liberal ideals do animate and inform much of US politics to some degree, and the populace (or much of it) exhibits a capacity for moral growth through political experience. The continued adherence of the regime to liberal justice ultimately depends on the support of the populace for liberal principles, and that support would be deepened and sharpened by approaching liberal virtues more closely. Liberal ideals are, finally, intrinsically worthy and so the US polity becomes better by striving to live up to them.

Cynicism can be unrealistic as well as corrosive. We need a balanced view of political behaviour in America.

COMPETITION AND CO-OPERATION: THE POLITICS OF INTERPRETATION

To break down the barriers dividing serious constitutional reflection and politics more broadly we must, according to some, first curb judicial activism. Long ago, James Bradley Thayer argued that the exercise of judicial review expressed 'distrust' of legislatures, effectively pre-empting and displacing legislative interpretations of the American Constitution:

The legislatures are growing accustomed to this distrust and are more and more readily inclined to justify it, and to shed the considerations of constitutional restraints. . . . The people, all this while, become careless as to whom they send to the legislature; too often they cheerfully vote for men whom they would not trust with an important private affair. . . . [T]he exercise of it [judicial review], even when unavoidable, is always attended with a serious evil, namely, that the correction of legislative mistakes comes from the outside, and the people lose the political experience, and the moral education and stimulus that comes from fighting the question out in the ordinary way, and correcting their own errors. The tendency of a common and easy resort to this great function, now lamentably too common, is to dwarf the political capacity of the people, and to deaden its sense of moral responsibility.[27]

Thayer's argument is a powerful one, forcefully restated by Felix Frankfurter and Alexander Bickel.[28] It is far from obvious, however, that judicial review discourages either legislative interpretation of the Constitution or popular moral responsibility. Even assuming the worst (legislators bent on pursuing their interests at the expense of justice) Hamilton, for one, expected that the threat of judicial review would curb rather than exacerbate legislative irresponsibility. Legislators, 'perceiving that "obstacles" to the success of iniquitous intentions are to be expected from the scruples of the courts, are in a manner compelled, by the very motives of the injustice they meditate, to qualify their attempts'.[29] Cardozo expressed a similar thought,

The utility of an external power restraining the legislative judgment is not to be measured by counting the occasions of its exercise. . . . By conscious or subconscious influence, the presence of this restraining power, aloof in the background, but none the less always in reserve, tends to stabilize and rationalize the legislative judgment, to infuse it with the glow of principle, to hold the standard aloft and visible for those who must run the race and keep the faith.[30]

It is, of course, difficult to measure the effects of the exercise of judicial review on the moral capacity of the legislature and the public. There is evidence to suggest, however, that when the US Supreme Court has taken a clear stand in favour of individual liberties it has often succeeded in shaping the views of politically sophisticated and active 'opinion leaders'. And when the Court has gained the support of other influential groups in the populace, it has shaped popular beliefs more

[27] James Bradley Thayer, *John Marshall* (Boston, Mass., 1901), 103–4, 106–7.
[28] See Frankfurter's opinions in *Dennis* v. *US* 341 *US* 494 (1951), and *West Virginia State Board of Education* v. *Barnette*, 319 US 624 (1943), and Alexander Bickel, *The Least Dangerous Branch* (New Haven, Conn., 1986), 16–23.
[29] *Federalist*, no. 78.
[30] Cardozo, *Judicial Process*, p. 93.

broadly.[31] With its landmark decision in *Brown v. Board of Education* the Supreme Court helped energize Congress and galvanize the support of other influential groups for civil rights, helping to make racial equality an effective principle in America's public morality. And here and elsewhere, the Court has provoked or continued debates, not cut them off, as it has in its recent decisions on flag-burning and abortion.

The force of Thayer's argument depends on depicting judicial review as a power that operates on democratic politics from the outside, precluding, when exercised, constitutional interpretation by the people and their representatives. But why should Supreme Court decisions preclude the interpretive efforts of other branches?

Most commentators wrongly suppose that the Supreme Court is the ultimate interpreter of the Constitution's meaning and that its judgments are binding on other political actors. This is a misconception. Judicial review should not be confused with judicial supremacy: the power of review in no way implies that Supreme Court interpretations of the Constitution are, beyond the disposition of the case at hand, binding on the Congress, the President, or the citizenry.[32] Supreme Court decisions should be regarded as final interpretations of the Constitution only for the cases that come before it and for lower courts, and they have, in fact, often and in a variety of ways been opposed by other branches.[33]

The Constitution declares itself to be supreme, and the justices are as much subject to its authority as any other public officials. Far from being an infallible interpreter of the Constitution, the Court acknowledges its own fallibility by

[31] McClosky and Zaller argue, 'On issues on which the Court has taken a strong libertarian position, community influentials and the politically sophisticated members of the general public are more tolerant than the less sophisticated. On issues on which the Court has not taken a clear libertarian stand, however, elites and the more sophisticated are not consistently more tolerant than the unsophisticated', *Ethos*, pp. 59–60, and see table 2-21.

[32] Having so roundly criticized New Right figures, I should mention here that former Attorney-General Edwin Meese was absolutely right in asserting that the Constitution and not decisions of the court is the supreme law of the land, see 'The Law of the Constitution', Speech by the Honourable Edwin Meese III, Attorney-General of the United States, Tulane University, 21 Oct. 1986, New Orleans, La.

[33] Louis Fisher provides an excellent overview of the various methods that political actors have used to oppose court decisions, *Constitutional Dialogues: Interpretation as Political Process* (Princeton, NJ, 1988).

reversing past decisions that it comes to regard as mistaken. The Constitution, furthermore, charges quite a large number of public officials with enforcing, not the judiciary's interpretation of the Constitution, but simply, the Constitution. The President takes an oath to 'preserve, protect, and defend the Constitution'.[34] And not only members of the US Congress, but also 'the Members of the several State Legislatures, and all executive and judicial Officers, both of the United States and of the several States, shall be bound by Oath or Affirmation, to support this Constitution'.[35]

The oaths and the co-ordinate status of members of Congress and the President oblige them to interpret the Constitution for themselves and not to defer to others. As President Andrew Jackson put it: 'Each public officer who takes an oath to support the Constitution swears that he will support it as he understands it, and not as it is understood by others.'[36] Presidents Jefferson and Lincoln also argued, albeit with some variations, for the President's status as co-ordinate interpreter.[37] And Jefferson and Madison, in the Virginia and Kentucky Resolutions of 1791, went so far as to suggest that state officials had a right to interpret the Constitution for themselves.[38]

Members of Congress have also defended their right to interpret the Constitution. Consider the colourful remarks of Senator Hernando D. Money of Mississippi:

I am not one of those who regard the judgment of the Supreme Court as an African regards his deity. I respect such a decision just exactly to the extent that it is founded in common sense and argued out on reasonable logic, but when it violates the law of common

[34] Article 2, Section 1.

[35] Article 6.

[36] Andrew Jackson, 'Veto Message', 10 July 1832, *Messages and Papers of the Presidents*, 2, ed. J. D. Richardson (Washington, DC, 1896), 582.

[37] See John Agresto's important discussion, *The Supreme Court and Constitutional Democracy* (Ithaca, NY, 1984), ch. 5.

[38] There have been a number of variations on the theme that the states play a proper role as interpreters of the Constitution. A state right to nullify federal laws or other national acts is inconsistent with the supremacy of the Constitution, the prerequisites of national unity, and the lessons of the Civil War. States may, however, monitor and comment upon the constitutionality of national acts by passing resolutions expressing their sense of constitutional meaning. See Barber's discussion, in *What the Constitution Means*, pp. 204–5.

sense, then I cease to so regard it, except as a citizen I am bound by it.[39]

As citizens we may be obliged to obey a court decision in a particular case while working politically to have it overturned.

The Supreme Court's decision in *Dred Scott* v. *Sandford* provoked an instructive exchange.[40] The Court held that Dred Scott, a slave, did not gain his freedom when his master took him into free territory because Congress lacked the power to prohibit slavery in a territory (as it had tried to do in the Missouri Compromise). Supreme Court decisions are, Stephen Douglas asserted, binding on all as final statements of what the Constitution means. Lincoln argued against regarding a Supreme Court decision

as a political rule, which shall be binding on the voter to vote for nobody who thinks it wrong, which shall be binding on the members of Congress or the President to favour no measure that does not actually concur with the principles of that decision. We do not propose to be bound by it as a political rule in that way. . . . We propose so resisting it as to have it reversed if we can, and a new judicial rule established upon this subject.[41]

And elsewhere Lincoln said, 'If I were in Congress and a vote should come up on a question whether slavery should be prohibited in a new territory, in spite of that Dred Scott decision, I would vote that it should'.[42]

The Supreme Court has only occasionally claimed to be the final interpreter of the Constitution, not only for the parties before it and for lower courts, but for Congress and the President as well.[43] And several Presidents have, as noted, stoutly defended their authority to interpret for themselves in carrying out their own constitutional powers. The idea

---

[39] Quoted in Bickel, *Least Dangerous*, p. 262.

[40] 19 How. 393 (1857).

[41] *Lincoln–Douglas Debates*, ed. Johannsen, p. 255.

[42] Ibid. 149. See also Bickel, *Least Dangerous*, p. 260. Presidents Jefferson and F. D. Roosevelt argued for the President's power to interpret the Constitution for himself; see Gerald Gunther, *Cases and Materials on Constitutional Law*, 11th edn. (Mineola, NY, 1980) 26–30.

[43] See *Cooper* v. *Aaron* 358 US 1 (1958), *Powell* v. *McCormick*, 395 US 486 (1969), *US* v. *Nixon* 418 US 683 (1974), and *Immigration and Naturalization Service* v. *Chadha* 462 US 919 (1983).

remains popular, nevertheless, that the meaning of the Constitution is ultimately determined by the Court.

Judicial activism properly understood, as opposed to judicial interpretive supremacy, is compatible with and indeed conducive to the establishment of a liberal community of interpreters. We should not curb the active judicial enforcement of constitutional rights and other requirements, but recognize that constitutional interpretation is an eminently political enterprise and that the courts' role (by no means the dominant role) exists within a larger political process of constitutional interpretation. The courts should not be criticized for actively enforcing the Constitution, rather, Congress, the President, and other political actors should take their own constitutional responsibilities more seriously.

To reject claims to interpretive supremacy made by or on behalf of the Supreme Court is to reject a hierarchy of constitutional interpreters. With Jackson, Lincoln, Senator Money, and others, we can understand the Constitution's distribution of powers among three co-ordinate branches and its levelling of authority to interpret as establishing a structured competition among interpreters. Structured competition gives institutional support and political impetus to the liberal ideal of a community of interpreters engaged in public justification.

In defending Lincoln's wartime suspension of habeas corpus, Attorney General Edward Bates provided an excellent defence of the 'competing interpreters' view. In a government of three co-ordinate branches, said Bates, 'If we allow one of the three to determine the extent of its own powers, and also the extent of the powers of the other two, that one can control the whole government, and has in fact achieved the sovereignty'.[44] According to Bates, each of the three branches

---

[44] Hon. Edward Bates, 'Opinion of the Attorney General on the Suspension of the Privilege of the Writ of Habeas Corpus', *Opinions of the Attorneys General of the United States*, 10, ed. J. Hubley Ashton (Washington, DC, 1868), 76. Bates here echoed Madison's similar statement, 'I beg to know, upon what principles it can be contended that any one department draws from the Constitution greater powers than another, in marking out the limits of the powers of the several departments? The Constitution is the charter of the people to the Government; it specifies certain great powers as absolutely granted, and marks out the departments to exercise them. If the Constitutional boundary of either be brought into question, I do not see that any one of these

is charged with making its own judgments about where the boundaries of its powers lie, and 'the judgment of one of them is not binding on the other two'.[45] Consequently, the very same question, such as whether a military emergency exists during wartime, may well be answered differently by each of the three branches:

it is quite possible for the same identical *question* (not *case*) to come up legitimately before each one of the three departments, and be determined in three different ways, and each decision stand irrevocable, binding upon the parties to each case; and that, for the simple reason that the departments *are* coordinate, and there is no ordained legal superior, with power to revise and reverse their decisions.[46]

The interpretive powers of the three branches are not 'preclusive': the power of one branch to decide upon a question or problem does not preclude other branches from ruling on the same question or issue in performing their own duties. Judicial review does not preclude the deliberations of legislators, executive branch officials, or the public. As Bickel put it,

The Court often provokes considerations of the most intricate issues of principle by the other branches, engaging them in dialogue. . . . Our government consists of discrete institutions, but the effectiveness of the whole depends on their involvement with one another, on their intimacy, even if it often is the sweaty intimacy of creatures locked in combat.[47]

Political conflicts may be redirected by court decisions, but the debates and political activities that swirl around constitutional controversies are hardly ever settled by the courts.

Political actors including the executive and Congress should not and often do not regard judicial interpretations of the Constitution as final for them. Chief Justice John Marshall produced one of his most impressive arguments on the constitutionality of a national bank in *McCulloch* v. *Maryland*, and the political debate raged on. The Supreme Court's elaborate commerce clause jurisprudence did not quell political debates

independent departments has more right than another to declare their sentiments on that point', *Annals of Congress*, 1 (8 June 1789), 500, quoted in Fisher, *Dialogues*, p. 236.

[45]   Bates, 'Opinion', p. 77.
[46]   Ibid., emphasis in original.
[47]   Bickel, *Least Dangerous*, p. 261.

in which Congress and the President participated.[48] *Dred Scott* tragically failed to settle the constitutional issue of black citizenship. Our long national struggle for racial justice is a continuing and broadly based quest for constitutional equality in which the President and Congress have often taken initiatives in the name of constitutional values.[49] All three branches, moreover, participate in defining the constitutional contours of executive, legislative, and judicial power. Abortion, busing, affirmative action, flag-burning—do not a host of political actors including Members of Congress and the executive branch continue debating, enacting legislation, and seeking support for their constitutional views on these issues long after the Supreme Court has spoken?[50]

The powers of the three branches of the federal government are by nature different in character and their spheres of action are largely distinct, but their duties overlap; they are involved in one another's business. What, then, defines the boundaries of the powers of the three great departments, the ebb and flow of the power of each? Not fixed rules or strict criteria but, as Bates put it, 'their mutual antagonism . . . [and] the system of checks and balances, to which our fathers were driven at the beginning by their fear of the unity of power'.[51]

Judicial review, properly understood, ought to be viewed as conclusive only where the arguments mustered and put forward by the courts actually convince other conscientious interpreters: the President, Members of the House and Senate,

[48] See the materials in William G. Andrews, ed., *Coordinate Magistrates: Constitutional Law by Congress and President* (New York, 1969), 65–95.

[49] The Civil Rights Act of 1964 is a constitutional landmark as important as *Brown* v. *Board of Education*. Ruth P. Morgan discusses the use of executive orders to advance the cause of civil rights, *The President and Civil Rights: Policy-making by Executive Order* (Lanham, Md., 1987).

[50] 1989 was marked by controversial Supreme Court decisions on political expression (flag-burning to be precise, *Texas* v. *Johnson*, no. 88–155, decided 21 June 1989) and abortion (*Webster* v. *Reproductive Health Services*, decided 3 July 1989). President Bush immediately proposed a constitutional amendment to reverse the flag-burning decision, and various Congressmen proposed legislation to counter the abortion decision: see Michael K. Frisby, 'House Democrats Prepare Bills to Counter High Court Rulings', *Boston Globe*, Friday 7 July 1989, p. 3. Fisher, *Dialogues*, discusses the ways in which numerous political bodies including the executive and legislative branches, state governments, and lower courts all participate in a dialogue with the court on constitutional meaning.

[51] Bates, 'Opinion', pp. 76–7.

scholars, and citizens, all play important roles in reviewing judicial decisions. All political actors have some role to play in judging whether the courts have interpreted the Constitution correctly, and where they believe a mistake has been made they should work to correct the courts through public arguments and the reasonable political means at their disposal.[52]

To accept the notion of co-ordinate interpreters is to invite political controversy on issues of constitutional principle. This political conflict will be structured and channelled by the overlapping nature of executive, legislative, and judicial powers.[53] Congress's 'power of the purse', and the Senate's right to confirm some executive branch appointments allows Congress to influence the executive. Congress has the power (of uncertain extent) to limit the jurisdiction of the courts (simply making noises in that direction may have some effect). The executive's veto allows it to participate in the legislative power, and both the courts and Congress depend on the executive faithfully to obey their writs and carry out their laws. Courts themselves dispose of cases contesting the constitutionality of executive actions and legislation. The political branches share the power of replacing justices and may alter the composition of the Supreme Court.

The President and the Senate both participate in constituting the Supreme Court. The President does not, as is sometimes said, have the power to 'appoint' justices: his is the power to nominate and the power to confirm is the Senate's. It is not enough for the Senate to ensure the competence and integrity of nominees to the federal bench. The confirmation process is a perfect opportunity, too often squandered, for the Senate critically to consider the substantive constitutional views of prospective nominees and to express its own sense of what range of constitutional interpretations is reasonable.[54]

---

[52] Even lower courts and state officials have an interpretive role and some proper leeway in applying and interpreting Supreme Court opinions, though this will be modest given the needs for a unified judicial system and a supreme national government.

[53] See Gary J. Schmitt, 'Executive Privilege: Presidential Power to Withhold Information from Congress', in J. Bessette and J. Tulis, eds., *The Presidency in the Constitutional Order* (Baton Rouge, La., 1981), esp. 176–8. I have benefited greatly from discussions with Professor Jeffrey Tulis on these issues.

[54] See Laurence H. Tribe, *God Save This Honorable Court: How the Choice of Supreme Court Justices Shapes Our History* (New York, 1985).

It might be objected that substantive Senate review would 'politicize' the appointment process. That process is already political, since presidents routinely choose nominees partly on grounds of their substantive constitutional positions. And while the President deserves a fair amount of ideological leeway in selecting his subordinates in the executive branch (whose special effectiveness depends on unity after all) no such deference is due when the appointment is to a co-ordinate branch and brings life tenure. Performing its duties in the confirmation process more conscientiously would be one way for the Senate to invigorate the constitutional dialogue that ought to be part of our politics.

The phrase '*separation* of powers' might be misleading. As Richard E. Neustadt famously pointed out, the Constitution gives America not separated powers but 'separated institutions *sharing* powers'.[55] The President is part of the legislative process, Congress and the courts take part in the administrative process. Each actor has the authority to make independent judgments about the conduct of the others and each should often act on those judgments.

Overlapping powers give each of the branches weapons to use in conflicts over interpretive issues. It was perfectly appropriate for President Jackson to veto on constitutional grounds a bill to renew the charter of the Bank of the United States even after a unanimous Supreme Court had declared it constitutional. And it was especially appropriate that Jackson accompanied his veto with a statement explaining his constitutional argument.[56] Members of Congress or state legislators might re-enact, perhaps in altered form, bills that courts have ruled unconstitutional, but they too should be sure to address judicial arguments and, where possible and reasonable, take account of judicial concerns. Constitutional interpretation may be political but it can and often does represent an elevated and elevating form of political activity, in which competing interpreters publicly address each other's reasons and arguments. This competitive process also demands a measure of co-operation and accommodation. Lincoln

---

[55] Richard E. Neustadt, *Presidential Power*, 2nd edn. (New York, 1980), 26, emphasis in original.
[56] See Agresto's helpful discussion, *Supreme Court*, pp. 92–5.

persuasively argued, for example, that court decisions judged erroneous by the President, while not regarded as binding future executive policymaking, should be enforced in the particular case being decided.[57]

All three branches of the national government (and sometimes state and local officials) participate in the process of constitutional interpretation. Serious conflicts on policy will often become disagreements over the extent of the powers of one of the branches (does Congress have power to establish a national bank? Can the President suspend habeas corpus?) The three branches can and do ultimately make their arguments to the public, drawing the citizens as a whole into the process of principled constitutional discourse. By throwing the weight of its support behind one branch or another, the public helps determine the eventual resolution of interpretive disputes.

Constitutional powers, institutions, and principles help structure these debates but no fixed rules resolve them and no particular branch has the final say. In place of the ordered simplicity of legislative or judicial supremacy, a system of competing interpreters allows for a clash of judgments and an outcome determined by political debate and contest. The constitutional separation of powers is a perpetual motion machine of public argument.

ODE TO THE SEPARATION OF POWERS

It would be inappropriate to give any one of the branches of the federal government the final say about what the US Constitution means, and that is because the perspective of each branch is narrower and more particular than that of the Constitution itself. It takes the combined qualities of the three branches, interacting appropriately in particular circumstances, to match the breadth of virtues a constitutional perspective entails.

---

[57] Ibid. 90–1. Lincoln did not regard this rule as absolute. In the extreme circumstances of the Civil War, having suspended the writ of habeas corpus in the communications zone between Philadelphia and Washington, Lincoln refused to honour a writ issued by Chief Justice Taney, see *Ex Parte Merryman* 17 F. Cas. 144 (1861).

The three branches of the federal government embody different (though not wholly distinct) sets of legislative, executive, and judicial virtues. And both constitutional structures and the relevant discussions in the *Federalist Papers* indicate that the three branches were crafted with these distinctive virtues in mind. While executive, legislative, and judicial tasks and qualities are only imperfectly separated, each branch has its own appropriate centre of gravity among the virtues. The nature of each institution effects the kinds of decisions it will reach. Good government was rightly held by the framers to require the mixing of both powers and correlative virtues in the various institutions of government, and the bringing to bear of the perspectives of all three branches of the federal government on particular problems.

The short terms and numerous, relatively small districts of the Members of the House of Representatives foster, according to Publius, 'an immediate dependence on, and an intimate sympathy with, the people'.[58] But even the House was not meant to mirror the wishes of the public, but rather 'to obtain for rulers men who possess most wisdom to discern, and most virtue to pursue, the common good of the society'.[59] And so, a Member of the House must be 25 years old and is provided with a two-year term with indefinite re-eligibility; these help insure at least a modicum of knowledge and experience.[60] The House is large enough so that the members know local circumstances, but not so numerous that it becomes a mob in which passion dominates reason.[61]

Senators, according to the Constitution, must be 30 years old and are elected two per state for six-year terms with indefinite re-eligibility.[62] As members of a 'temperate and respectable' lawmaking body, the Senate was expected, by the authors of the *Federalist* at least, to be a repository of the 'cool and deliberate sense of the community'.[63] The Senate was structured so as to encourage not only legislative experience, but also a measure of judicial detachment. As Madison explained.

there are particular moments in public affairs when the people,

---

[58] *Federalist*, no. 52.   [59] *Federalist*, no. 57.   [60] *Federalist*, no. 53.
[61] Ibid., no. 55.   [62] Ibid., no. 62.   [63] Ibid., no. 63.

stimulated by some irregular passion, or some illicit advantage, or misled by the artful misrepresentations of interested men, may call for measures which they themselves will afterwards be the most ready to lament and condemn. In these critical moments, how salutary will be the interference of some temperate and respectable body of citizens, in order to check the misguided career and to suspend the blow meditated by the people against themselves, until reason, justice, and truth can regain their authority over the public mind? What bitter anguish would not the people of Athens have often escaped if their government had contained so provident a safeguard against the tyranny of their own passions? Popular liberty might then have escaped the indelible reproach of decreeing to the same citizens the hemlock on one day and statutes on the next.[64]

The presidency was structured to allow the chief executive to act as an enforcer of constitutional rights and principles, even against popular sentiment if need be. In order to protect the nation from foreign threats, provide for the steady administration of the laws, protect property against 'irregular and high-handed combinations which sometimes interrupt' the course of justice, and preserve 'the security of liberty against the enterprises and assaults of ambition, of faction, and of anarchy', the executive branch must be capable of acting with 'decision, activity, secrecy, and dispatch'. According to the *Federalist*, no. 70, 'Energy in the executive is a leading character in the definition of good government'.

The executive branch should combine energy with independent judgment: the capacity for 'cool and sedate reflection' in the face of 'sudden breezes' of passion and 'transient impulses' that sometimes move a majority of the populace to press for measures at odds with constitutional rights or the real interests of the nation. And so, 'it is certainly desirable', said Hamilton, 'that the executive should be in a situation to dare to act his own opinion with vigour and decision'.[65] Executive energy and independence from day-to-day reliance on popular support are fostered by the unification of authority and responsibility in a single individual. The President's salary cannot be lowered by Congress during an incumbent's term of

---

[64] *Federalist*, no. 63.
[65] Ibid., no. 70.

office; in addition to this safeguard the veto gives him 'constitutional arms' for his defence. A four-year term, Publius thought, would provide duration in office adequate to withstanding temporary popular pressures, and re-eligibility would set ambition in support of duty by holding out the possibility of a long tenure with adequate time to pursue great projects.

The judiciary, as Hamilton said in *Federalist*, no. 78, has 'neither FORCE nor WILL but merely judgment'. In order to guarantee the independence of that judgment, Supreme Court justices are granted lifetime tenure and a 'fixed provision for their support'.[66] The courts should be 'bulwarks of a limited Constitution' and the judicial office is crafted to encourage that 'independent spirit in the judges which must be essential to the faithful performance of so arduous a duty', namely, the enforcement of constitutional provisions even against 'the major voice in the community' as expressed through legislation.

It is sometimes said that the call for judicial restraint is politically neutral. Nothing could be further from the truth. To argue for judicial restraint but not legislative or executive restraint is to favour particular constitutional virtues, elevating collective power over individual rights. The nature of the forum influences the decisions reached. In court, individuals challenging government acts appear as the equals of those who represent the state. The Supreme Court's prophylactic remoteness from public opinion helps insure the fair consideration of arguments and reasons on their own merits.

The institutional characteristics of the three branches represent distinct sets of virtues, aptitudes for particular tasks, and differing perspectives on the requirements of good government. But each department is also involved in the business of the others. A fair amount of agreement and co-operation is necessary, but a conflict of perspectives is guaranteed and a tendency toward different kinds of political solutions is inevitable. The legislature's concern with openness and deliberation is bound to conflict in many cases with

---

[66] Ibid., nos. 78, 79.

the executive's special preoccupation with secrecy and speedy action. The courts are likely to be especially interested in respect for rights, reasonableness, and due process, which will place them at odds with the legislative tendency toward compromise and majority rule and the executive's pursuit of order and security. Good government requires all three sets of virtues, combined in different measures on different issues. No particular branch should always win out because no branch represents a comprehensive or unbiased perspective on good constitutional government.

The conflicts among the branches and their perspectives are most strikingly evident in times of constitutional crisis, which elicit emergency executive powers deeply at odds with due process and open deliberation. The legislature is a collective body not always in session, acting with deliberate slowness and via general prospective rules, but the energized executive concentrates authority in a single person always on duty and capable of acting with speed, specificity, and secrecy. The normal execution of the law requires a kind of particularized judgment and discretion (is this a case of larceny? should I pull down this house to stop that fire?), out of which the executive's emergency power grows.[67] The problem of executive power is that of accepting the need for specialized initiatives undertaken without or even against the usual rules of conduct, while trying to insure that the ultimate ends served by these extraordinary means are those of normal politics.[68]

It would be wrong to think, on the one hand, that permissible emergency executive power could be reduced to rules or fully contained by the other branches of government. The Supreme Court once held (after peace had been restored at the end of the Civil War) that the President could not authorize the suspension of habeas corpus without prior Congressional approval, or subject citizens to military jurisdiction until the courts themselves abandon the field. The court declared in *Ex Parte Milligan* that the Constitution, 'is a law for rulers and people, equally in war and in peace, and covers with the shield of its protection all classes of men, at all times, and under all

---

[67] See Locke, *Second Treatise*, paras. 159–60.
[68] See Locke's discussion of prerogative, *Second Treatise*, chap. 14.

circumstances'.[69] The President, according to the court, 'is controlled by law'; his job 'is to execute, not to make, the laws'.

It is of doubtful wisdom to define in advance what the executive may or may not do in particular crises: crises are by their nature unpredictable. The 'messenger boy' theory of executive power is a way of reconciling that office with America's commitment to due process and government by rules, but in its fear of a government 'too *strong* for the liberties of its own people', it risks committing the nation to a form of government 'too *weak* to maintain its own existence'.[70] While it is certainly valuable for Congress and the Supreme Court to keep a close eye on the Executive, we should not regard his power as subordinate to theirs or as exhausted by a timid, rule-bound understanding of what it means to execute the law.

A different danger is exemplified by Justice Robert Jackson's remarkable dissent in the Japanese–American wartime exclusion case, *Korematsu* v. *United States*.[71] Jackson worried that the military judgments on which the exclusion order was based were simply beyond the cognizance of a court:

In the very nature of things, military decisions are not susceptible of intelligent judicial appraisal. They do not pretend to rest on evidence, but are made on information that often would not be admissible and on assumptions that could not be proved. . . . [C]ourts can never have any real alternative to accepting the mere declaration of the authority that issued the order that it was reasonably necessary from a military viewpoint.[72]

Courts cannot make reasonable judgments about military necessity, so they should not try to do so. Those making military decisions should be responsible 'to the political judgments of their contemporaries and to the moral judgments of history'. If it is a danger to defer to military judgments it is, for Jackson, a greater danger to 'validate the principle' underlying the emergency order by bringing it within the bounds of

---

[69] *Ex Parte Milligan* 71 US 2 (1866).
[70] Abraham Lincoln, 'Message to Congress in Special Session', 4 July 1861, *Collected Works of Abraham Lincoln*, iv, ed. Roy P. Basler (New Brunswick, NJ, 1953), 426.
[71] 323 US 214 (1944).
[72] *Korematsu*, p. 245.

constitutionality, for it then 'lies about like a loaded weapon ready for the hand of any authority that can bring forward a plausible claim of an urgent need'.

The underlying premiss of Jackson's argument, that claims of military necessity cannot as such be assessed by the courts, is itself a 'loaded weapon': it excuses military decisions with broad political impact from the responsibility for public justification in court. To announce that the courts will refuse to hear cases involving difficult military judgments (in circumstances which Jackson does not specify) is to close the courts, in advance, against individuals like Gordon Hirabayashi who believe that their rights have been violated (and to masses of individuals: the exclusion order at stake in *Korematsu* incarcerated 100,000 people for several years). The problems of evidence and judgment that Jackson points to are real, but so are the ugly phenomena of wartime hysteria and prejudice. Consider the remarks in a House subcommittee hearing of General DeWitt, the man responsible for the exclusion order:

You needn't worry about the Italians at all except in certain cases. Also, the same for the Germans except in individual cases. But we must worry about the Japanese all the time until he is wiped off the map. Sabotage and espionage will make problems as long as he is allowed in this area—problems which I don't want to have to worry about.[73]

It may be that special precautions need to be taken to protect military intelligence in court (most military decisions will not, in any case, raise justiciable controversies). If, however, the exercise of judicial review is rendered most difficult by the circumstances and passions of war, those same circumstances and passions threaten the gravest injustices.

The Supreme Court may need to exercise a very political form of prudence in wartime and some other times as well, but a blanket allowance that military judgment (or what purports to be) is beyond the critical competence of courts creates a most dangerous division of constitutional authority. Individual rights, due process, and public reasonableness are

[73] *Hearings before Subcommittee of House Committee on Naval Affairs* on HR 30, 78th Cong., 1st Sess. 739–40 (1943), quoted in Eugene V. Rostow, *The Sovereign Prerogative* (New Haven, Conn., 1963), 260–1.

claims whose weight is not eliminated by the circumstances of war, and then least of all should executive institutions be given a *carte blanche* to dispose of minority rights at will. If one cannot trust the executive branch to protect the full range of constitutional values on its own, far less can one trust the military to do so. We do better to require, as Justice Murphy insisted in his *Korematsu* dissent, that even the military be subjected to tests of public reasonableness in impartial and independent courts wherever possible. Whatever else we do, we should resist the mindset that subordinates all moral considerations to winning a war (an attitude that will tend to characterize the executive branch and its partisans). There are many ways for a constitutional regime to be destroyed; winning wars in the wrong way is one of them.

The constitutional executive is not a messenger-boy, and the courtroom is not a fair-weather forum. The qualities represented by the executive may be needed most in wartime and other times of crisis, but so too the potential for executive unreasonableness may be greatest where the banner of national security flies. Only together do the three branches represent entire the virtues of constitutional self-government, and even in the most inhospitable conditions (or perhaps especially there) courts make a vital contribution to liberal, that is reasonable, self-government.

When co-ordinate interpreters disagree about constitutional meaning, each must hope for (even if it does not directly solicit) popular support. The President and members of the legislative branches conduct a continuous campaign for public support: a constant exercise in explaining to and persuading the public. The political branches participate in the process of interpretation and so should share the virtues of conscientious interpreters. The courts participate in politics (in their own way) and the political virtues.

The Supreme Court is immune from the immediate press-ures of electoral accountability but not from the need for sufficient public support to impress the co-ordinate branches. The Court's core commitment to the enforcement of individual rights, constitutional limits, and public reasonable-ness must be tempered by principled moderation: rights vindicated in court face further political hurdles in which the judiciary's own capital will be at stake. The court should, and in any case will, consider not only what is reasonable in constitutional terms, but what is capable of being seen to be reasonable by the public.[74]

The process of resolving interbranch interpretive disputes is essentially not hierarchical but competitive, not vertical but horizontal, not rule-governed but guided by constitutional structures, powers, and principles, as well as existing political forces. No extra-political authority imposes constitutional norms on the politics of interpretation. In any given instance, the outcome is contingent, depending on the particularities of circumstance and the political support that the opposing sides can muster. The institution and interpretation that win out in a given instance can always be challenged by public officials or by groups of citizens with a variety of means at their disposal (including civil disobedience). Constitutional meaning emerges from this dynamic political process and is, at any given point in time, constantly changing and moving, more quickly in some areas than in others, in response to a host of pressures from courts, legislatures, executive branch officials, the states, interest groups acting through litigation or other means, citizen pressures, academic and other intellectual commentators, and so on.[75]

When there is an interbranch dispute, all three branches must ultimately press their cases at 'the bar of politics'.[76] For the eventual resolution of interbranch disputes will, given the power of persistent, concerted majorities in America's system of government, depend on the will of the public. This is not, of course, to say that whatever the public decides is right but only that as a matter of fact no branch or combination of branches can forever persist in an unpopular course of action.

If the American Constitution and its liberal principles are to be supreme, they must be honoured by citizens charged with reviewing the records of all three branches in periodic elections. By favouring one branch over another on a constitu-

---

[74] Many studies emphasize the political sensitivity of the Supreme Court. Walter F. Murphy argues that the Court responds to Congressional attacks on its decisions, *Congress and the Court* (Chicago, Ill., 1962), pp. 245–6.

[75] As Bessette and Tulis emphasize in 'The Constitution, Politics, and the Presidency', in Bessette and Tulis, *Presidency*, pp. 3–30.

[76] Bickel's phrase, see *Least Dangerous*, ch. 6.

tional dispute (say, in favouring the New Deal over the *Lochner* Court) citizens help determine the authoritative meaning of the Constitution and America's public morality. By engaging in public arguments with one another, the three branches help facilitate and broaden the popular understanding of their different perspectives and thereby promote the public's participation in the qualities each branch contributes to good government. Citizens must be capable of sharing the particular perspectives of the three branches. To exercise their political power properly citizens must become conscientious interpreters of constitutional morality.

CONCLUSION

The political process of interpretation I have described might seem like a messy and inefficient way of deciding disputes about the meaning of the fundamental law. Messy it may be, but when considering its efficiency we should remember that widespread participation in debate about the US Constitution's meaning is part of the desired output.

The virtues of liberal citizenship are a function of the expectations and opportunities provided by the complex, competitive process of interpretation set in motion by the separation of powers. It is a commonplace of legal thought that no party should judge its own case. Judicial review is often defended on the ground that when the issue is one between majority power and minority rights the usual workings of democratic politics cannot be relied upon because that would entail the majority acting as judge in its own case. And yet, because judicial review operates within rather than outside the political process properly understood, citizens and other political actors are not really exempted from judging their own cases.

The exercise of judicial review may temporarily check a popular but unjust legislative or executive act, but the judiciary cannot long withstand the concerted political efforts of the more democratic branches. Even Supreme Court justices are not immortal; they occasionally die and are replaced by others nominated and confirmed by popularly elected

Presidents and Senators. If the constitutional polity is to be liberal, citizens must govern themselves by liberal principles.

Judicial review need not deaden the moral sense of citizens, because judicial decisions should themselves be reviewed by citizens. The exercise of judicial power is *typically* accompanied by reasoned public argument and explorations of issues of political morality, and for that reason this branch has a special capacity to infuse issues of principle into our politics. Judicial review can serve, and often has served, as a stimulus to popular moral deliberation.[77] The judiciary should call upon the other branches and the citizenry to meet its reasons with better reasons, in so doing it summons the liberal political virtues of reflectiveness and self-critical reason-giving.

Constitutional issues are political in the deepest sense of that term. Liberal politics is, at its best, infused with constitutional principle. Principled constitutional politics can be initiated by courts, other public officials, or by a group of citizens impatient with perceived injustice. The Supreme Court is a vital player in constitutionalism's quest for reasonable self-government, a quest that calls for Court, Congress, Executive, and citizens all to act with vigour as conscientious interpreters of America's liberal public morality.

[77] Stephen Holmes puts it well: 'Liberal constitutionalism is not only an obstruction and a safety-valve: it is also a mobilizer. It can serve as a stimulant as well as a depressant, enlisting the energies, imagination, and knowledge of citizens in formulating policy and solving common problems'; *Benjamin Constant and The Making of Modern Liberalism* (New Haven, Conn., 1984), 141.

5

The Constitution of Liberalism

INTRODUCTION

Contemporary constitutional argument provides an example of a version of communitarianism that has succeeded in gaining a share of political power. We revisit the conservative communitarianism of the American New Right, discussed briefly in previous chapters, because it directly denies the constitutional relevance of public justification. Conservative communitarians claim the legacy of the founders and the authority of the Constitution for a vision of American public life radically at odds with the ideals of liberal community, a vision that provides a hint of what communitarian politics could look like in practice. In place of liberal commitments to principled interpretation, individual liberty, and public justification, the New Right's Constitution is informed by historical intentions, majority power, and moral scepticism.

MORALITY AND CONSTITUTIONAL LAW

As we have seen, New Right scholar and jurist Robert H. Bork, like Lord Devlin, depicts the enforcement of liberal rights as tantamount to the 'privatization of morality'. And Terry Eastland, another New Right figure, worries about the triumph of a 'culture of rights' in an America,

so awash in rights that we are virtually unable to pass legislation reflecting traditional religious and moral views. Moral relativism will then be the rule, at law; and what is true at law will shape what is practised. For when morality is strictly up to the individual, with no judgment possible by communities, it is likely that everyone will do what is right in his own eyes. . . . America will then become a land of strangers whose religion, if any, is a private matter, and who are bound by no social ties or common aspirations.[1]

New Right constitutionalism is a reaction against the breadth of liberal constitutional rights and the relative vigour of liberal judicial review. New Right scholars view road individual rights and an unelected Supreme Court as morally suspect in what they understand to be a basically democratic system of government. Most strikingly, New Right scholars seek not only to confine liberal rights and judicial review, but also to supplant liberalism's insistence on the political authority of moral principles and imperative of public reasonableness.

Bork insists that judicial decisions must rest on 'reasoned opinions'. A 'legitimate' court must have 'a valid theory, derived from the Constitution' to justify its actions.[2] Fair enough. But Bork's view of what constitutes a valid constitutional principle is extremely narrow. For Bork, constitutional principles should be drawn only from the text interpreted in light of specific historical intentions: the 'framers' intentions with respect to freedoms are the sole legitimate premise from which constitutional analysis may proceed'.[3]

Cut loose from plain text and historical intentions there is, for Bork, 'no principled way of saying which . . . inequalities are permissible'.[4] Beyond text and intention are 'matters of morality' which 'belong . . . to the political community'.[5] Political morality is of no help in deciding what constitutional rights people have because, says Bork, any system of 'moral and ethical values . . . has no objective or intrinsic validity of its own . . .'.[6] To invoke a principle is merely to state a preference. As if to make moral scepticism or subjectivism official US government policy, then Attorney General Meese approvingly quoted Judge Bork's aphorism: 'the judge who

[1] Terry Eastland, 'The Politics of Morality and Religion: A Primer', in Carl Horn, ed., *Whose Values?* (Ann Arbor, Mich., 1985), 17. I have explored and criticized New Right jurisprudence at much greater length in *The New Right v. The Constitution*, 2nd edn. (Washington, DC, 1987). A powerful defence of New Right jurisprudence can be found in McDowell, *Constitution*.

[2] Robert H. Bork, 'Neutral Principles and Some First Amendment Problems', *Indiana Law Journal*, 47 (1971), 3.

[3] Bork, *Tradition*, p. 10.   [4] Bork, 'Neutral Principles', p. 11.   [5] Ibid. 12.

[6] I have benefited from Sotirios Barber's excellent 'Judge Bork's Constitution', in *Courts, Judges, and Politics*, eds. Murphy and Pritchett, pp. 691–5.

looks outside the Constitution always looks inside himself and nowhere else.'[7]

Bork's scepticism turns to cynicism when he reduces all moral arguments to claims for 'gratification': 'Every clash between a minority claiming freedom and a majority claiming power to regulate involves a choice between the gratifications of two groups.'[8] When examining *Griswold* v. *Connecticut*, in which married couples asserted, as a matter of constitutional and political morality, the right to use contraceptives in the privacy of their own home, Bork sees no serious moral problem but only a question of 'sexual gratification'. And since there is no principled way, according to Bork, to discriminate between kinds of 'gratification', the majority should have its way.

On its face, the resort to framers' intentions seems reasonable enough. A broadly worded Constitution is, after all, hard to interpret. The First Amendment seems straightforward enough: 'Congress shall make no law . . . abridging freedom of speech, or of the press. . . .' But what forms of expression does speech include? Words that libel or offend? Obscenity? Exotic dancing? The interpretive puzzles posed by the Fourteenth Amendment are truly gargantuan:

No State shall make or enforce any law which shall abridge the privileges or immunities of citizens of the United States; nor shall any State deprive any person of life, liberty, or property, without due process of law; nor deny to any person within its jurisdiction the equal protection of the laws.

Deciding what these majestic phrases require is no easy task. In spite of the deliberate breadth of the language of the Amendment, New Right scholars would have interpreters seek the specific intentions of those who framed the Amendment. The reasoning then goes something like this: segregated schooling was a common and accepted policy when the Fourteenth Amendment was drafted and passed, so (as Raoul Berger argues, with more courage than often accompanies

---

[7] Edwin Meese, III, Address before the District of Columbia Chapter of the Federalist Society Lawyers Division, 15 November 1985, Washington, DC.

[8] Bork, 'Neutral Principles', p. 9.

New Right convictions) segregated schooling must be regarded as constitutionally permissible.[9]

On its face, there is something quite implausible about interpreting sweeping constitutional language in light of particular intentions or practices that framers could have written into the law if they had wanted. The very search for 'framers' intentions' is, however, fraught with difficulties never adequately addressed by its proponents. It is difficult even to identify who the framers were. It is easy to read Madison's record of the Philadelphia Convention but extremely difficult to distil unified intentions from the remarks of a disparate group who could barely agree on the text of the Constitution, let alone other and more specific matters. It was ratification, in any case, that gave the Constitution the force of law, and over 1,600 delegates attended the thirteen state ratifying conventions.[10]

What, moreover, is to count as an intention? Immediate expectations or long-term hopes and aspirations? To fix intentions in the actual practices of the founders denies the aspirational quality of their project. The Constitution is law, but it is not a tax code: it contains not only rules but reasons and values to explore, aspire to, and progressively realize. Recall Lincoln's understanding of constitutional principles as standards constantly to strive for.[11] Among the framers were men who believed that slavery was at odds with fundamental constitutional principles, but who saw no immediate way to get rid of the practice. Honouring the highest aspirations of the framers may require ignoring their immediate intentions.

What, finally, is to count as evidence of intentions? Public records only or private correspondence as well? And what do we make of the fact that no official record of the Philadelphia Convention was kept? All we have are edited versions of the personal notes of several of the delegates. Of these, only Madison's notes appear to approach completeness but we have no way to verify their accuracy: he published his notes only

[9] Raoul Berger, *Government By Judiciary* (Cambridge, Mass., 1977), ch. 7.

[10] My criticisms of original intent rely on two excellent discussions: Walter F. Murphy, 'Constitutional Interpretation: The Art of the Historian, Magician, or Statesman?' *Yale Law Review*, 87 (1978), 1752–71, and Dworkin, 'Forum of Principle' in *A Matter of Principle*.

[11] Johannsen, ed., *Lincoln–Douglas Debates*, p. 304.

posthumously, after everyone who had attended the Convention was dead.[12] If the framers intended us to be guided by intentions not apparent in the Constitution's text and structure they chose a most roundabout means of conveying those intentions to us.

The inherent difficulty of discerning original intentions makes it reasonable to consider from whence comes the appeal of this approach to interpretation. Original intentions are typically invoked selectively: as ways of narrowly constructing individual rights rather than government powers. A political preference for political majorities and a basic scepticism toward moral principles and individual rights help motivate the quest for historical intentions. Bork makes much of preferring the 'common sense of the people' to the 'theorists of moral abstraction', 'intellectuals', and to 'what-have-you philosophy'.[13] But Bork and other New Right sceptics never submit their own implicit moral judgments to the cynical wash they pour on liberal constitutionalism. If all moral principles are mere preferences then what but an arbitrary preference is New Right majoritarianism? Why not interpret the Constitution's grant of government powers with the narrow historicism applied to those provisions dealing with individual rights? What Bork gives us is selective moral scepticism in service of a basic majoritarianism unrooted in the Constitution or its history.

The odd combination of moral scepticism and majoritarianism that bolster the search for historical intentions compose a problematic and improbable way of reading the founding document. Quite apart from the moral defensibility of majoritarianism, Bork and company never address the well-known imperfections of the democratic processes whose outcomes they identify with 'the will of the majority'. The mechanisms of social choice (primaries, general elections, committee votes, floor votes, conferences, executive vetoes, and so on) are replete with opportunities for vote trading, agenda control, manipulation, and preference shaping. 'Outcomes of voting cannot, in general', William Riker argues, 'be

[12] See Winton U. Solberg, *The Federal Convention and the Formation of the Union of the American States* (Indianapolis, Ind., 1976), 67–70.
[13] Bork, *Tradition*, pp. 7–11.

regarded as accurate amalgamations of voters' values.
Sometimes they may be accurate, sometimes not; but since we
seldom know which situation exists, we cannot, in general,
expect accuracy. Hence we cannot expect fairness either.'[14]
This is not to say that the ballot should be scrapped. However,
we should avoid misleadingly identifying elections or legislation with the 'voice of the people' or even the majority. Laws
duly propounded often reflect no more than the will of a well-
positioned, well-financed, or otherwise powerful minority.
The electoral process often merits respect, but not undue
sanctity. And we should never forget that majority tyranny
was the great vice feared by the framers of America's
fundamental law.[15]

The jurisprudence of conservative communitarianism
creates a moral void at the heart of the US Constitution. Bork,
Eastland, and others see a community concerned with rights
as one whose members are drifting apart, growing weary
'with turmoil and relativism', and becoming 'strangers' to one
another. The point of this exercise for at least some on the
New Right is clear enough: to fill the moral vacuum
established in liberal constitutionalism with a Christian communitarianism. As Terry Eastland puts it,

Protestant Christianity . . . tutored the first generations of Americans. It provided what we today would call the value system of the
society. . . . Christianity provided an attitude toward law that law
itself could not provide. It instilled in Americans the civic virtues of
respect for legitimate authority and obedience to it. By strengthen-
ing the legal order, Christianity in turn strengthened the social order
and thus the bonds of community from which emerge still other
civic virtues—those of altruism, neighbourliness, and patriotism.[16]

No doubt, many religious values may support liberal citizenship. But the Constitution itself neither invokes nor seeks to
inculcate religious values, and cannot be read as the vehicle of
religious communitarianism.

Religion is mentioned only twice in the Constitution. Just
before its ratification provisions and signing, the original
Constitution says 'no religious Test shall ever be required as

---

[14] William H. Riker, *Liberalism Against Populism* (Prospect Heights, Ill., 1982), 236.
[15] See the *Federalist*, no. 10.
[16] Eastland, 'Politics of Morality', pp. 14–15.

Qualification to any Office or public Trust under the United States', and in the opening words of the First Amendment, 'Congress shall make no law respecting an establishment of religion, or prohibiting the free exercise thereof. . . .' The public morality which the Constitution embodies, while it surely accommodates free religious practice, does not rest on particular religious beliefs or on the presumption of religious agreement. Rather than seeking political virtues in religious sources, we would do better to investigate how a widespread popular commitment to liberal justice in a pluralistic society may itself generate the attitudes and virtues necessary to support a moral community.

Conservative communitarians err in identifying individual rights with moral relativism. To recognize the moral force of individuality is to recognize that reasonable persons can and do pursue widely divergent personal goals and projects. This is especially true in a vast, diverse nation like the United States. This 'extended republic' embraces people with a dizzying array of faiths, cultures, goals, and lifestyles. Liberals hold that persons derive their common dignity and right to liberty not from any particular allegiance or commitment shared by a nation, class, sect, clan, or caste, but from their capacity to reflect and understand, to choose and act and be held responsible, to settle on projects and pursue them, to change their minds and begin again, and to restrain their desires and the pursuit of their goals when other people's rights are at stake.

Liberal rights and norms constitute a public morality. Law and the other liberal institutions embody commitments to public reasonableness. These beliefs and practices together constitute the kinds of resources liberals need to defeat communitarian charges. They also help inform an understanding of the Constitution more adequate and valuable than the problematic programme advanced by the New Right. It is time to make a fresh start.

CONSTITUTING LIBERALISM

New Right proponents of original intentions are at least correct in asserting that interpreters must not forget the past.

Constitutional interpretation, properly construed, partakes in public justification without being a pure and simple exercise in that project. Public justification embraces a fellowship with other reasonable people. The conscientious interpreter also enters, at least tentatively, into a certain kind of fellowship with the past: with the framers of our basic law and the political thinkers who informed their work, and with those subsequent interpreters, thinkers, and statesmen who have added to or subtracted from that complex body of material (interpretive utterances and expressive acts) that constitute our basic law.

'Not in entire forgetfulness, / And not in utter nakedness' do we come to face the future.[17] The interpreter looks backward in expectation, hoping to understand the meaning of his inheritance but determined to make it the best it can be by applying his own critical lights. The refusal of blind acceptance does not place one outside the constitutional tradition, because that tradition points beyond itself to moral ideals not yet attained and perhaps not fully attainable.

Critical interpreters take the American Constitution as icon, and not as idol or token. An idol, in Jaroslav Pelikan's instructive discussion, purports to embody that which it represents, it 'makes the preservation and the repetition of the past an end in itself; it claims to have the transcendent reality and truth captive and encapsulated in that past, and it requires an idolatrous submission to the authority of tradition, since truth would not dare to appear outside it'.[18] A token, on the other hand, is 'an altogether accidental representation that does not embody what it represents'. An authentic image or icon, however, 'is what it represents; nevertheless, it bids us look at it, but through it and beyond it, to the living reality of which it is an embodiment'.[19]

Worship of Original Intentions and uncritical submission to the handiwork of the 'Founding Fathers' can be forms of constitutional idolatry. Tradition as icon invites us to interact

[17] '. . . But trailing clouds of glory do we come from God, who is our home', William Wordsworth, 'Ode: Intimations of Immortality from Recollections of Early Childhood'.
[18] Jaroslav Pelikan, *The Vindication of Tradition* (New Haven, Conn., 1984), 55.
[19] Ibid.

critically with our past, interpreting that past in light of the ideals to which it, and we, aspire. As critical interpreters we seek to respect, but also to participate in the project of the framers: provisionally entertaining and then proceeding critically to vindicate (if possible) the authority of their legacy. Constitution as icon invites us to read the letter in light of the spirit of the whole—the moral ideals of justice, liberty, and equality—preserving if we can both our loyalty and our moral integrity.

The critical interpreter seeks, in effect, to respect tradition rather than history. A nation's history is simply the record of its past, some good, some bad. America's history includes lynching and racism and other practices that no decent and reasonable person could be proud of. Her tradition, on the other hand, is made up of those practices and ideals that her people properly take pride in. Tradition is a critical distillation of the past, a rendering that seeks to be true not to the past entire but to what is best in it, to what is most honourable and most worth carrying forward.[20] History has no necessary moral authority, but in most places it will be possible to discern a tradition worthy of allegiance.

What does the Constitution mean, and why should Americans be governed by it?[21] These are questions that citizens and other constitutional interpreters cannot avoid. The Constitution's status as supreme law is not self-validating, that status cannot be established by noting the age and origin of the document, or the *de facto* power of the institutions it establishes. For liberal citizens who are critically reflective about the justice of their political institutions (as they should be) the Constitution, in order to be authoritative, must be capable of being read as a reasonable approximation to principles that pass the test of public justification.

As supreme law the Constitution needs to be both vindicated and justified by interpreters. That is, interpreters must both make sense of the Constitution's language and see it as a

[20] I draw here on Sotirios Barber's discussion of tradition, *On What the Constitution Means*, pp. 84–5.

[21] There are many important questions of constitutional interpretation that I cannot address here. For an overview of the questions an interpreter must pose, see Walter F. Murphy, 'The Art of Constitutional Interpretation', in M. J. Harmon, ed., *Essays on the Constitution* (Port Washington, NY, 1978), 130–59.

reasonably successful embodiment of principles by which the populace ought to be governed. And so, the interpretation of a constitution must be a moral enterprise. The best way of affirming the Constitution's supremacy is self-consciously, self-critically, and on the basis of reasons that can be publicly articulated and widely seen to support the contention that this Constitution really is a good way of setting in motion a government capable of pursuing ends that governments ought to pursue and of respecting the rights and limits they ought to respect.

A principled approach to constitutional interpretation accords not only with the best way of being committed to liberal justice, but also with the Constitution itself. Beginning with the words, 'We, The People of the United States', the preamble announces the authority of popular consent and helps engage the public's responsibility for sustaining the project of constitutionalism. The document's purposes and aspirations are immediately set out in terms that are broad, strikingly moral and liberal: 'in Order to form a more perfect Union, establish Justice, insure domestic Tranquility, provide for the common defense, promote the general Welfare, and secure the Blessings of Liberty to ourselves and our Posterity', we the people 'do ordain and establish this CONSTITUTION . . .'. The preamble frames what is to follow: setting out the terms in which the Constitution seeks to justify itself, the standards against which we ought to measure the framers' success.[22]

The Constitution has long (though not always) been read in the spirit of critical moral seriousness. Unlike Bork and other conservative communitarians, the framers were neither moral sceptics nor derisive of abstract ideas. For what else but abstract ideas are the 'self-evident' truths of the Declaration of Independence? What else but philosophical principles are 'unalienable Rights' that belong naturally to all men? And how else, except as the assertion of an abstract moral claim, can we understand the *Federalist*, no. 51's assertion that 'Justice is the end of government'.

The framers feared the 'passions' of the people, and argued

---

[22] On the importance of preambles see Plato, *Laws*, Bk. 4.

that 'the reason, alone, of the public . . . ought to control and regulate the government'.[23] The framers were not simple democrats but republicans, who rejected the idea that popular government was necessarily good government. They sought to ensure that political power would be in the hands of the wisest members of the community and not those most responsive to popular will: 'the republican principle demands that the deliberate sense of the community should govern'.[24]

The Constitution itself does not claim to create or confer rights, it only 'secures' them. And the Ninth Amendment explicitly calls upon constitutional interpreters not to 'deny or disparage' the existence of rights not stated explicitly in the Constitution's text. By implication, then, the Constitution itself calls upon citizens and officials to reflect upon the rights that persons have even in the absence of explicit political acknowledgement. The Ninth Amendment calls upon conscientious interpreters to reflect upon our moral rights, and so to engage in moral reflection. Neither the founders nor the Constitution support moral scepticism or a disparaging attitude toward rights not explicitly stated in the founding document.

Judicially enforceable moral principles, even those not explicitly stated in the Constitution's text, have played an important role throughout our history. Early on, Justice Samuel Chase invoked, in *Calder* v. *Bull*, 'the general principles of law and reason' which constrain legislators even in the absence of explicit constitutional provisions.[25]

Chief Justice John Marshall, an ardent nationalist, could have struck down Georgia's revocation of a land grant in *Fletcher* v. *Peck* by invoking only the Constitution's contracts clause.[26] Instead, he went beyond the text of the Constitution and engaged in a considerable discussion of 'the great principles of justice, whose authority is universally acknowledged'. Seventeen years later in *Ogden* v. *Saunders*, Marshall invoked the 'abstract philosophy' of natural rights: 'Individuals do not derive from government their right to contract, but

[23] *Federalist*, no. 49.
[24] Ibid., no. 71.
[25] 3 Dall. 395 (1798).
[26] 3 L. Ed. 162 (1810).

bring that right with them into society . . . every man retains [the right] to acquire property, to dispose of that property according to his own judgment, and to pledge himself for a future act.'[27]

When we think of the American political tradition at its best, the name of Abraham Lincoln must rank along with the greatest of the founders. Lincoln's political morality sprang from a basic concern with human equality, and, in the Gettysburg Address, Lincoln described the central proposition of the Declaration of Independence, to which the nation was, at its birth, dedicated, as 'an abstract truth applicable to all men and all times'. Lincoln, unlike Bork, held that right and wrong depend on standards of judgment independent of mere opinion. What Lincoln would have thought of the assertion that the gratifications of slave-traders and slaves, for instance, are not morally distinguishable or distinguishable only quantitatively, may easily be inferred from his Peoria speech of 1854:

All these free blacks are the descendants of slaves, or have been slaves themselves, and they would be now, but for something which has operated on their white owners, inducing them, at vast pecuniary sacrifices, to liberate them. What is that something? Is there any mistaking it? In all these cases it is your sense of justice, and human sympathy, continually telling you, that the poor negro has some natural right to himself—that those who deny it, and make merchandise of him, deserve kicking, contempt, and death.[28]

After the Civil War, the development of the doctrine of 'substantive due process' carried forward the 'higher law' tradition in the form of judicially protected economic liberties. Now the Supreme Court has stopped protecting economic liberties, but cases like *Griswold* keep alive the substantive due process doctrine in the service of constitutional privacy.

America has a prominent tradition of respecting moral rights and invoking moral principles in legal and other politi-

---

[27] 2 Wheaton 213 (1827).

[28] Abraham Lincoln, Peoria Speech of 1854, quoted in Harry V. Jaffa, *Crisis of the House Divided* (Seattle, Wash., 173), 312. For a discussion of Lincoln's view of the moral status of the Declaration of Independence see Jaffa, ch. 14, and Gary J. Jacobsohn's excellent 'Abraham Lincoln "On this Question of Judicial Authority": The Theory of Constitutional Aspiration', *Western Political Quarterly*, 36 (1983), 52–70.

cal institutions, and so history and social practice cannot be invoked against moral rights or the project of public justification. Constitutional law, frequently infused with moral theory, has helped shape and elevate her political life. Martin Luther King recognized the capacity of a morally informed Constitution, when taken in hand not only by judges but by citizens as well, to elevate a polity:

One day the South will know that when these disinherited children of God sat down at lunch counters they were in reality standing up for the best in the American dream and the most sacred values in our Judeo-Christian heritage, and thusly, carrying our whole nation back to those great wells of democracy which were dug deep by the founding fathers in the formulation of the Constitution and the Declaration of Independence.[29]

It is not my aim to argue that liberal theory best fits the 'facts' of American history, or that liberal constitutionalism is the most felicitous model of our practices. America has a chequered history that includes racism, sexism, and other forms of prejudice that do not and could not become justified by mere persistence or deep-rootedness. To situate liberal values in history and practices does not justify them. Like any normative theory, liberalism properly endorses certain aspects of America's history and provides the grounds for criticizing other aspects: it attempts to separate the grain of valuable tradition from the chaff of mere history. From inherited practices interpreters craft a heritage worth affirming and carrying forward.

Establishing just political practices and institutions is no easy thing. It is reasonable for political moralists and critics to begin by putting the basic political institutions we do have in their best light, trying to discern the ideals implicit in these institutions viewed in light of our best understanding of justice. It is not unreasonable to favour ideals that have a place in our historical practices so long as those practices are in reasonable accord with our basic political values.

What then, is the morality that animates the American

[29] Martin Luther King, 'Letter from Birmingham City Jail', in Bedau, ed., *Civil Disobedience*, p. 88.

Constitution? Innumerable analyses begin with the assumption that America is basically a democratic polity, in which judicially enforceable constitutional rights are to be construed narrowly and legislative powers broadly. As Alexander Bickel put it, 'judicial review is a deviant institution in the American democracy'.[30] Not only legal scholars like Bickel and John Hart Ely but also, as we have seen, political theorists like Michael Walzer contend that America is basically a democratic regime. We must begin, therefore, by establishing the liberal pedigree of the Constitution.

Conservatives like Bork argue, in effect, that judges should enforce only explicit rights, rights plainly stated in the Constitution's text or very clearly implied in it. Legislators, on the other hand, may do anything that is not plainly forbidden by the Constitution's text and its clear implications. This stark divergence of standards can only be justified by a strong background assumption that the overall purpose or point of the Constitution is to empower majoritarian institutions. Bork quotes Chesterton:

'What is the good of telling a community that it has every liberty except the liberty to make laws? The liberty to make laws is what constitutes a free people.' The makers of our Constitution thought so too, for they provided wide powers to representative assemblies and ruled only a few subjects off limits by the Constitution.[31]

But neither Bork's majoritarianism, nor the more elevated and egalitarian democratic theories of Ely and Walzer, comport with the Constitution itself. The Constitution is not simply democratic, but republican and liberal, it pledges the national government to securing for every state, not a democratic, but a 'republican form of government'; it guarantees substantive liberal rights well beyond those that maintain the openness and fairness of democratic processes. The governmental process must meet basic standards of reasonableness, and some things are not permitted irrespective of the process followed.

The institutions and processes established by the Constitution filter and check popular sentiment, and do not simply

---

[30] Bickel, *Least Dangerous*, p. 18.
[31] Bork, *Tradition*, p. 9.

transmit it. Senators were originally chosen by state legislators and not until 1913, with the passage of the Seventeenth Amendment, were they chosen by direct popular election. And, most importantly, each state continues to have two Senators regardless of population. State legislatures were given the power to choose presidential electors, and the electoral college continues to overrepresent the less populous states. The President and the upper chamber have a prophylactic remoteness from popular passions that has been only partially eroded. The bicameral legislature, staggered elections, long terms for Senators and the President, the system of separated powers, and the embrace by one national government of a large or 'extended' republic were all designed to make it difficult for a national majority to gain effective control of the government. It was hoped that, in this way, ample room would be left for deliberation, statesmanship, and the rule of justice. On the 'input' side, therefore, democracy is tempered and compromised by many 'checks and balances', including the power of the courts.

Bickel, Bork, and many others argue that the Supreme Court must exercise its review powers with circumspection because of its anomalous status in a basically democratic or majoritarian scheme of government. This presumption against the Court finds no warrant in the Constitution. The Supreme Court is a branch of the federal government co-ordinate with, and not subordinate to, the legislative and executive branches. The Constitution extends the judicial power 'to all Cases, in Law and Equity, arising under this Constitution'.[32] Judges take an oath to support the Constitution; and in declaring itself supreme the Constitution adds, in the next breath, that judges should take special notice: 'This Constitution, and the Laws of the United States which shall be made in pursuance thereof . . . shall be the supreme Law of the Land; and the judges in every State shall be bound thereby. . . .'[33]

In *Federalist* no. 78, Hamilton defined limited government as that which protects individual rights through courts even against 'legislative invasions . . . instigated by the major voice

[32] Article 3, sect. 2.
[33] Article 6.

of the community'. And in the first Congress Madison proposed and led the passage of the Bill of Rights, explaining that once passed and 'incorporated into the Constitution, independent tribunals of justice will consider themselves in a peculiar manner the guardians of those rights'. The courts, Madison continued, will be an 'impenetrable bulwark against every assumption of power in the legislative or executive' branches and 'be naturally led to resist every encroachment upon rights expressly stipulated for in the Constitution by the declaration of rights'.[34]

So much for the claims of democracy on the 'input' (or process) side. The Constitution also imposes a number of substantive limitations on the ends the federal government may pursue. The Constitution explicitly denies Congress power to, among other things, suspend habeas corpus in peacetime, to pass bills of attainder, *ex post facto* laws.[35] The Constitution also explicitly denies to the states power to conduct their own foreign policies, grant titles of nobility, emit bills of credit, make paper money legal tender, pass bills of attainder or *ex post facto* laws, or impair the obligation of contracts.

Now the Constitution's specific prohibitions may seem rather thin. And, indeed, one of the chief complaints of those who opposed ratification of the Constitution was the absence of a bill of rights limiting the power of the national government in the name of fundamental rights and liberties. This absence had, however, nothing to do with any scepticism on the part of the framers about the existence of broad natural rights. In the logic of the *Federalist Papers*, the security of individual rights is ranked higher than the support of republican institutions.[36] There was probably nothing in politics that

[34] James Madison, *The Papers of James Madison*, ed. W. T. Hutchinson *et al.*, 13 vol. to date (Chicago, Ill., and Charlottesville, Jo., 1962–??), xi. 297. See also R. Rutland, 'How the Constitution Secures Rights: A Look at the Seminal Years', Robert Goldwin and William Schambra, eds., *How Does the Constitution Secure Rights* (Washington, DC, 1985), 1–14.

[35] Article 1, sect. 9.

[36] See, for example, the first paragraph of the *Federalist*, no. 70, where Hamilton considers the charge that 'a vigorous executive is inconsistent with the genius of republican government', Republicans who level the charge, Hamilton says, had better hope not, because if the two are incompatible, republican institutions must be sacrificed. A strong executive is 'essential' to certain protections which are, implicitly,

the founding generation was more certain of than the existence of natural rights.

As Alexander Hamilton explained in *Federalist* no. 84, the enumeration of rights in a constitution could, paradoxically, be harmful to rights. The founders distrusted the 'aphorisms' that tended to be embodied in bills of rights and, more importantly, they positively opposed the natural implication of an enumeration of rights: to specify the rights to be protected against oppressive majorities might imply, wrongly, that these rights are exceptions to a general grant of government powers.[37]

A government of enumerated powers need not specify the rights to be protected against the power of majorities. And so, 'The Constitution is itself', as Hamilton put it in *Federalist* no. 84, 'in every rational sense, and to every useful purpose, a BILL OF RIGHTS'.

To help quiet the fears of the Anti-Federalists, the proponents of the Constitution did eventually propose a Bill of Rights in the first Congress. The logic of limited government was not overturned but nailed down by Madison in the Bill of Rights itself. Thus, to the first eight amendments, which specify various liberties to be protected against government, was added the Ninth Amendment, which explicitly denies that popular rights can be limited to those enumerated in the Constitution: 'The enumeration in the Constitution, of certain rights, shall not be construed to deny or disparage others retained by the people.' The Bill of Rights closes with the Tenth Amendment, emphasizing the logic of limited powers, 'The powers not delegated to the United States by the Constitution, nor prohibited by it to the States, are reserved to the States respectively, or to the people.'

One need hardly recite the textual support in the Bill of Rights for a broad range of liberal freedoms, including religious freedom, freedom of speech, of the press, and of assembly. The founding document also protects the many

---

more basic and important than those served by republic institutions: 'the protection of property . . . [and] the security of liberty against the enterprises and assaults of ambition, of faction, and of anarchy'.

[37] See Herbert Storing's discussion, 'The Constitution and the Bill of Rights', in M. J. Harmon, ed., *Essays*, pp. 32–48.

privileges and immunities associated with the rule of law and with fair proceedings in criminal cases, in the Fifth, Sixth, Seventh, and Eighth Amendments.

It should also be noted that the Constitution lends explicit support to the values of economic freedom, private security, property rights, and liberty of contract. Article I, section 10 prohibits any state 'Law impairing the Obligation of Contracts'. The Third Amendment protects the sanctity of the home against the quartering of troops, and the Fourth protects 'The right of the people to be secure in their persons, houses, papers, and effects, against unreasonable searches and seizures'. Personal security and privacy are thus clearly linked with the ownership of personal property. The Fifth Amendment brings 'life, liberty and property' under the protection of 'due process of law', and this guarantee is explicitly extended to the states by the Fourteenth Amendment. The Fifth also requires that private property may only be taken for public use and with 'just compensation'.

The founders originally believed that the need for a Bill of Rights had been pre-empted by the limited nature of national government powers (and by bills of rights in state constitutions). Constitutional interpreters should not overemphasize the Bill of Rights at the expense of the power-limiting logic of the Constitution itself. Whereas the President is granted 'The Executive Power' and the courts 'The Judicial Power', the Congress is, conspicuously, given only 'all legislative powers herein granted'. Legislative powers are enumerated and not general.

The Constitution's language with respect to rights is at least as sweeping as Article 1, Section 8's enumeration of Congress's powers. The first eight powers concern commerce broadly: the power to tax, to borrow money on credit, regulate commerce, establish uniform rules for naturalization and bankruptcy, to coin money, punish counterfeiting, establish post offices, and grant exclusive patents and copyrights. Congress is also given power to provide for establishment of lower courts, for governing of the District of Columbia, and, most importantly, for national security. At the end of Section 8 stands the 'necessary and proper' clause: Congress may 'make all laws which shall be necessary and proper for carrying into Execution the foregoing Powers, and all other Powers vested by this Constitution in the Government of the United States. . . .'

The 'necessary and proper' clause certainly allows Congress to do many things incidentally required to carry out the enumerated powers. The enumerated powers are strikingly concerned with commerce broadly: the regulation of trade, rules for bankruptcy, coining money, punishment of counterfeiting, patents, copyrights, post offices—all these are provided for, implying a vision of the general welfare that suggests a 'commercial republic'. If, however, judges stuck 'close to the text and its clear implications' when interpreting powers, as Bork says they should do when interpreting rights, then the national government would be very severely constrained indeed.

The Constitution is concerned not simply with empowering the people's representatives to govern, but with checking and limiting the powers of legislative majorities in a host of important ways, both procedurally and substantively (or on both the 'input' and the 'output' sides). The preoccupation of democratic theorists and conservatives with the legitimacy of judicial review ignores the fact that in a system of limited government the exercise of legislative power itself demands positive constitutional support.

Legislators and executives are bound, no less than judges, to carry out their constitutional mandate. All who take an oath to support the Constitution as supreme law have an obligation to strive conscientiously toward its ends and purposes and not just to avoid breaking its most obvious commands. All of these offices are empowered by the Constitution and not simply limited by it. There is no presumption in the Constitution in favour of legislatures and against judges, or in favour of majority power and against individual rights and liberties. The Constitution gives Congress no general grant of power, but even if it did, conscientious legislators would have both constitutional and moral reasons for insuring that the exercise of their power could be squared with the requirements of justice and the limits imposed by liberal rights. Judicial review is not an anomalous blotch on a democratic scheme of government. Contrary to what the democratic and conservative communitarians hold, judicial review is an integral part of a scheme of constitutionally limited government.

The Constitution, I have argued, is not a basically democratic or majoritarian document. It is just as basically concerned with protecting rights and imposing certain limits on government as with empowering elected officials to govern. This argument, it is sometimes said, neglects a constitutional provision that ultimately places America's fundamental law in the camp of popular sovereignty and democratic rule: the amendment provision. An amending majority following appropriate procedures can, presumably, alter any feature of the document including its commitment to basic liberties and constitutional forms. Surely, then, the voice of the people so expressed has ultimate constitutional authority.

The amending provision may appear to be the democrat's *coup de grace*. But not so fast. The constitutionalist has one last available move. The Constitution's many provisions and principles are not equally basic. It guarantees a trial by jury, but also commits the President to preserving the constitutional order as a whole. If there is a conflict in a given instance between these or other provisions of the Constitution, one would reasonably think that the more basic or important should prevail. The Constitution, as Walter F. Murphy has argued, presents not simply a set but an ordering or hierarchy of constitutional values.[38]

The exercise of the amending provision might come into conflict with the most basic values and commitments of America's fundamental law, with principles that underlie *many* specific provisions and constitutional structures. Imagine, as Murphy suggests, that an ugly wave of racism sweeps the country after which an amendment is passed that states: 'Members of the coloured race are inferior to Caucasians in moral worth.'[39] The amendment goes on to deny blacks a host of basic civil and political rights. Why should the Supreme Court allow that amendment to override the Constitution's basic and pervasive commitment to equality? Why should the amendment provision be read as overriding the basic commitment of constitutionalism, that is, to *reasonable*

[38] Murphy, 'Ordering'.
[39] Ibid. 755.

self-government? There are, admittedly, few explicit limitations on the amending provision, but much constitutional interpretation is and must be a matter of tracing implications.

Constitutions contain hierarchies of values and implicit unities which interpreters seek to elicit and apply. An amendment could be so out of keeping with the basic commitments of the whole document that it would not be recognizable as an amendment to the document and so would be an unintelligible constitutional anomaly.[40] The values of liberal constitutionalism, then, do not fully give way to those of democracy or popular sovereignty even via amending provisions.

Consider another example. The American Constitution exhibits a basic commitment to liberal public justification: the election of many public officials, the dialogue required by separated powers, bicameralism, and judicial review, the 'first freedoms' of speech and the press, the requirement of warrants for police searches, the right to confront witnesses, and to a trial by jury, even the elaborate procedures required to amend the Constitution, all these provisions and more represent basic structural commitments to institutionalizing a process of free and reasonable self-government. An 'amendment' which sought to expunge that basic commitment and to wipe out basic political and personal freedoms intrinsic to reasonable self-government suggests a desire to revolutionize rather than correct and amend. It would be unintelligible and revolting from the perspective of the Constitution as a whole. It would not be faintly recognizable as reasonable in constitutional terms and so it would properly be held by the Supreme Court to be a nullity.

THE CONSTITUTIONAL DOUBLE STANDARD

The jurisprudence of the modern Supreme Court developed in response to the perceived illegitimacy of the Court's efforts, over many years, to develop principled ways of limiting the

---

[40] Ibid. 755–6. Constitutional courts in Bavaria and India have confronted constitutionally offensive amendments and partially invalidated them: see the materials in Walter F. Murphy and J. Tanenhaus, *Comparative Constitutional Law: Cases and Commentaries* (New York, 1977), 209.

regulatory powers of the federal and state governments in the economic sphere. The Supreme Court's efforts in the economic sphere were directed at imposing limits on Congress's regulatory powers under the commerce clause, and at defining individual economic liberties enforceable against the states under the Fourteenth Amendment's due process clause. Despite the fact that most constitutional scholars on both the left and the right now agree that the courts should give Congress and the states a free hand in the economic sphere, the Supreme Court's efforts there, while far from perfect, were, on the whole, legitimate and principled exercises in constitutional interpretation.[41]

In the late nineteenth and early twentieth centuries, the Supreme Court forged distinctions to define and limit Congress's power to 'regulate Commerce . . . among the several States'.[42] Of particular importance was the distinction between commerce and production, which placed the regulation of the latter beyond Congress's power, and among the reserved powers of the states.[43] These distinctions were swept away when the Court moved to accept the constitutionality of the New Deal.[44] But any conscientious interpreter of the Constitution must feel uncomfortable with a commerce power so extensive that it sacrifices other values with high constitutional standing, or with a commerce power used pretextually to pursue ends unrelated to commerce.[45]

Consider *Wickard* v. *Filburn*, the case of an Ohio farmer who sowed 23 acres of wheat wholly for consumption on his farm.[46] He was fined by the Department of Agriculture, however, for harvesting in excess of his quota, which the Department had set at 11.1 acres. The New Deal's Agri-

---

[41] Exceptions to the overwhelming, but I believe ill-founded, consensus on this point are Richard Epstein, *Takings* (Cambridge, Mass., 1985), Bernard Seigan, *Economic Liberties and the Constitution* (Chicago, Ill., 1980), and Martin Schapiro, 'The Constitution and Economic Liberties', in Harmon, ed., *Essays*, pp. 74–98.

[42] Article 1, sect. 8.

[43] See *US* v. *E. C. Knight* 156 US 1 (1895).

[44] See *NLRB* v. *Jones & Laughlin Steel Co.* 301 US 1 (1937) and *US* v. *Darby* 312 US 100 (1941).

[45] For a pretextual use of the commerce power, to suppress lotteries and thereby to pursue an end subsumed by the states' reserved police powers, see *Champion* v. *Ames* 188 US 321 (1903).

[46] *Wickard* v. *Filburn* 317 US 111 (1942).

cultural Adjustment Act of 1938 gave the Secretary of Agriculture the power to establish these allotments for the sake of regulating supply and stabilizing prices. Although there was no 'commerce' involved in Filburn's activity, the Court ruled that his activities 'effected commerce' because excess supply constituted an 'obstruction to commerce'.

The problem with *Wickard*, of course, is that it cavalierly dismisses property rights closely connected with domestic privacy and personal liberty to a policy rather loosely related to Congress's commerce power. Long before *Wickard*, Justice Holmes had warned that the logic of indirect effects on a 'national market' had no limit: 'Almost anything—marriage, birth, death, may in some manner effect commerce. . . .'[47] But without the sorts of defining and limiting distinctions which the Supreme Court has abandoned, it is hard to see why marriage and divorce should not fall under commercial regulation as well.

Besides the limits placed on the commerce power, the Courts also deployed, against the states, the doctrine of 'substantive due process', a doctrine now identified most closely with the case of *Lochner* v. *New York*.[48] In *Lochner* the Court struck down a New York statute limiting the working hours of bakery employees as an abridgement of 'liberty of contract'. The modern Court has not abandoned the idea that the Fourteenth Amendment (which says 'No state shall . . . deprive any person of life, liberty, or property without due process of law') implies that there are substantive limits on the ways in which the state can interfere with private relations. The Court has simply shifted its inquiries away from the economic sphere. When it comes to state economic regulation, the Court requires nothing more than the merest 'rationality' to justify restrictions on individual liberty. And where no rational basis for restrictions on economic liberty have been put forward by the legislators themselves, the Court has simply hypothesized its own rationale.[49]

Cases like *Lee Optical* and *Skrupka* not only neglect economic

---

[47] *Northern Securities Co.* v. *US* 193 US 197 (1904).

[48] 198 US 45 (1905).

[49] See *Williamson* v. *Lee Optical* 348 US 343 (1955), and *Ferguson* v. *Skrupka* 372 US 726 (1963).

liberties, they also sanction the abandonment of reason-giving by state legislators, who are themselves sworn to uphold the Constitution. Legislators, as much as judges, ought to be able to justify their actions publicly. Legislators, citizens, and all other political actors are required by liberal justice and their constitutional oaths to provide dissenters and those whose lives and property are at stake with public justifications for controversial interpretations of the Constitution.

Lee Optical and *Skrupka* stand for the judicial acceptance of laws which have no apparent basis but the interests or will of the majority. *Lee Optical* contested an Oklahoma bill that required a prescription from an optometrist or ophthalmologist before having lenses replaced or even just fitted in new frames by opticians. The law gave every appearance of being a victory of the interest of optometrists and ophthalmologist over opticians and consumers. The law was unsupported by any legislative reasons linking the added income of eye doctors with the general good of the state. Justice Douglas admitted the apparent 'needless' and 'wasteful' character of the Oklahoma law, but then proceeded to invent hypothetical reasons, one might say a rationalization, for the legislature.[50]

Legislators may often be justified in overriding the economic liberties of particular business groups in order to pursue a conscientious vision of the common good. But in order to justify restrictions on liberty of any kind, under their liberal Constitution, Americans must at least expect legislators to present public reasons for their actions. Legislators ought to be expected, no less than judges, to participate in the process of constitutional reason-giving.

The Supreme Court has largely abandoned the protection of substantive economic values, but it has not abandoned fundamental values. The modern Court closely scrutinizes legislation touching on a list of 'preferred freedoms', such as the right to freedom of speech, of religion, of the press, and more recently to privacy and the equal protection of the laws.

As noted above, the Constitution manifests a basic concern with protecting a wide range of human freedoms, and in this

---

[50] See Barber, *What the Constitution Means*, pp. 132–3.

way reflects basically liberal commitments. Governmental powers are limited while the Ninth Amendment tells us that people have rights not explicitly mentioned in the document. Judges who wish to remain faithful to their oaths of office cannot flinch, therefore, at the task of applying the same expansive logic to individual rights that has been applied to government powers.

Griswold v. *Connecticut*, which Bork and Ely deride as an arbitrary judicial creation of a new right, is an excellent case in point.[51] *Griswold* struck down a Connecticut statute that made it illegal for married couples to use contraceptives. The court based its decision on an implicit constitutional right to zones of privacy, which emanate from and form 'penumbras' around the specific guarantees of the Bill of Rights. As Justice Douglas argued, these implicit, penumbral rights, including one protecting the privacy of the marriage relationship, help give life and substance to express guarantees:

Various guarantees create zones of privacy. The right of association contained in the penumbra of the First Amendment is one, as we have seen. The Third Amendment in its prohibition against the quartering of soldiers 'in any house' in time of peace without the consent of the owner is another facet of that privacy. The Fourth Amendment explicitly affirms the 'right of the people to be secure in their persons, houses, papers, and effects against unreasonable searches and seizures'. The Fifth Amendment in its Self-Incrimination Clause enables the citizen to create a zone of privacy which government may not force him to surrender to his detriment.

Justice Goldberg, concurring, emphasized that the Ninth Amendment testifies to the existence of fundamental rights not expressly enumerated.

Most commentators on the liberal left applaud the Supreme Court's shift from protecting economic values to protecting non-economic ones such as privacy. Conservatives like Bork and democrats like Ely, on the other hand, see the new jurisprudence as no better than the old. They want the Court to abandon the protection, not just of economic liberties, but of all 'fundamental' interests or 'substantive' values other than, in Bork's case, those explicitly stated in the constitutional text

[51] 381 US 479 (1965).

and originally intended by the text's framers, or those, in the democrats' case, which secure the continued working of democratic procedures.

Critics of recent liberal judicial activism have a point. Both the new 'activist' jurisprudence and the old are flawed: in both cases the choice of values to be protected is partial and unjustified. The 'Old Men' of the *Lochner* era failed adequately to recognize the high place that the Constitution gives to non-economic liberties like freedom of speech.[52] Modern courts err, likewise, in neglecting economic liberties that have a substantial place in the Constitution's scheme of values. But these flaws can be rectified without abandoning the active judicial protection of individual rights. The old Court and the new err not by protecting constitutional liberties, but by failing to protect them all.

The underlying logic of *Griswold* is essentially correct, though Justice Douglas's execution leaves something to be desired. *Griswold* fleshes out the meaning of the Constitution's general phrases by articulating the principles and purposes that underlie specific guarantees and structures in the text. Proceeding in this way permits us to see specific guarantees of rights or allocations of powers as attempts to realize the broader ends of the preamble (including justice, liberty, and the general welfare). From explicit constitutional rights and limits on government, and purposes stated and implied in the Constitution, we establish a principled basis for the unstated rights guaranteed by the Ninth Amendment, a constitutional basis capable of supporting the full panoply of liberal rights. The implicit right to privacy is at least as well founded as various implicit national powers, such as the power to create a national bank.[53] The Constitution can and should be read as an attempt to protect the whole range of liberal freedoms.

Constitutional interpretation should help answer a basic question of political morality: 'Why should the nation affirm this Constitution as supreme law?' By proceeding in a manner similar to *Griswold*, interpreters can vindicate the Constitu-

---

[52] See, among other cases, *Schenck* v. *US* 249 US 47 (1919), *Abrams* v. *US* 250 US 616 (1919), and *Whitney* v. *California* 274 US 357 (1927).

[53] See *McCulloch* v. *Maryland* 4 Wheaton 316 (1819).

tion's authority by establishing its rightness. The authority of supreme law depends, at least in part, on its approximation to political principles that pass the test of public justification. In fusing constitutional interpretation and moral theory, the polity helps institutionalize the practice of moral criticism and improvement, and thereby helps guarantee that the republic will remain worthy of allegiance.

The method of critical and principled interpretation employed in *Griswold* helps clarify the relation between morality and constitutional law. Natural law or 'higher law' notions are not pulled from the sky and slotted into constitutional gaps and openings. Rather, interpreters read an open-ended and complex document in a certain spirit: searching for the principles that seem to underlie its specific phrases and larger structures, principles that help complete and justify the document's more specific aspects, and interpreting those principles in a morally critical light. The point is to read this document as the best it can be, completing its meaning by drawing out the document's latent principles, understanding the whole as attempting to realize the preamble's ends of justice, liberty, and the general welfare.

PUBLIC REASONABLENESS AND PRINCIPLED ACTIVISM

The US Supreme Court has, on occasion, seemed to be heading toward a principled insistence on the value of respecting the whole range of constitutional rights. The Court of the *Lochner* era may justly be accused of inadequate concern with non-economic liberties; it did take the important step of holding that the word liberty in the Fourteenth Amendment's due process clause protects freedom of speech.[54] And even the crustiest of the 'Old Men' recognized the close relation between economic and other personal liberties, and thus pointed the way toward a principled synthesis. In *Meyer* v. *Nebraska* the Court overturned the conviction of a German language teacher under a statute prohibiting the teaching of foreign languages to young children. For the Court, Justice

---

[54] *Gitlow* v. *New York* 268 US 652 (1925).

McReynolds articulated a broad conception of the liberty protected by the Fourteenth Amendment:

> Without doubt, it denotes not merely freedom from bodily restraint but also the right of the individual to contract, to engage in any of the common occupations of life, to acquire useful knowledge, to marry, establish a home and bring up children, to worship God according to the dictates of his conscience, and generally to enjoy those privileges long recognized at common law as essential to the orderly pursuit of happiness by free men.[55]

Justice McReynolds links the autonomy and intellectual freedom of parents and students with the 'economic' right of language teachers to pursue their calling.[56] The Old Court displayed a capacity for principled growth that is yet to be matched by the modern Court.

The Supreme Court has recently moved, albeit haltingly, to infuse a measure of substantive 'bite' into the minimal reasonableness standard that it applies in the sphere of economic policy. In *City of Cleburne* v. *Cleburne Living Center*, the Court struck down a municipal ordinance requiring special permits for the establishment of homes for the mentally retarded.[57] Instead of hypothesizing possible reasons for singling out homes for the retarded, the Court critically examined the reasons offered by the City Council.

The Court found all of the council's arguments specious, and charged that requiring a special permit only for housing for the retarded appears to rest 'on an irrational prejudice against the mentally retarded'.[58]

> mere negative attitudes, or fear, unsubstantiated by factors which are properly cognizable in a zoning proceeding, are not permissible bases for treating a home for the mentally retarded differently from apartment houses, multiple dwellings, and the like. . . . 'Private

---

[55] 262 US 390 (1923), p. 399.

[56] See also *Pierce* v. *Society of Sisters* 268 US 510 (1925).

[57] US 432 (1985). For another harbinger of the beefed up minimum rationality standard see *Plyler* v. *Doe* 457 US 202, 224 (1984). *Plyler* concerned a Texas law denying a free public education to the children of illegal aliens. The court held that although alien children are not a 'suspect' class and the right to education is not 'fundamental', nevertheless, the challenged classification 'can hardly be considered rational unless it furthers some substantial goal of the state': ibid. 224.

[58] *Cleburne*, p. 450.

biases may be outside the reach of the law, but the law cannot, directly or indirectly, give them effect'.[59]

In his concurring opinion in *Cleburne*, Justice Stevens argued that the Equal Protection Clause should be interpreted as imposing a duty on legislators always 'to govern impartially'. This duty to govern impartially or reasonably embodies the core values of constitutionalism: to have a government of laws rather than of men is to have government based on reasons that all ought to be able to accept. And so, Stevens objected, 'I cannot believe that a rational member of this disadvantaged class could ever approve of the discriminatory application of the city's ordinance in this case'.[60] Stevens properly asserted, in effect, that Justices must put themselves in the shoes of those being discriminated against and ask whether a restriction or burden could be judged to be reasonable. To adopt the perspective of the victim of discrimination is to insist that laws be made on the basis of public reasons, reasons good for both the politically powerless and weak as well as the strong.

Stevens's concurring opinion in *Cleburne* adopts precisely the right moral perspective; he ascribes to legislators a pervasive obligation to act reasonably. A critical standard of reasonableness ought to be applied to all cases, whether involving civil rights or any other issue, including economic regulation. Stevens's defence of judicial scrutiny on equal protection grounds across the whole range of possible challenges to state laws is an important step toward principled activism and a publicly reasonable legislative process.[61]

Dissenting Justices Marshall, Brennan, and Blackmun fully appreciated the import of the strengthened rationality test of *Cleburne*: 'the rational basis test invoked today is most assuredly not the rational basis test of *Williamson* v. *Lee Optical*. . . . In normal circumstances, the burden is not on the legislature to convince the Court that the lines it has drawn are sensible.'[62] Nothing could better sum up the paltriness of the usual minimum review standard than Marshall's admission

[59] Ibid. 448.
[60] Ibid. 455.
[61] See also Steven's opinion in *Craig* v. *Boren* 429 US 190 (1976).
[62] *Cleburne*, pp. 458–9.

that it sanctions laws not shown to be 'sensible'. Marshall's fear is precisely that beefing up the minimal reasonableness test opens the way to principled activism, the careful review of the reasons advanced to support restrictions on economic as well as civil and political freedom. The review standard of *Cleburne* 'creates precedent', Marshall said, 'for this Court and lower courts to subject economic and commercial classifications to similar and searching "ordinary" rational basis review—a small and regrettable step back toward the days of *Lochner* v. *New York*. . . .'[63]

Marshall correctly gauges the implications of *Cleburne*, but these implications should be embraced. Economic liberty is a constitutional value, property rights have a place in, and deserve some weight in deliberations upon, hard questions of constitutional interpretation. This does not mean that *laissez-faire* must always triumph over competing values, including the undoubted right of Congress and the states to a range of discretion in making policy on many commercial matters. But conscientious adjudicators must not mark off the economic realm as the no man's land of unreasonableness, a domain of unfettered legislative discretion. At the very least, the reasons and evidence needed to justify restrictions on economic liberty should never be left to the imagination: a burden of justification should rest on legislatures; the justifications actually offered by legislators should be scrutinized; not only reasons and arguments but a measure of empirical support should be required to make the case for economic regulations.

Economic liberties are not the only ones threatened by misguided judicial deference. There is a growing danger that the Supreme Court will abandon the relatively (but not excessively) robust standards of review it has deployed in the non-economic sphere. The Court erred, for example, in refusing to extend the privacy right to homosexuals, and in doing so it ignored the imperatives of liberal public justification.

In cases following *Griswold*'s recognition of a constitutional right to privacy, the Court banned prosecution for possessing obscene materials in the home, and later overturned a convic-

---

[63] *Cleburne*, 459–60.

tion under a state law banning the distribution of contraceptives to an unmarried person.[64] The constitutional right to privacy was extended from the use of contraceptives by married couples to unmarried couples, and to reading pornography at home.

Justice White's opinion for the Court in *Bowers* v. *Hardwick* construed the privacy right as extending only to matters involving 'family, marriage, and procreation': 'None of the rights announced in those [the previous] cases', said White, 'bears any resemblance to the claimed constitutional right of homosexuals to engage in acts of sodomy. . . . No connection between family, marriage, or procreation on the one hand and homosexual activity on the other has been demonstrated.'[65] Constitutional protections extend, the Court majority argued, only to family decisions broadly speaking. Is this, however, the best interpretation of constitutional privacy? How do we decide?

White's opinion displays all the distinguishing features of New Right jurisprudence. He is defensive about the power of the Supreme Court in a democracy, and insists that judges stay close to the 'express' language of the Constitution when interpreting rights.[66] Gesturing toward the authority of Original Intent, White pointed out that sodomy was a common law crime in all of the thirteen original colonies and that anti-sodomy statutes were in force in thirty-two of the thirty-seven states in the Union at the time the Fourteenth Amendment was ratified.[67] White's whole opinion, finally, relies on a broad moral scepticism. That scepticism is announced most loudly by his unwillingness to advance critical moral reasons for distinguishing privacy rights associated with family life from those claimed by homosexuals: 'to claim that a right to engage in such conduct [namely sodomy] is "deeply rooted in this nation's history or tradition" or "implicit in the concept of ordered liberty" is, at best, facetious.'[68]

An adequate basis for the Georgia ban on sodomy is found,

[64] *Eisenstadt* v. *Baird* 405 US 438 (1972); *Stanley* v. *Georgia*, 394 US 557 (1969).
[65] *Bowers*, 106 S. Ct. 2841 (1986), p. 2844.
[66] Ibid. 2846.
[67] Ibid. 2844–5.
[68] Ibid. 2846.

White said, in 'the presumed belief of a majority of the electorate in Georgia that homosexual sodomy is immoral and unacceptable', in presumed 'majority sentiments about the morality of homosexuality'.[69] In place of an examination of the reasons for banning sodomy *per se*, or a discussion of the morality of homosexuality, both White and Chief Justice Burger (in a concurring opinion) simply accept the 'ancient roots' of proscriptions on homosexuality as adequate.[70]

Gesturing toward what no one disputes, that homosexuals have often been subject to discrimination and prejudice, does not constitute a reason for continuing to discriminate. Not all historical practices are good, and prejudices often persist. To recommend or condemn a practice one must say something about its reasonableness or goodness; referring to 'ages of moral teaching' is not enough.[71] The Court in *Bowers* failed to provide real public reasons justifying its refusal to recognize an extremely important constitutional claim.

Justice Blackmun's dissent characterized the right at stake in *Bowers* more generally and more abstractly than the majority: the case, he said, is not about sodomy but about the 'right to be let alone'. Blackmun also correctly insisted that Georgia and the Supreme Court majority had failed to live up to the demands of public reasonableness: 'It is revolting', said Blackmun quoting Holmes, 'to have no better reason for a rule of law than that so it was first laid down in the time of Henry IV. It is still more revolting if the grounds upon which it was laid down have vanished long since, and the rule simply persists from blind imitation of the past.'[72] If constitutional rights stand for anything, Blackmun contends, they 'must mean that, before Georgia can prosecute its citizens for making

---

[69]   *Bowers*, 2846.

[70]   Burger probably got his history wrong on several counts. According to John Boswell, homosexuality has been subject to active state intervention not for millenia but only since the latter half of the twelfth century; it was accepted as natural by the classical Greeks; it was accepted by the Romans of the Republic and in the Empire until the beginning of its decline in third century. See Boswell, *Christianity, Social Tolerance, and Homosexuality* (Chicago, Ill., 1981), 71 and *passim*.

[71]   Here again, it is worth noting that Justice Stevens has recognized that principled constitutional interpretation requires rising above 'stereotyped thinking', which often relies on mere prejudice, on 'habit rather than analysis' or reflection; see *Mathews* v. *Lucas* 427 US 495 (1976), in his dissenting opinion on p. 520.

[72]   *Bowers*, p. 2848.

choices about the most intimate aspects of their lives, it must do more than assert that the choice they have made is . . . an "abominable crime not fit to be named among Christians.""[73] Only public reasons that all ought to be able to accept can count as good reasons for lawmaking. Religiously grounded intolerance, historically persistent practices of prejudice and discrimination, and simple feelings of disapproval cannot be invoked by public officials to support state infringements on individual liberty.[74]

Previous privacy cases should, Blackmun insisted, be understood as resting on broad guarantees of individual freedom: freedom in our intimate associations with others provides the 'ability independently to define one's identity', and 'is central to any concept of liberty'.[75] The previous cases protect certain intimate decisions and also certain *places*. The privacy of intimate association in the home implicates the more general right of privacy associated with home owner-ship. The Fourth Amendment speaks explicitly of 'The right of the people to be secure in their . . . houses . . .'—the most explicit of the various provisions supporting the privacy right announced in *Griswold*. The liberty of consenting adults to engage in intimate relations at home is, Blackmun argues, the heart of the privacy right articulated in previous cases and so the right claimed by Michael Hardwick is indeed justified.

There are, it must be said, problems with Blackmun's defence of homosexual privacy.[76] The freedom to 'define one's identity' is too broad in its sweep and too narrowly individual-istic in its moral pedigree. The goods embodied in human relationships are not entirely reducible to the value of individual choice and free self-definition. There is no need to deny, as Blackmun seems to do, that the family as such embodies certain goods worth protecting. The point is that homosexual relationships embody many of those same goods: friendship, care, affection, intimate society, all of these goods and more are promoted through homosexual as well as

[73] Ibid.
[74] Ibid. 2854–5.
[75] Ibid.
[76] My remarks here are indebted to conversations with Sotirios A. Barber and Michael J. Sandel.

heterosexual relationships, and for most homosexuals these goods are not available through the conventional marriage bond.

The opinions of White and Burger might be taken as statements about the virtues the Constitution stands for. They imply that at their best Americans are intolerant and mistrustful, that they act on sentiments and feelings rather than reasons, that they fear that the effort to rise above prejudice will dissolve the fragile and unreasoned bonds that hold society together. Such attitudes nurture the anxious fear that American politics is held together by no more than prejudice, sentiment, and belief. Expectations such as these foster the 'minimal rationality' standard of constitutional review which, as we have seen, stands for precious little review. These attitudes represent the antithesis of those appropriate to constitutionalists, to those determined to honour the rule of law in the spirit of public justification.

Blackmun's dissenting opinion in *Bowers* implies a vision of constitutional virtue much superior to that of the Court majority: a striving to be governed by impartial reasons, a resolve to protect the victims of prejudice, a recognition that freedom leads naturally to a diversity that should be tolerated rather than suppressed—these are, suggests Blackmun, the moral core of America's constitutional aspirations.[77]

Bowers v. *Hardwick* poses hard questions for constitutionalists: which values have pride of place in the Constitution's scheme of values? What sort of freedom and privacy does the Constitution stand for? These questions cannot, as I have argued, be answered by reference to the words of the Constitution, past cases, and history alone; this case confronts us with inescapable moral questions about the rights that individuals ought to have against state interference. Deciding which interpretation of the case law and history is *better* requires a judgment both about which interpretations adequately fit received legal materials and also about which interpretation shows that material in an honourable and morally worthy light. Constitutional interpretation cannot flee

---

[77] The same thing, I might add, is implied in *Federalist*, no. 10, where Madison notes that diversity is the natural result of liberty.

from hard moral judgments, it can either make them and defend them or stumble into them or past them. While there is more to be said on both sides of this difficult issue, on the strength of the arguments examined here one must conclude that homosexuals have the right denied to them by the courts.

Principled activism stands for the idea, suggested by Justice Stevens in *Cleburne*, that legislators have a *pervasive* duty to act on public reasons, to offer good reasons to the public for *all* restrictions on liberties. This broad duty finds support in the Constitution's concern with economic as well as human rights, and with the commitment to reasonable self-government. To absolve state legislators from the need to justify restrictions on economic liberty or the privacy of disfavoured groups is inconsistent with a conscientious desire to apply and enforce the Constitution's own values. Judicial review exercised with vigour and consistency can be good for liberty and for public reasonableness.

One argument often put forward in defence of the 'double standard' in constitutional law is the claim that political and regulatory processes, without meaningful judicial review, can be trusted to act fairly with regard to economic affairs. This claim cannot withstand scrutiny. In elections and the policy-making process, narrow and self-seeking *economic* interests are often at work. The benefits derived from government programmes or regulations are often highly concentrated on a few individuals or groups whereas the costs can be dispersed over millions of taxpayers or consumers who hardly notice if at all. Politics presents innumerable opportunities for the pursuit of private interests at the expense of other people: exclusionary zoning laws, regulations that disadvantage competitors, licensing requirements that keep potential competitors out of a market—the list could be expanded *ad infinitum*.[78]

The effective non-review of economic legislation at work in the minimum rationality standard as applied flies in the face of what we know about politics. The notion that the US

---

[78] For an excellent recent study of the misuse of licensing laws see S. David Young, *The Rule of Experts* (Washington, DC, 1987). Gabriel Kolko's study of the private interests behind the rise of business regulation is still a classic, see *The Triumph of Conservatism* (New York, 1963).

Constitution speaks only to political and civil rights and not to economic liberty cannot, moreover, withstand even a cursory reading of the founding document. The Constitution exhibits a concern with individual liberty in general, and that is not hard to explain or justify. Free economic activity sustains a productive society, and provides outlets for human energy and creativity; it also allows people to build and preserve spheres of autonomy and personal security which are supportive of all other liberties.

Vocations, professions—even common trades and occupations—represent more than an investment of time and effort: these are choices of ways of life. Our occupations often shape our identities as deeply as what we read or take in through the media, as deeply as the intimate choices we make. Economic liberty is bound up with personal security as well as personal liberty and self-definition. The security of the home and personal effects protects not only privacy or 'property', but an investment of time and care spent building a worthwhile way of life. The home shields our intimate associations with others and, like our occupations, shapes and is shaped by our personalities.

Property rights and economic liberties often converge with other personal values—the security of the home, the survival of valuable communities and associations, the maintenance of freely chosen ways of life. My claim is that judges should critically review the reasons put forward for economic regulations, and that the value of economic liberty and private property must be allowed their due weight in the admittedly difficult process of weighing competing constitutional values. Specifying this weight in particular cases is a difficult but inescapable task.

Economic security and property rights shield some of the deepest and most valuable aspects of free human existence. Judges should, therefore, begin by scrutinizing legislation touching on those forms of free economic activity and property ownership most closely related to liberty interests already being protected: the right to engage in an occupation and the security of the home would be good places to start. These personality-protecting and autonomy-nurturing economic rights merit judicial scrutiny for many of the same reasons that other 'personal rights' (like privacy) do.[79] Those forms of economic liberty and property less closely connected with personal life and individual autonomy still deserve at least some judicial protection, because the Constitution exhibits a measure of support for free market values, because corrupt motives of self-interest are at work in political activities concerned with all economic matters, and because public reasonableness is a pervasive political duty.

I am not arguing that we must leap boldly back to *Lochner*, invalidating the welfare state as unconstitutional. Some of the factors I have cited, indeed, might be thought to *support* certain forms of economic redistribution. The value of economic liberty, even when politically contested, cannot be ignored by constitutional interpreters any more than the value of free speech. The shape and nature of First Amendment rights depend upon contestable arguments about the intrinsic importance of free speech to human life and the consequences of free speech for society more broadly. Economic liberties raise similarly tough issues, and these must be addressed by conscientious adjudicators. In neither instance should liberty interests be left entirely to legislators.

CONCLUSION

Liberal ideals, far from being opposed to what is distinctive in American politics, help illumine (and are illumined by) what is best in the American political tradition. The US Constitution provides grounds for challenging acts of government, and the power of the courts stands not only for the nation's commitment to rights but also for the special form of respect paid to those on the losing side of legislative battles or those who feel victimized by executives carrying out the law. Judicial review dramatizes the commitment to treat even the weak and powerless in a reasonable and justifiable manner; it embodies a determination to be governed by more than mere force. Non-activists of the New Right and the selective activists of the left

---

[79] Judges should begin, that is, by overturning decisions like *Wickard*, *Poletown*, and *Lee Optical*.

threaten the core commitment of the liberal, constitutional order: the promise of reasonable self-government.

When judges properly exercise their review power, demanding real reasons and evidence before allowing restrictions on individual liberty, judicial review helps ensure that majorities treat minorities as fellow citizens worthy of liberal respect. Judicial review helps create a certain especially valuable form of political community: a political community based on reasoned self-government, a community of citizens committed to the practice of public reason-giving. When the Supreme Court announces, however, that restrictions on economic and other disfavoured liberties will pass muster without a meaningful inquiry into the quality of the case for these restrictions it provides a cloak for unjust power: arbitrary power unsupported by good, impartial reasons beyond the particular interests of the politically well connected.

Principled judicial activism would require, at the very least, that governments provide a 'real and substantial' justification for restrictions on the full array of liberties that find a place in the Constitution's scheme of values.[80] Principled activism would help both protect liberty and ensure reasonableness in all spheres of government; under its banner the Supreme Court would enlist in the service of liberal public justification. On the procedural side, judges would critically examine the reasons and the evidence offered to support restrictions on liberty; a measure of real critical 'bite' would be infused into examinations of the rationality of *all* government restrictions on constitutional liberty.[81] On the substantive side, principled activism would give greater weight to the interest in economic liberty, and thus offer greater judicial protection to the whole range of individual liberty, economic as well as civil and personal.

It is surely unrealistic to expect that the citizens of such a diverse nation as the USA will ever settle on a single vision of

---

[80] The theoretically still-operative standard of *Nebbia* v. *New York* 291 US 502 (1934).

[81] I have benefited from Gerald Gunther's discussion of ways to infuse some critical 'bite' into the minimal rationality standard of judicial review, see *Constitutional Law*, pp. 472–5.

the good life. We can neither hope nor expect that one way of life will ever secure the allegiance of both Jerry Falwell and Jane Fonda, of urban yuppies and suburban families, of Midwestern farmers and Vietnamese immigrants. To grant supreme political status to the preferences of the greatest number, rather than to public moral norms protecting the liberty of all, constitutes oppression and invites social conflict.

Like liberal justice itself, the American Constitution does not merely embrace a heterogeneous array of interests and lifestyles, it also draws this array together, organizing it under a supreme and regulative set of moral principles and practices of public justification. By its very embrace of a vast, heterogeneous, 'extended republic', the Constitution embodies a point of view and a conception of justice, capable of rising above and uniting all these differences. It provides a unifying and moral focus for a pluralistic society, for a union, as Lincoln said, dedicated to a certain proposition, namely, the supremacy of the basic values embodied in its supreme law: liberal rights and justice and a conception of the general welfare consistent with these.

Few communitarian critics of liberalism would endorse the politics of the moral majority, and few would support the repeal of the Bill of Rights. But what except liberal justice and individual rights stands between communitarianism and the political enforcement of the preferences of the moral majority or other powerful groups?[82] This question is worth pondering. For if we were to cast aside liberal individualism, the political vision of the New Right would be a leading contender in the contest to supply the content of a more exacting common morality.

The rights that define associative freedoms, and those that provide for basic individual autonomy and personal security, are part of the constitution of any good community. The enforcement of liberal freedoms is not a way of supplanting the value of community, it is a way of constituting a community that is valuable. And among the values enforced and promoted in a community constituted by respect for liberal rights are, if the argument of the next two chapters is sound,

[82] As Amy Gutmann asks in her important discussion, 'Communitarian Critics'.

ideals of character and citizenship, of virtue and community—values that add up to a positive rejoinder to liberalism's communitarian critics.

Rejecting the constitutional vision of the conservative and democratic communitarians should not be confused with a wholesale rejection of conservative sentiments or of patriotism. Only a blind conservatism is without reasons for valuing what it seeks to preserve. Only an uncritical patriotism ('my country right or wrong') forgets that it is in aspiring to worthy principles and ideals that government, constitution, and community become worthy of loyalty, allegiance, and self-sacrifice. Instead of uncritical conservatism or communitarianism, we would do far better to aspire to the virtues and ideals of public justification and liberal community that ennoble our constitutions and sustain free self-government.

6

Freedom, Autonomy and Liberal Community

INTRODUCTION

Liberalism is, first and foremost, about certain political values and institutions, and so that is where my argument began. We have, to this point, been concerned with articulating and defending liberal institutions committed to preserving freedom and promoting public reasonableness. These dual commitments run through the complex practices and institutions of liberal constitutionalism.

I have avoided prejudging the nature of the liberal personality but will, here and in the next chapter, consider the personal traits liberalism presupposes and the attributes conducive to flourishing in a liberal milieu. Laying down metaphysical or universal foundations for liberal politics is not my aim. I proceed from what has already been said about liberal politics, not from a special theory of the 'nature' of persons in the abstract. My aim is not to disparage or deflect all communitarian concerns, but to argue that liberal ideals accommodate reasonable and attractive forms of shared identity, interpersonal commitment, and community. Communitarian values are implicit in the idea of a pluralistic community governed properly by liberal justice.

The liberal project is to find regulative political principles for people who disagree. Disagreement about ends, goals, and the good life is a basic precondition of liberalism, generating scarcity even among altruists. Liberal justice is best understood, I have argued, as a public morality that all citizens have a duty to interpret, criticize, and support in their own conduct and against the possible transgressions of public officials. Liberal politics protects the equal right of persons to devise, criticize, revise, and pursue a plan of life, and it furnishes institutional settings for the activity of public justification.

Liberalism also embodies, somewhat ambivalently, an ideal of persons as self-determining and unpredictably self-transforming creatures. As inhabitants of pluralistic, tolerant societies they are confronted with a variety of different ways of life and called upon to choose. And having chosen, they yet may choose again; they may engage in critical self-examination, revise their plans and projects, and, in some ways, even alter or shape their very character. Their ends and purposes, roles, occupations, and lifestyles are not given and never fixed. Liberal politics, the rule of impersonal law and individual rights, protects the liberty to explore various ways of realizing the good life, and to exercise self-critical, self-transforming reflective capacities. For liberalism, autonomy is something more than one personal ideal among others.

Communitarians advance pictures of liberal man and society rather different from the brief sketch of the preceding paragraphs. They argue that liberal man is naturally isolated, 'atomistic', and 'self-sufficient alone'.[1] The liberal self, say communitarians, is an empty locus of will confronting a myriad of open possibilities with no objective moral guideposts and no basis for choosing. Called upon to choose all its attachments and even its own attributes, the liberal self is unable to do so because bereft of 'constitutive' commitments to other persons, ends, or projects. Liberal theory, communitarians say, depicts liberal citizens as 'radically detached' strangers; liberal individualism is a 'vision of society as an association of radically separated individuals fated to struggle against one another'.[2] Liberal justice, with its emphasis on individual rights, impersonal law, and liberty, protects the aimless and solitary freedom of atomistic liberal individuals.

I shall not, as you may have guessed, accept the communitarian critique of liberal man. The purpose of this chapter is to show that liberal political theory can avoid the pitfalls attributed to it by its communitarian critics: Liberal theory is

---

[1] Charles Taylor, 'Atomism', in Taylor, *Philosophy and the Human Sciences: Philosophical Papers, 2* (Cambridge, 1985).

[2] Walzer, 'Philosophy and Democracy', pp. 379, Sandel, *Limits*, p. 183, Roberto Unger, *Knowledge and Politics* (New York, 1975), 155.

not confined to an 'instrumental' conception of reason or a sceptical or subjective view of the ends of life; liberal individualism should not be identified with atomism or a superficial conception of community. By freeing liberal theory of these unnecessary encumbrances, I hope to show that liberals can articulate worthy and attainable ideals of human flourishing, virtue, and community.

I shall begin by considering some of the theoretical baggage liberalism does not require, and will then explore the personal capacities and characteristics liberalism does presuppose and promote. Certain basic reflective capacities define liberal moral persons. The fuller development of those capacities is both encouraged by life in a pluralistic liberal regime and characteristic of a distinctively liberal form of personal flourishing, one that draws on the critical and reflective capacities that nurture liberal citizenship. My aim is not to defend a comprehensive theory of freedom and personal identity, but rather to consider one way of combining basic liberal political values with communitarian concerns and higher liberal aspirations.

INSTRUMENTAL REASON AND SUBJECTIVE VALUE

One of the leading planks of the communitarian platform is the rejection of the 'instrumental' conception of reason which liberal theory purportedly relies upon.[3] The instrumental conception of reason was congenial to the anti-Aristotelian attitude of many early modern philosophers and scientists, who separated facts and values and held that reason does not comprehend essences or ends inhering in a purposive universe. In Hobbes's metaphor: 'the thoughts, are to the desires, as Scouts, and Spies, to range abroad, and find the way to the things Desired.'[4] 'Reason is, and ought only to be', in Hume's well-known formulation, 'the slave of the passions, and can never pretend to any other office than to serve and

---

[3] MacIntyre, *After Virtue*, pp. 51–2, and Sandel, *Limits*, p. 175, Unger, *Knowledge*, p. 39.
[4] Hobbes, *Leviathan*, ch. 8.

obey them'.[5] Reason, said Hume, can neither determine nor rank ends: "Tis not contrary to reason to prefer the destruction of the whole world to the scratching of my finger.' Bentham provided another well-known statement of reason's subordinate role:

Nature has placed mankind under the governance of two sovereign masters, *pain* and *pleasure*. It is for them alone to point out what we ought to do, as well as to determine what we shall do. . . . In words a man may pretend to abjure their empire: but in reality he will remain subject to it all the while.[6]

The instrumental view of reason was deployed against Aristotelianism and medieval natural law theories which held that reason is capable of discovering what is good for man by nature. Politics, it was thought, should be concerned with facilitating the attainment of human goods broadly understood. In contrast, many modern thinkers hold that reason does not lead us to converge on a common vision of the good life, but is compatible with the pursuit of a wide range of religious and other personal values. At the extreme there is no objective good and bad, and ethics is invented.[7] Many fear that this rather lonesome view of the moral universe culminates in Nietzsche: 'Can you give yourself your own evil and your own good and hang your own will over yourself as a law? Can you be your own judge and avenger of your law?'[8]

Communitarians take instrumental rationality to be part of the liberal view of man as essentially isolated from his fellows: liberals recognize, it is said, many individual rights but no common duties. If preferences and standards are merely subjective and men are moved by arbitrary desires, then their final ends are independent of one another and their relations with others are of merely instrumental, not intrinsic, importance. But while many early and contemporary liberals are

---

[5] David Hume, *A Treatise of Human Nature*, ed. L. A. Selby-Bigge (Oxford, 1968), 415.

[6] Jeremy Bentham, *Introduction to the Principles of Morals and Legislation*, ed. Wilfrid Harrison (New York, 1948), 1.

[7] As John Mackie puts it in *Ethics: Inventing Right and Wrong* (Harmondsworth, 1979).

[8] Friederick Nietzsche, *Thus Spoke Zarathustra*, First Part, 'On the Way of the Creator', in *The Portable Nietzsche*, trans. and ed. Walter Kaufmann (New York, 1968), 175.

sceptics who depict reason as a mere instrument of desire or the passions, these ideas are not necessary features of liberal thought. It is not, therefore, at all clear that a critique of instrumental rationality has any necessary bearing on liberalism (as opposed to certain defences of liberalism).

Critiques of liberalism that proceed at too abstract a level risk being beside the point. It is, first of all, hazardous to jump from deep philosophical claims about the nature of human values to psychological or sociological assertions: values may be arbitrary and reason instrumental and persons still desperately interdependent or highly sociable. Liberalism is not first and foremost a theory of the relation between the 'self and its ends', it is most directly a way of organizing political life that stresses the importance of freedom, individual rights, law, limited government, and public reasonableness. There are, of course, a number of ways of understanding the often disparate complex of ideas and claims that go under the label 'liberal'; one reliable approach is to look for the characteristic features of personality and reasonableness linked to recognizable liberal political institutions and practices.

Liberalism holds that reasonable persons properly pursue a wide variety of lifestyles, goals, projects, and commitments. Indeed, one of the great attractions of liberal politics and its view of man is that they liberate persons from inherited roles, fixed hierarchies, and conventions that narrowly constrain individuality and the scope of choice. Liberal reasonableness must be broad enough to encompass variety: it must accommodate liberal diversity, public reasonableness, and critical reflection on personal roles and allegiances.

As an alternative to instrumentalism, several communitarians exhibit a nostalgia for a social world governed by a politically authoritative conception of the good life, but they are more than a little elusive about what they believe the human good consists in. There is no reason why a belief in common or objective human goods should lead one away from liberalism. It may be, after all, that the good life is importantly linked to human freedom, as in MacIntyre's description of it as 'the life spent seeking the good life for man'. Tolerant, pluralistic, liberal communities are just the right places for exploring the variety of ways people seek to live well. Liberal rights to speak, publish, associate with whom you please, travel, and secure privacy for intimate relations among consenting adults, all protect a search for the good life conditioned by equal respect for the rights of others.

The liberal theory I am defending holds that individual freedom is politically central, and that rights normally take priority over the collective pursuit of common goods. This priority does not (as should become clear) depend on value subjectivism or on scepticism about human goods, and it does not require an instrumental conception of reason. Liberalism supposes that beings with the reflective capacity to form plans of life and act justly are moral persons with a claim on our respect and an equal right to a wide range of basic freedoms. The claim to respect of liberal persons does not, however, require the flattening of all judgments about the good life. To say that persons have a right to be free to make a broad range of choices about their lives does not imply that whatever anyone wants or whatever gives a person pleasure is good; nor does it imply that nothing can be said about what is good as such or good for all men. Subjectivism and scepticism about the good are compatible with, but not presupposed by, the priority of liberal rights.

Some confusion probably stems from liberal theory itself. Liberal rights are often thought of as 'trump cards' which can be played to defeat perfectionist and paternalist political measures. The metaphor is somewhat misleading: it is not the case that rights can only be overridden by other, weightier rights. Liberal rights establish presumptions, of varying strengths, against the legitimacy of policies and other government acts that would interfere with their free exercise. These presumptions may often be very strong, but they are not absolute. One of the most basic rights is to not be deprived of liberty or property without due process of law. And yet, liberal citizens may sometimes be deprived of due process justifiably: the denial of normal due process to suspected conspirators during the Civil War was probably justified, the denial of such rights to Japanese Americans during World War II was almost certainly not.[9] Moreover, people should, argu-

[9] See Allan Nevins, 'The Case of the Copperhead Conspirator', in John A. Garraty, ed., *Quarrels that Have Shaped the Constitution* (New York, 1966), 90–108.

ably, be prevented from destroying those basic rational capacities that make them moral beings worthy of respect. Whatever one says of particular examples, however, it is difficult to see the reasonableness of holding that due process and other liberal rights never could be justifiably overridden except by other rights. Rights can be overridden by measures carefully tailored to advance very pressing policy goals.[10]

Rights and collective goals compete at various points, and this is not surprising: the grounds that justify both rights and political goals are mixes of consequentialist, non-consequentialist, and perfectionist reasons. We insist on certain rights partly because we believe that persons inherently merit certain forms of respect, quite apart from whatever good consequences are promoted. It is also important, however, that many of those same rights advance certain valued goals (such as prosperity) and contribute to good character traits (personal responsibility and energy). The contours of our rights are sensitive to various kinds of reasons, and are re-examined and refined as we confront particular cases.

Liberals need not be rights absolutists; most would permit, for example, certain minimal forms of political paternalism. Social insurance, drug laws, and automobile safety requirements are among the ways that modern states require people to do or buy things for their own good. It is not part of my agenda to specify what range of paternalistic measures, if any, is justified. Liberals are certainly people who try to minimize interferences with personal freedom, including risk-taking, but liberals need not be people who categorically reject every vestige of paternalism and perfectionism.

This may seem a bit messy. It would be simpler if liberalism were treated as the view that political means should be employed only to defend individual rights or liberty. It would be easier if liberal rights and freedom could be thought of as based on the priority of 'the right' over 'the good', that is, on the absolute priority of reasons that flow from the imperative

---

[10] One might want to say that rights are not really being overridden, but rather, that a careful description of rights would include certain exceptions, it makes little difference: the exceptions will be various and open-ended, and justified not only by reference to other rights and the reasons that support rights, but also by reference to broader policy goals and collective aims.

of respecting moral persons, whatever the consequences may be. In practice, however, the contours and substance of our rights are sometimes affected by consequentialist and perfectionist considerations, and from a philosophical standpoint that seems appropriate. No one category of moral reasons is powerful enough always to override the others. The moral value and actual shape of rights does not flow only from the imperative of equal respect for persons even if that imperative has great force, but neither are they simple functions of the good consequences rights promote. Considerations of respect for persons and for good consequences cannot be reduced to one another, and neither takes absolute priority over the other in politics or anywhere else. Or so it seems to me (I cannot here expound a complete moral theory of liberalism).

The question of whether 'the right' is prior to 'the good' or vice versa is unhelpful. Moral life is complex, the ultimate sources of moral value are plural.[11] Political arguments, such as Locke's argument for toleration, properly deploy a repertoire of reasons: consequentialist, right-based, and otherwise. Rawls's argument for justice cannot be said to be based on the priority of the right: certain basic goods play an elemental role in his theory.[12] The reasons that support our political arrangements must be openly stated and publicly accessible in order to compose a scheme of public justification; that said, the basic categories of value that support the liberal settlement will remain plural.

One prominent alternative to either the morally complex liberalism I am defending or a simpler rights-based liberalism would be a more robustly Aristotelian or perfectionist approach. Reasons of political morality, on this view, would reduce one way or another to ways of participating in general human goods or aspects of human flourishing. It seems to me reasonable enough to say, as proponents of natural law do, that life, knowledge, play, friendship, and practical reasonableness are among the basic things that are good for human

[11] For their discussions of the heterogeneity of morality, I am much indebted to Nagel, *The View from Nowhere* (New York, 1986), chs. 9 and 10, and 'The Fragmentation of Value', *Mortal Questions* (Cambridge, 1986), and Larmore, *Patterns*, ch. 6.

[12] For an insightful discussion, see Will Kymlicka, 'Rawls on Teleology and Deontology', *Philosophy and Public Affairs*, 17 (1988), 173–90.

beings.[13] The problem is that these categories are extremely abstract and a long way from yielding publicly justifiable solutions to specific practical controversies.

When a natural lawyer such as John Finnis turns to the issue of sexual morality, we see just how great is the gap between the first principles of natural law and practical ethical judgments. He offers a variety of reasonable arguments showing that masturbation forgoes opportunities to participate in human goods.[14] Masturbation uses the body for mere pleasure and involves a person in fantasy rather than in valuable experiences of real friendship, play, and other goods. Fair enough; few would disagree. Finnis goes on to argue, however, that extra-marital sex, homosexuality, and indeed contracepted conjugal sex, are essentially mere variations on masturbation, and there he is unconvincing.

Finnis claims that only sexual relations in heterosexual marriages for the purpose of procreation integrate and express full participation in human goods. The problem with his argument is not that he mischaracterizes the goods involved in rearing children in a stable marriage relationship: those goods are real and profound. It is far from clear, however, that sexuality divorced from procreation is quite so thoroughly a distraction from real human goods as Finnis holds. Finnis gives short shrift to the possibilities inherent in many kinds of human sexual relationships. Non-promiscuous homosexual relationships, for example, also participate in real human goods (friendship, play, knowledge). And for those whose attractions nature has directed toward members of the same sex, homosexual love may be the best way to participate in the goods of intimate friendship.

A larger problem hovers over natural law: in many of its versions, natural law is incompatible with the political morality of public justification. Because there is such a large gap between the first principles of natural law and actual moral norms (such as those found in the Ten Commandments) much work needs to be done by a process of inference. And Finnis

---

[13] I rely on John Finnis's lucid and powerful account, *Natural Law and Natural Rights* (Oxford, 1980). And see below, pp. 233–4.

[14] John M. Finnis, 'Personal Integrity, Sexual Morality, and Responsible Parenthood', *Anthropos*, 1 (1985), 43–55.

acknowledges that in many cases the moral inference will require a wisdom or reasonableness 'not found in everyone or even in most people'.[15] Natural law may be incompatible with the equality of respect that liberalism attempts to embody in its canons of public justification. As a public, political matter, inferences beyond the capacities of 'most people' are not proper grounds for law. Natural law might try to save itself from élitism by licensing not public reasons but popular prejudices about how human beings should behave. Natural law would, then, deflect the charge of élitism only to fall into an unreasoned populism of the kind deployed by Lord Devlin and Robert Bork.

Let us proceed on the working assumption, admittedly only partially established here, that the sources of moral value are complex, and that liberalism regards respect for persons and rights as central and very weighty political principles but not as absolutes. A significant if subordinate part of the case for liberal politics is the quality of personal and communal life that it promotes. In what follows I shall argue that the instrumental conception of reason is compatible with liberalism but not required by it. Implicit in the idea of liberal justice governing a pluralistic community is an ideal of autonomy that transcends instrumental reason.

Freedom as autonomy is linked most closely with Kant's moral thought, but it is not his version of autonomy that I want to develop here. Kant linked freedom with the active exercise of reason in human conduct, but in doing so opened a gap between reason on one side and nature or desire on the other.[16] To be autonomous or fully free, according to Kant, it is not enough merely to be unimpeded in the pursuit of desire, our will must be determined by pure reason rather than desire or any other external or contingent factor. Kantian freedom avoids a crude dependence on passions and desires, but at the cost of a radical dissociation of reason from nature, desire, and social context. And Kantian abstract reason is notoriously incapable of generating specific, substantive moral impera-

---

[15] Finnis, 'Personal Integrity' p. 52.
[16] Immanuel Kant, *Groundwork*, pp. 114–31.

tives. The problems generated by Kantian autonomy might drive liberals back, after all, to merely instrumental conception of reason. We can, however, preserve the idea of autonomy as the critical capacity to interpret and shape nature and desire, a capacity most at home in and nurtured by a free and pluralistic society.

Part of the case for liberalism (though perhaps not the most important part) is that it promotes types of character that may be esteemed virtuous and kinds of community that are attractive as communities. The liberal ideal of 'situated autonomy' avoids, as I shall try to argue, the shortcomings and pitfalls of both the instrumental and the Kantian conceptions of reason.

LIBERAL PERSONS AND LIBERAL AUTONOMY

Liberalism is often associated with what is called the 'negative' conception of liberty, of which the canonical definition is Isaiah Berlin's: 'political liberty in this sense is simply the area within which a man can act unobstructed by others', and it is checked not by personal inabilities but by the 'deliberate interference' of others.[17] The positive conception of liberty consists of self-mastery, of being 'conscious of myself as a thinking, willing, active being, bearing responsibility for my choices and able to explain them by references to my own ideas and purposes'.[18] Positive liberty, unlike negative liberty, can fail for 'internal' reasons.

We should be careful not to mistake Berlin's point. He does not mean to deny that persons are distinguished by positive capacities that justify the ascription of moral dignity or worth, capacities requiring us to 'count' these as beings worthy of full respect. We do not care about, or even sensibly speak of, the freedom of turnips or lampshades. Berlin himself argues that at least a minimum rationality requirement must be met before an agent can be considered free: among those we should disqualify are the delirious, the insane, and hypnotized

---

[17] Isaiah Berlin, 'Two Concepts of Liberty', in *Four Essays on Liberty* (Oxford, 1979), 122.
[18] Ibid. 131.

agents.[19] No defence of liberty can dispense with positive criteria needed to distinguish 'consenting adults' from children and various incompetents.

Berlin does not deny, furthermore, that developing our capacity for critical thought and autonomous choice is good. His point is that freedom should not be conflated with other genuine values such as goodness, social solidarity, 'objective reason', or particular conceptions of valuable ends. To be free is not necessarily to be fully autonomous or enlightened. Liberals avoid raising the hurdles of rationality too high because they believe that all normally competent adults share a moral dignity justified by the ability to reflect and choose not by the substantive quality or worth of the choices made. To say that in coercing people in the name of authenticity or their higher selves or true interests, we are making them free, is to paper over the real moral costs of interfering in other people's lives. Negative freedom is not an absolute, it may be outweighed and overridden, and even many liberals will allow that sometimes the law should make people do things for their own good. The language of negative liberty makes clear that something of value is lost when people's choices are interfered with, and it provides a prophylactic against equating the consummation of tyranny with the culmination of freedom.

Liberal theory distinguishes between responsible, competent adults, on the one hand, and immature minors and less than fully competent adults, on the other. Members of the former category, let us say, by virtue of possessing 'normal' mental and intellectual capacities all qualify for the full respect and forbearance owed to moral persons: they merit the full panoply of civil and political rights. Members of the latter category lack, to one degree or another, one or more of the relevant capacities distinguishing personhood, and for that reason liberals think it right and proper to treat their choices and preferences with less than the full respect owed to moral persons. The latter category includes the mentally incapacitated and the incompetent, and ranges from unconscious

---

[19] See Isaiah Berlin, 'Rationality of Value Judgments', in C. J. Friederich, ed., *Nomos VII: Rational Decision* (New York, 1967), 221–3.

human vegetables and the insane, to adolescents and the slightly retarded or senile.

There is no sharp divide or simple bifurcation between competent moral persons and others. Even where it seems clear that a human being is not appropriately respected as a full moral person capable of forming plans and giving justice, nevertheless he or she may merit certain forms of appropriate concern and respect, which will vary depending on the impairment. Indeed, where human beings suffer a mental incapacity we often think them the appropriate objects of special concern.

That liberal practice is as much concerned as liberal theory with distinguishing moral persons from others, is illustrated by our intense political debates over the right to life of the unborn, and the permissibility of withdrawing the seriously and permanently incapacitated from life support systems. The categories and distinctions at issue in these moral debates are rooted in liberal practice, though only imperfectly and sometimes unselfconsciously. In both liberal theory and practice there are a number of complex and open questions concerning personal competence, rights, and respect, questions I shall not try to settle.

'Normal' persons (in the moral sense) have, say liberals, a claim upon our respect, a moral claim to forbearance, an equal right to freedom. Persons are capable of reflective choice, of formulating, pursuing, and revising goals, projects, and a plan of life. Persons have a degree of practical and cognitive rationality, and are 'self-governing' or 'autarchic'; they recognize themselves as continuous over time.[20] The reflective capacities of self-governing persons can be impaired by defects including various forms of compulsive behaviour, paranoia, schizophrenia, and other conditions we need not pause to catalogue. The important point here is that liberals commonly recognize a principle of respect for persons and object in principle to manipulation, coercion, paternalism, and perfectionism.

Liberals believe that persons merit respect and that consequently

[20] See S. I. Benn's excellent essay, 'Freedom, Autonomy, and the Concept of a Person', *Proceedings of the Aristotelian Society, New Series* 76, 1975/76 (London, 1976), 109–30, esp. pp. 112–6.

they should be free to choose their own ideals or to live without ideals. While respecting the freedom to choose, liberals need not, however, regard all choices as equally valuable or as equally compatible with a liberal form of excellence. To develop more fully the reflective capacities associated with normal personhood leads one toward an ideal of character, an ideal we may call 'autonomy'.

The autarchic person has the capacity to reflect upon, choose among, defer, and shape desires to some degree, and so is self-governing, but he or she may lack the discipline to resist desires and inclinations for the sake of valued long-term projects and commitments. Autarchic persons may still be conformists or 'slaves' to fashion or to conventions, acting from standards, ideals, and values taken over uncritically from others. That is, an autarchic person may lack the ability or propensity critically to weigh and judge conventions for him or herself.[21] A merely autarchic person does not act from values, ideals, and aspirations that have been critically assessed and reasonably integrated. An autarchic person with only instrumental rationality still qualifies for basic forms of respect; flourishing as a liberal requires reflective capacities beyond instrumental rationality.

A crucial feature in the move from autarchy to autonomy is the development of the capacity critically to assess and even actively shape not simply one's actions, but one's character itself, the source of our actions. The capacity for 'strong evaluation' offers a way of thinking about autonomy without relying on the troublesome dichotomies that plague Kantian autonomy: in deliberating we can evaluate and shape our desires themselves and, thus, reflection and desire remain closely linked rather than opposed. Strong evaluation allows us, as we shall see, to situate autonomy in a social context by emphasizing the roles played by language and articulation in the process of deliberation.

Strong evaluation rejects Kantian or situationless autonomy, accommodating, instead, the communitarian concern to see reflective deliberation as fully situated in a certain kind of social context. Liberal 'situated autonomy', thought of in

---

[21] See Mill's discussion of the 'despotism of custom', *On Liberty*, p. 66.

terms of strong evaluation, allows us to appreciate the kind of critical reflectiveness that is encouraged in a liberal pluralistic society, one in which many visions of the good life compete for attention and allegiance.

Strong evaluation is marked by the capacity for what Harry Frankfurt calls 'second-order' desires:

> Besides wanting and choosing and being moved *to do* this or that, men may also want to have (or not to have) certain desires and motives. They are capable of wanting to be different, in their preferences and purposes, from what they are. Many animals appear to have the capacity for what I shall call 'first-order desires' . . . which are simply desires to do or not to do one thing or another. No animal other than man, however, appears to have the capacity for reflective self-evaluation that is manifested in the formation of second-order desires.[22]

Autarchic persons may be either strong evaluators or what Charles Taylor calls 'simple weighters'.[23] The utilitarian (or, at least, the Benthamite utilitarian) exemplifies the 'simple weighter' who contrasts alternative courses of action only quantitatively. This 'weak evaluator' exhibits 'shallowness of character'. He knows only first-order desires distinguished by their strength or magnitude on a simple scale; he does not evaluate the 'worth' or quality of desires, he lacks depth. The 'simple weighter' is a 'wanton' with only 'calculative rationality': he can weigh his different desires and forgo the weaker for the stronger, 'but he does not care which of his inclinations is the strongest'.[24]

The strong evaluator on the other hand, distinguishes between desires according to their worth and not just their strength and acts on the basis of this evaluation. The strong evaluator 'aspires to a certain way of life which consists in certain acts'. That is, the strong evaluator fashions a coherent pattern of second-order desires into an ideal of character, and is capable of weighing one ideal against another. Stuart Hampshire expresses this familiar idea well:

---

[22] Harry Frankfurt, 'Freedom of the Will and the Concept of a Person', *Journal of Philosophy*, 67 (1971), 7.

[23] Charles Taylor, 'What is Human Agency?', in *Human Agency and Language: Philosophical Papers,1* (Cambridge, 1985), 1–44, and Sandel, *Limits*, pp. 160–3.

[24] Frankfurt, 'Freedom', p. 11.

A man may on reflection want to be the kind of man who has certain interests and desires; he may cultivate certain interests in himself, and may try to smother or divert others, in pursuit of some ideal of character. This reflectiveness—the desire not to have certain desires—is unavoidable in anyone who reflects and criticizes.[25]

Significantly, the strong evaluator is able to articulate the superiority of his choices in a richer language than that available to the simple weighter. The opportunity to indulge some appetite, for instance, can only be a matter of assessing the relative strengths of desires for the simple weighter. But for the strong evaluator, appetites themselves can be evaluated as 'higher or lower, noble or base, courageous and cowardly, integrated and fragmented'.

The strong evaluator can test, shape, and perhaps reject his dispositions and desires by reference to competing norms, ideals, and qualitative evaluations. Strong evaluation is not Kantian 'situationless' autonomy, which presupposes a transcendental subject inhabiting a realm beyond all contingency and able to act from pure reason. The ideal of autonomy is the autonomy of one informed by different standards and ideals. It stems from the ability to establish a reflective distance from our desires and to deliberate on them and on ourselves more broadly. Deliberation is conducted in an inherited moral language: the repository of a shared culture composed of a plurality of communities and ideals. Liberal autonomy is not a matter of transcending contingency or of inhabiting a world beyond our own; it is not a matter of standing outside one's community, much less all communities. Autonomy is a way of comporting ourselves in our liberal, pluralistic, community—critically playing off one aspect of our culture against other aspects and against our own experience. As Benn puts it, 'To be autonomous one must have reasons for acting, and be capable of second thoughts in light of new reasons; it is not to have a capacity for conjuring criteria out of nowhere'.[26]

Strong evaluation 'is a condition of articulacy', as Taylor puts it, 'and to acquire a strongly evaluative language is to become (more) articulate about one's preferences'.[27] To

---

[25] Stuart Hampshire, *Freedom of the Individual* (London, 1965), 93.
[26] Benn, 'Freedom', p. 126.
[27] Taylor, 'Human Agency', pp. 24–5.

acquire an evaluative language is also to add a dimension to our experience, because different ways of life are 'sustained' or perhaps constituted by the qualitative contrasts and distinctions possessed by the users of a rich moral language. To acquire a richer set of contrasts is to acquire a richer set of options: 'where there is articulacy there is the possibility of a plurality of visions which there was not before.'[28] If the value of liberty is partly a function of the breadth and distinctiveness of the options available to an agent, then the liberty of the strong evaluator is more valuable than that of the simple weighter: the world of the strong evaluator is one of richer, deeper contrasts than any the simple weighter can comprehend.

If our world really is one of incommensurable basic goods then one who is knowledgeable and articulate about these different basic values, one who possesses a language of qualitative contrasts and a broad experience of the nature of basic goods and the different ways of participating in them, understands the world better than shallow reductionists and those uncritically wedded to a narrow, parochial way of life. The autonomous individual is a socially embedded individual, one who understands his intellectual and cultural inheritance but is determined to make that inheritance his own by fashioning an individual character and lifeplan, and by turning his participation in social practices into performances expressive of his individuality.[29]

We are most likely to engage in strong evaluation when faced with a 'deep' or very difficult choice, one that calls into question values of basic importance. Consider Sartre's well-known example of a young man who must choose, during wartime, between remaining with his ailing mother or going

---

[28] Ibid. 26.

[29] As Oakeshott puts it: '[W]hat is called "moral autonomy" does not require moral choice to be a gratuitous, criterionless exercise of a so-called "will" (an isolated *meum*) in which a lonely agent simultaneously recognizes or even creates a "value" for which he is wholly responsible and places himself under its command, thus miraculously releasing himself from organic impulse, rational contingency, and authoritative rules of conduct. . . . [H]is "moral autonomy" lies, first, in his character as an agent (that is, in his action or utterance being a response to an understood want and not the consequence of an organic impulse), and secondly, in his action or utterance as self-disclosure and self-enactment in a contingent subscription of his own to the conditions of a practice. . . .' *Human Conduct*, p. 79.

off to join the Resistance. These alternatives present, arguably, such radically different kinds of actions, each noble in its
own way, that it would be impossible to weigh them on any
simple scale, or perhaps even to have any reasons at all for
choosing. Must one, then, simply 'plump' or 'leap' one way or
the other, by force of sheer will unguided by reasons,
unencumbered by personal history and values, prior commitments, plans, projects, and propensities, as the existentialist
suggests? Radical freedom is not situated autonomy.

Achieving autonomy is not a matter of detaching one's 'self'
from all one's commitments and aspirations and from social
understandings and ideals, choosing as a purely abstract subject constituted only by 'reason' or sheer arbitrary will.
Situated autonomy involves critical reflection on inherited
values, personal commitments, and basic goods, not a flight
from and abandonment of them. Liberal autonomy engages
our understanding and responsibility at a deep level by engaging the capacity critically to reflect upon morality and personal
identity, itself already constituted by projects, plans, commitments, and strong evaluations.

In making difficult choices we draw upon an already existing sense of what is fundamentally important, and further
articulate and shape that sense. Reflection, spurred by
fundamental conflicts of moral values, leads me to consider the
sort of person I am and the sort I wish to be. Looking back
over my life, I critically examine my current plans, projects,
and aspirations. I engage in a project of self-interpretation and
self-criticism. I recognize that my personality has a definite if
not absolutely fixed shape; I have invested time and effort in
developing certain traits and have neglected others. The story
of my life is already partly written and I want to continue it in
the best way that I can; it can proceed in any number of ways
but not any old way. My personal history is also embedded in
and illumined by the long course of human experience and the
deep tendencies of human nature; most of us have some sense
of the lessons and limits of these.

A person, reflecting on a difficult personal choice, finds
himself already defined by strong evaluations, basic convictions, propensities, weaknesses, ideals, and, of course, convictions of political morality that condition and shape all his other

values. The autonomous self is never a disembodied ego or perfectly detached will choosing in a state of radical freedom as the existentialists claim. Rather, a core of basic evaluations and commitments form the horizons or foundations, the provisionally fixed background 'character', out of which we reflect upon or evaluate some particular choice or project or commitment or value.

Our choices are grounded in a way that is incompatible with the existentialist idea of radical choice. The fact that we possess a provisionally settled character, a set of values and dispositions to act in certain ways, for which we have presumably summoned up reasons of some sort over time, ballasts our deliberations, providing an initial basis for choosing, a set of relatively fixed points with which deliberation begins. Our descriptions, as Taylor says, are 'not simply arbitrary, such that anything goes'.[30] Some things are more or less given: we cannot choose our parents, decide not to be mortal, or escape the taxman (though we can adopt different postures toward and understandings of even these apparently 'fixed' constraints). Some settled assumptions, beliefs, and dispositions would be difficult to examine critically and reshape, and some might be nearly impossible to renounce without great trauma or an 'identity crisis'. In addition to the constraints arising from a given character, we value integrity, a certain consistency of action, or at least a unity or connectedness between parts of a life, or what MacIntyre calls the 'narrative unity' of a good life.[31]

Personal identity provides provisional baselines for choosing, we begin from where we are and not from nowhere; we have other less personal guideposts as well. To articulate a given predicament in terms of a rich evaluative language is to invoke values that count as reasons for acting one way or the other. An autonomous person will 'apprise one aspect of his tradition by critical canons derived from another'.[32] We cannot arbitrarily apply the ideas we have learned (if we have learned them) or make of our situations whatever we wish. We may imaginatively create options and alternatives, but we

[30] Taylor, 'Human Agency', p. 38.
[31] MacIntyre, *After Virtue*, pp. 203–5.
[32] Benn, 'Freedom', p. 126.

remain critical interpreters of our situations and discriminating inheritors of standards of evaluation.

We understand our achieved identity and options in terms of a public moral language, something over which no individual is sovereign (whatever subjectivists like Hobbes and Humpty Dumpty may have thought).[33] Moral words and paradigms cannot mean whatever we choose them to mean. As Taylor says, 'there are more or less adequate, more or less truthful . . . interpretations . . . an articulation can be *wrong*', and this is not only because a person can mistake his or her own inclinations, but also because a person can have an inadequate or confused grasp of ideals, values, and goods which are not merely personal and not dreamt up by each new individual or generation.[34]

Self-interpretation and self-criticism should involve looking, not only 'inward', but also 'outward' toward ideals of nobility and baseness, of courage and cowardice, of success and failure, faithfulness, fiendishness, and so forth. We are guided, not only by fresh insight into our own character but also by public ideals that naturally furnish the sources and models (always capable of being creatively individualized and made one's own rather than slavishly imitated) of one's most personal aspirations.

As moral agents who acknowledge an overriding commitment to liberal justice, citizens are morally self-critical, and admit that their projects and plans must be revised and perhaps scrapped if they fail to pass the impersonal test of liberal justice, which reconciles the freedom of each with the freedom of all. But the reasons of liberal justice are not external impositions foisted upon liberal citizens; justice is not only a

---

[33] As Julius Kovesi puts it: 'The proper description of an act depends upon the relevant facts of the situation. . . . [I]n so far as the agent's intention can feature among the relevant facts it must be publicly knowable or accessible, either through the agent's avowal, or through the pattern of his behavior which makes his act intelligible and meaningful for us. . . . When an appeal to a personal intention does succeed in changing the proper description of an act it succeeds in virtue of interpersonal rules that govern these procedures, and not by virtue of the fact that the agent knows what he intends to do in a way that nobody else can know it.' *Moral Notions* (London, 1967), 131–2. One must wonder, however, whether the publicity condition will act to filter out aspects of real human goods.

[34] Taylor, 'Human Agency', p. 38.

public test of our actions but is, in a well-ordered society, a constitutive feature of the lives of liberal citizens, shaping their projects and commitments right from the start.

Our basic, strong evaluations, constitutive of personal identity, are never fixed. One does not simply confront or discover one's fundamental judgments, these features are not just 'there', waiting to be uncovered and disclosed. In choosing I must understand and articulate my basic convictions, and, as Taylor puts it, 'to give articulation is to shape our desires . . . self-interpretation is partly constitutive of experience'. And crucially, 'it is always possible that fresh insight might alter my evaluations and hence even myself for the better. . . . No formulations are considered unreviseable'.[35] The desires, convictions, and even the identity of the autonomous liberal subject are never fixed or closed: they are to some degree malleable and open to revision in response to the broad vista of human experience.

Strong evaluation does not, of course, provide a method or technique for arriving at objectively 'right answers' or even determinate answers to the Sartrian situation of choice and others like it. The range of relevant considerations in Sartre's example are quite broad: are there others who could stay with mother? Is the young man capable of helping the Resistance? Is the Resistance making any difference? And what does mother think about the whole business? Strong evaluation and liberal autonomy constitute a self-consciously reflective and clear-eyed stance for making difficult choices, but they prescribe no simple or obvious solutions.

I cannot choose my character, but I can shape and revise it piecemeal. Critical self-reflection is an active engagement; it is something we do, and it is always up to us to do it. In this way, says Taylor, 'our responsibility is engaged . . . the limits of a man's insights are taken as a judgment on him'.[36] John Rawls expresses a similar idea, when he says that 'members of a well-ordered society are viewed as responsible for their fundamental interests and ends' and this is because 'they view themselves as capable of revising and changing their final ends'.[37] Persons

[35] Ibid. 39–40.
[36] Ibid.
[37] John Rawls, 'A Kantian Conception of Equality', *Cambridge Review* (1975) 96.

ought to reflect upon the deep commitments from which their actions flow, for the sake of conforming with justice. The politics of liberal justice is, as we have seen, a dynamic, critically evolving set of values and practices whose progressive development requires the active participation of citizens and public officials. There are substantive moral reasons closely related to the demands of justice for developing critical capacities, and those capacities are likely to be deployed in personal as well as political matters.

Language mediates between the freedom and the social context of the strong evaluator in a threefold way. First, articulate, self-critical, self-analysis allows a person to gain some distance from his own desires, dispositions, and character, to hold himself up for critical analysis (though not all at once). Persons with this articulate capacity can shape their own desires and character and possess the *autonomy* of strong evaluators. Second, self-criticism can only be undertaken in a language already a part of the social world into which we were born; language offers the key to the *situatedness* of the strong evaluator. Finally, because strong evaluation is conducted in a language shaped by countless others over centuries, a language drawn upon and reshaped by others all at once, our self-judgments can be shared with others and criticized by them; language offers the key to the *interrelatedness* of strong evaluators.[38]

As articulate beings we exist in a larger linguistic order which has no master. Language exhibits the characteristics of what Hayek calls 'spontaneous order': we can never comprehend it as a whole (there is an inevitable tacit element) or predict its future course; it is not designed but emerges out of the interaction of individual speakers; it is dynamic or constantly remade as it is used in the life of the community; and it has no single purpose but serves the manifold purposes of unseen millions.[39] As the crucial medium of man's self-shaping understanding of himself and his predicaments, language is largely given or received; short of an Orwellian

---

[38] See Hampshire, *Freedom*, p. 38.
[39] Hayek, *Law, Legislation and Liberty*, vol. i, *Rules and Order* (Chicago, Ill., 1973), ch. 2.

nightmare, public meanings are beyond conscious control of a centralized authority.

We can control our actions but not the public meanings of our actions, for we act in a context largely given. We are not autonomous in the sense of being 'radically free' or able to create the values that define the moral problems we face, or to make words mean whatever we choose. Our freedom and the autonomy we strive for are not the consequence of an ability to extricate ourselves from this network of public meanings. We are objects and not only agents of critical interpretation, and it is natural for us to care about other people's interpretations of us and our actions (at least some others most of the time). The better we understand the context of our actions, the better able we are to negotiate our way in the world.

We are at once both empowered by, and dependent upon, this ever and unpredictably changing system of public meanings. Liberalism, at a deep level, rests upon a policy of 'linguistic *laissez-faire*', on an ordered context of meaningful interaction perpetuating itself with everyone's participation and influence but no one's exclusive control. Without this 'spontaneous order' of public meanings we would be at the mercy of the most radical power of a Hobbesian sovereign, whom Sheldon Wolin calls 'the Great Definer'.[40] We have a framework of public meanings beyond the control of public authorities, which in a free society they, as we, accept. We are all both agents within and subjects of that public order of meaning, shaping it and shaped by it.

The active power of persons to shape who they are, to understand, control, and shape their desires, is what strong evaluation is all about. When a person also has the resolve, the fortitude, to act from the results of such deliberations, we may think of him or her as autonomous. These are the dimensions of the full positive ideal of autonomy: the possession of critical self-directedness, a mastery of language and cultural ideals, a capacity to conform with impersonal rules and moral norms, and the requisite resolve and fortitude to act from on the basis of personal deliberations.

---

[40] Sheldon Wolin, *Politics and Vision* (Boston, Mass., 1960), 265–72.

The ideal of situated autonomy depicts the fully human agent as a 'mover' and not simply 'moved' by the force of desires or the currents of history, genetics, socialization, and community or economic pressure. This model allows us to affirm man's protean nature, our openness to many possibilities, without falling prey to MacIntyre's pessimism. Our very identity may be open to revision, but we are not simply adrift, as MacIntyre charges, because autonomous persons are not passive but active centres of self-direction, always constituted by a range of commitments, attachments, and allegiances, some deeply, some tentatively, but none so dogmatically that it is beyond reflective limitation in light of the reasons of justice. We may, with Oakeshott, recognize, 'this condition as the emblem of human dignity and as a condition for each individual to explore, to cultivate, to make the most of, and to enjoy as an opportunity rather than suffer as a burden'.[41]

Just as the search for the best reasons of political morality is a never-ending process, so the identities of liberal persons are never closed, our self-shaping basic judgments are never unrevisable. As Taylor emphasizes, 'full responsibility comes from the ability to change myself by fresh insight'.[42] To borrow loosely from Popper, we might say the openness to self-criticism and the 'falsification' of even our basic judgments embodies a peculiarly liberal attitude; this is the way that autonomous liberal citizens ideally support both liberal justice and their personal commitments and values.

Liberal, situated autonomy stems from the ability to use the resources of a pluralistic and tolerant culture critically to develop a valuable individuality. The culture of a reflectively, self-critical, liberal community, its poetry, history, literature, and moral philosophy, as well as its more popular media, offers resources and stimulation for this self-interpretive process. As free private persons then as much as citizens, autonomous liberals are immanent, interpretive critics of themselves, others, and their culture.

Openness to change in the face of an unpredictable future calls for a measure of clear-eyed fortitude. But because liberal political values are more uniform and permanent than the

[41] Oakeshott, *Human Conduct*, p. 236.
[42] Taylor, 'Human Agency', p. 41.

ever-changing diversity of the projects, goals, and commitments of liberal individuals, Oakeshott's famous metaphor is more aptly applied to personal than to political life: 'men sail a boundless and bottomless sea; there is neither harbour for shelter nor floor for anchorage, neither starting place nor appointed destination. . . .'[43]

PLURALISM AND LIBERAL PERSONHOOD

Autarchy incorporates those reflective capacities which/distinguish free agency from insanity, delirium, and other conditions falling short of it. Liberals avoid building further substantive conditions into the criteria of normal personhood; the logic of respect for the rights of persons is independent of substantive judgments about the value of what persons choose. Persons, say liberals, merit our respect for their choices so long as they respect the equal rights of others; liberal freedom importantly includes the right to define, revise, and pursue a vision of the good life, and the right to be a layabout.

Dissatisfaction with the 'thin' conception of rationality defining liberal personhood leads some critics of liberalism, including communitarians, to broaden and render more substantive the hurdles that must be cleared before an action or an agent is considered free and worthy of respect. According to Taylor, liberals ignore three ways that freedom can be obstructed: by desires with which an agent does not identify (usually desires which run counter to settled plans and projects), by 'inauthentic' desires, and by desires that are relatively insignificant. By introducing elements of the ideal of autonomy into the conditions of liberal respect, Taylor attempts to transcend liberal personhood without relying upon the claim that rational persons necessarily pursue certain specifiable conceptions of the good life.

Taylor claims to develop a theory of positive freedom while avoiding 'the metaphysic . . . of a higher and lower self'.[44] And yet he contends that within conflict-ridden individuals, persons torn in different directions by incompatible desires,

---

[43] Oakeshott, 'Political Education', in *Rationalism*, p. 127.
[44] Charles Taylor, 'What's Wrong With Negative Liberty?', in *Papers, 2*, p. 216.

there is a 'true self' that we can identify as the locus of 'authentic' desires. Now the idea of an authentic self may simply draw attention to the provisionally settled character forming the background against which strong evaluation takes place, a character composed of fairly settled propensities, habits, values, and a broad lifeplan. Certainly, a degree of constancy in our judgments, personal stability, and resolve in the pursuit of our projects are important traits; we cannot call all of our values and ideals into question at once, and we cannot live well if our deep evaluations are highly unstable. There is nothing objectionable in observing that one's settled character may come into conflict with relatively transitory desires, impulses, or temptations. Taylor wants us to go further, however, and regard desires that conflict with projects as 'obstacles to freedom'.

To the extent we feel beset by transient desires, says Taylor, we are not free; 'we can experience some desires as fetters, because we can experience them as not ours'. Our true self is what we identify with, generally, our reflectively adopted plans and purposes, and 'desires may frustrate our deeper purposes . . . [and] may be inner obstacles to freedom'.[45] Taylor never clarifies precisely what work is done by the term 'authentic' or why the 'authentic' self should be equated with reflective plans. The notion of authenticity seems to suggest that under the surface of conflicting desires or interests lies not simply a relatively stable set of commitments and propensities, but a fixed, true or higher self. Taylor seems to posit a harmonious core of individuality and to equate freedom with action based on accurate self-knowledge, inflating the 'cognitive' element in strong evaluation without clarifying the nature of that fixed inner core of propensities, much less substantiating its existence.[46]

No doubt, desires that overwhelm or 'underwhelm' the capacity for reflection and choice constitute inner obstacles to freedom. To be moved by an obsession that overrides the capacity for reflection is not really 'acting' at all: it is more like

---

[45] Taylor, 'Negative Liberty', pp. 225–6.
[46] I am indebted to the discussion of the 'cognitive' and 'voluntarist' ideas of agency in M. M. Bick, 'Conceptions of the Self and the Community: Rawls and Sandel', M.Phil. Thesis, Politics (Oxford, 1984).

being blown off a cliff by a high wind than jumping off. In other cases, persons may be unaware of what they are doing, their capacity for reflection is short-circuited or under-whelmed and, again, they do not really act. What they do is more like an involuntary blink than a wink. A person may be anomic, or completely lacking in the sort of internal regula-tion that permits one to establish order among desires; like Plato's 'tyrannic soul' such a person is, as Joel Feinberg puts it, 'free of external shackles, but tied in knots by the strands of his own wants . . . his options overwhelm his capacity to order them in hierarchies of preference. . . . To be unfree is to be constrained and in the absence of internal rules, desires will constrain each other in jams and collisions'.[47] We need not catalogue the various ways that the capacities which define normal persons can be overwhelmed, underwhelmed, and otherwise defeated. I only wish to note that we typically recognize such cases as abnormal. As Thomas Nagel puts it, 'Most people do not regard themselves as passengers in their bodies, and are motivated rather than assaulted by their natural impulses.'[48]

Cases in which desires defeat the attainment of the basic capacities defining personhood should be carefully dis-tinguished from cases in which what is defeated is the achieve-ment of the ideal of autonomy or some other ideal; something other than freedom is at stake in the latter case. Many personal traits or habits might defeat or thwart the ability or the inclination to strive for the ideal of autonomy, but while the ideal of autonomy helps us live up to the demands of liberal citizenship and helps us flourish in a diverse and open society, it is not mandatory. We should respect persons, those capable of making lifeplans and acting justly, and not only those who successfully strive toward the ideal of autonomy. One who unquestioningly and single-mindedly pursues a career marked out for him by his parents rather than experimenting with different projects and reflecting critically on other possible goals and aspirations, forgoes the liberal ideal of autonomy, but not the status of responsible personhood. On the liberal

---

[47] Joel Feinberg, *Social Philosophy* (Englewood Cliffs, NJ, 1973), 15.
[48] Thomas Nagel, *The Possibility of Altruism* (Princeton, NJ, 1970), 126.

model, only obstacles to autarchy (not obstacles to autonomy) are obstacles to freedom.

'[I]s freedom not at stake', Taylor asks, 'when we find ourselves carried away by a less significant goal to override a highly significant one? Or when we are led to act out of a motive we consider bad or despicable?'[49] Among the obstacles to freedom, Taylor would include desires that conflict with projects, goals that conflict with more important goals, and bad motives that conflict with good ones. But is free action confined to the good-natured and reflective pursuit of important projects? Should all these judgments be built into the hurdles that must be cleared before one is considered free? Or are they, rather, hurdles that a free act must pass before it can also be considered good, significant, authentic, or in accord with the ideal of autonomy or some other ideal? Is the temptation to break my resolution to give up smoking not 'mine', and an obstacle to freedom just because it conflicts with my project to become healthier?

Critics of liberalism may claim that 'acting out of some motives negates freedom'. But it would be better to say that acting out of some motives may defeat the attainment of autonomy or of an autonomously chosen project. 'Purposes can', as Taylor says, 'be checked by desires experienced as fetters.' These desires (and also the less significant goals and bad motives mentioned above) are not obstacles to freedom unless they thwart the basic capacities of personhood; the claim of unfreedom depends on what is being fettered. As long as desires contrary to long-standing projects or 'purposes' allow a choice to be made, and both the desire and the project are 'mine', then I am free whichever way I choose, and my choices merit the respect owed to the acts of a free man.

Taylor accords projects and 'vocations' a highly privileged status relative to desires that conflict with them. The boundaries of the self are narrowed so as to include projects but not contrary desires; the threshold of personhood is raised so that 'free' persons choose important projects over whimsical desires. To be free, for Taylor, ·it is not enough to be a reflective agent unimpeded in the pursuit of a valued aim, one must make the 'right' choice: opt for rational plans over flights of fancy, for significant over insignificant plans, and for good over bad motives; 'freedom now involves being able to recognize my important purposes.'

We should not substantively limit the sorts of ends that free and responsible (if not wise and good) persons can pursue. Freedom is at stake in a narrower range of cases than Taylor contends; to be free is to be capable of making choices, of making mistaken or even bad choices.[50] It makes no sense to put freedom at stake when one gives in to whims or flights of fancy.[51]

In a defensible theory of the good life, Taylor's emphasis on choosing important projects over desires would be of only limited help. His identification of authenticity with reflection commits him to a kind of hyper-rationalism, setting the 'true self' at odds not only with 'transient desires' but spontaneity. In political life we have a responsibility to act on the basis of articulate public reasons. But were every private action to be so carefully planned and thought through, every flight of fancy rejected, the result would be a cold and stifling lack of spontaneity. Without spontaneity, it would be difficult to make sense of the good of play, and it would be hard to find room for the 'divine madness' of love. I am not defending utterly arbitrary, random, unreflective behaviour. We need not go that far to hold that free action accommodates and a good life requires space for spontaneity.

To suppose that free, responsible persons always do things that are good, significant, and respectful of others is to inflate the concept of personhood to the point where very few human beings would qualify. And if to be free and responsible is to be good, there would be no real evil in the world, only weakness of will, sickness, and failures of practical rationality. But it

---

[50] See Jeremy Waldron's 'A Right to Do Wrong', *Ethics*, 92 (1981), 21–37, and William Galston, 'On the Alleged Right to Do Wrong: A Response to Waldron', *Ethics*, 93 (1983), 320–4, followed by Waldron's 'Galston on Rights', *Ethics*, 93 (1983), 325–7.

[51] Taylor may be influenced by Aristotle's opposition between the disciplined deliberateness and inner harmony of a free man acting in accord with a plan, and the slave who acts mostly at random, see *Metaphysics*, 1075[b].

seems wildly naïve to deny that people may do wrong in a coldly calculating, even reflective way (and that such persons ought to be restrained or punished and not just corrected).

Taylor's communitarian project is permeated by an ambivalence toward liberal diversity similar to MacIntyre's. On the one hand, Taylor suggests that people have no right to lead 'truncated' lives: we cannot 'sensibly claim the morality of a truncated form of life for people on the ground of defending their rights'.[52] On the other hand, he is not eager to use his rather broad category of 'internal' obstacles to freedom to justify political intervention, or to substantively limit the choices that free persons can make. As he says, the freedom associated with 'self-realization': 'can fail for internal reasons, but . . . no valid guidance can be provided in principle by social authority, because of human diversity and originality . . . the attempt to impose such guidance will destroy the other necessary conditions of freedom.'[53] Does Taylor believe that a person has a right to lead either a silly or a serious life? To spend his free time either watching TV and drinking beer or cultivating 'higher' pleasures? Raising the threshold of person-hood too high, or building in thick, substantive criteria, sacrifices the logic of respect for persons to the logics of perfectionism and paternalism, and risks, as Berlin warns, equating freedom with despotism. Ultimately, as the above quotation indicates, Taylor seems to allow that autonomy itself is best promoted in a liberal environment in which people are free to lead 'truncated' lives.

The ideal of autonomy has more to do with the style than the substance of a way of life. The manner of a person's engagement in his projects is crucial: self-critically and self-consciously making projects and commitments one's own are highly personal and complex matters. Whether an activity is chosen autonomously will depend on whether it is actively or passively engaged in, and how it fits in with a larger pattern of activity, or even a broad lifeplan. None of this means that individual choices can never be wrong or that second-guessing the choices of a close friend is never justified. To claim that a

---

[52] Taylor, 'Atomism', p. 199.
[53] Ibid. 217.

person acts autonomously is not, moreover, to immunize him from criticism, because autonomy is not a complete ideal; it is amenable to, but not a guarantor of, other virtues, it is one moral value among others.

It is difficult to bring abstract basic human goods to bear on particular choices. Allowing that there are real human goods does not make it easy to understand the ways in which lives that are strange to us may be ways of participating in those goods. Emphasizing the public nature of language and the role of articulateness in deliberation should not blind us to the fact that each of us is shaped by highly personal, even intimate, experiences and subtle influences: we are never perfectly transparent to ourselves let alone to others. The place and meaning of the projects and pursuits that compose one's life depend in part on the peculiar experiences that have shaped that person. A Catholic priest will have a hard time knowing what it is like to be a lesbian, and vice versa.

Human goods are abstract and open-textured, admitting of an illimitable variety of ways of participating in them; there is always a degree of presumption in passing judgment on others: always room for doubt, always ignorance, always cause to wonder whether we have seen clearly the real quality and import of other people's choices. No life is an 'open book'.

My friend is dead, my neighbour is dead, my love, the darling of my soul, is dead; it is the inexorable consolidation and perpetuation of the secret that was always in that individuality, and which I shall carry in mine to my life's end. In any of the burial places of this city through which I pass, is there a sleeper more inscrutable than its busy inhabitants are in their innermost personality, to me, or than I am to them?[54]

People are not totally mysterious and we must, of course, call them to account for certain ways in which their actions and lives impinge on others (when they violate the rights of others, harm, or offend in certain ways). Requiring people publicly to account for their lives in a fuller sense, for the quality of their choices and the nobility and worth of their projects, may be a

---

[54] Charles Dickens, *Tale of Two Cities* (New York, undated), ch. 3, p. 112.

vain and presumptuous assault on an inevitable, and by no means valueless, residuum of personal opacity.[55]

Liberal respect for diversity is based, here at least, less on scepticism about the existence of real human goods than on the legitimate variety of ways of participating in those goods and the difficulty of entering into the experiences of others in a way that would be adequate to fathom and evaluate their personal projects and choices. These difficulties are bound to be in important ways insurmountable in a large, open, dynamic, and tolerant liberal society, where most of our fellow citizens will of necessity be strangers to us. We confront the problem of moral opacity by requiring all to refrain from various forms of harm and self-destruction (it is often much easier to identify and publicly justify basic prohibitions than the features of a good life that all ought to strive for[56]) and by supporting educational and other institutions that promote in a gentle and relatively unobtrusive way certain goods (such as autonomy) closely related to liberal politics.

SOCIAL PLURALISM AND VALUE CONFLICT

Disagreement about what the good life consists in is a basic condition of liberal justice. Liberal politics may seem, at first, to be a response to the 'problem' of disagreement and pluralism, a *modus vivendi* or a compromise imposed on persons who would prefer to dominate others if they had the power to do so. In fact, a pluralistic social milieu positively encourages the reflective capacities defining moral personhood and those more extensive capacities composing the ideal of liberal autonomy.

When thinking about the prerequisites of autarchy and autonomy, one can become preoccupied with the realm of ideas and the language of 'qualitative contrasts' and neglect, as

[55] Iris Murdoch has some interesting remarks about the limits of public articulateness in *The Sovereignty of the Good* (Oxford, 1969), 20–45. Murdoch argues that articulation and speech must give way at some point to perception and discernment, to an 'attention' to the good better thought of in terms of 'vision', as a 'just and loving gaze directed at an individual reality', p. 34.

[56] I have learned much on this theme from conversations with Judith N. Shklar about her forthcoming book on injustice.

Taylor sometimes does, the importance of social pluralism. The mere existence of a language of qualitative contrasts is not enough to support the flourishing of strong evaluation; the development of reflective capacities also requires the existence of a number of 'live' ethical options. In a pluralistic and sufficiently tolerant social milieu one may seriously consider and actually choose among a variety of options and lifestyles. Unless a plurality of conceptions of the good life compete respectfully in a society, unless many voices converse about the good, and liberal citizens can imagine themselves changing their lives, individuals will not be stimulated to reflect upon their own commitments and values. We possess the language required to describe the lifestyle of the chivalrous knight errant, but if this ideal is regarded as dead, not a real option for us, it can spur amusement or wonderment but not soul-searching.

Only live options spur strong evaluation. Strong evaluators need both the right personal attitude (of understanding, sympathy for diverse ideals of life, and an openness to change) and a supportive social environment, one in which there are many live options and in which changes are tolerated. The capacities of the strong evaluator are, as Taylor says, 'unavailable to one whose sympathies and horizons are so narrow that he can conceive of only one way of life.'[57] What is needed is not only competition among ideals, but respectful competition and a certain attitude toward change: a mutual willingness to try new things, to entertain various ideals. This attitude will exist in one whose mental life reflects the value conflicts that characterize the pluralistic polity itself.

One might resist linking freedom and autonomy with the internalization of value conflict by identifying the self with a closed core of individuality and by isolating that harmonious core from social pluralism. Romantic individualists, like Humboldt and Mill, link freedom with a striving to remain faithful to a deep, fixed core of originality or individuality.[58] And Taylor, as we saw above, invokes an idea of authenticity tied to a harmonious core of individuality. This manœuvre creates a tension between persons whose freedom consists in

---

[57] Taylor, 'Negative Liberty', p. 204.
[58] See Mill, *On Liberty*, ch. 3.

striving to remain true to an inner harmonious essence and a pluralistic social milieu that constantly assaults them with new alternatives, conflicting ideals, and a wide variety of conceptions of the good life.

The plurality of values might be seen as either a superficial or a radical phenomenon. On Berlin's account, the 'clash of values at once absolute and incommensurable' is knit into the fabric of the universe, making 'the very concept of an ideal life, a life in which nothing of value need ever be lost or sacrificed . . . not merely utopian, but incoherent'.[59] The pluralist's *bête noire* is the doctrine that a 'single criterion' can be found which reconciles all values in a 'final solution' or a 'vision of some future perfection'.[60] Against this view Berlin holds that 'ultimate values are irreconcilable'. Choosing among ultimate values is inescapable, and in choosing persons exercise and explore their individuality; 'the ends of men are many'. The exercise of judgment and choice are intrinsically valuable. And so liberal pluralists encourage the proliferation of new options by recommending Millian 'experiments in living'.[61]

In contrast with the pluralist's emphasis on the inescapability of choosing between ultimate values, Taylor argues that we are presented with a 'plurality of moral perspectives', rather than a plurality of competing values within the same perspective. Once a perspective is chosen, the experience of value conflict is overcome. The result is a kind of moral perspectivism: normal moral reflection operates out of a settled, coherent perspective but is interrupted by extraordinary periods of unsettled questioning and deep reflection. Berlin's pluralism cuts deeper, it stems from the irreconcilability of ultimate values, not perspectives:

since some values may conflict intrinsically, the very notion that a pattern must in principle be discoverable in which they are all rendered harmonious is founded on a false a priori view of what the world is like . . . the need to choose, to sacrifice some ultimate values to others, turns out to be a permanent characteristic of the human predicament.[62]

---

[59] Berlin, *Four Essays*, pp. l–li.
[60] Ibid. 167–70.
[61] Ibid. 169–70.
[62] Ibid., p. li.

Radical pluralism seems to me a truer picture of the nature of moral value and the experience of living in a liberal pluralistic society. The impossibility of a harmonious moral life is not a modern discovery. Sophocles recognized an ineradicable element of tragedy in the human predicament: people are sometimes forced, like Antigone, to choose between ultimate values. For Sophocles the conflict of 'good with good' is 'prior to and independent of any individual characteristics', as MacIntyre notes; tragedy is stitched into the fabric of the universe, it does not arise from some flaw in a person's character.[63]

For liberals value conflict is normal and usually tolerable, and that is in part because these conflicts are overarched by political values insuring toleration and peace. The normalization of value conflict may be what leads MacIntyre to the liberal conclusion that the good life is the life spent seeking the good life. Likewise, despite his initially hostile attitude to liberalism's 'open' conception of the self, MacIntyre eventually denies that freedom depends upon remaining true to our settled plans, propensities, and projects: 'rebellion against my identity is always one possible way of expressing it.'[64]

The argument for positive freedom entails isolating the self from its pluralistic social context. It is as though an inner, rational, harmonious, closed core of character or individuality can be isolated from a periphery beset and disrupted by external, heteronomous, and ever-changing stimuli. But human personality is not so easily lifted out of its social context. Once these divisions within persons and between persons and social context are denied, the argument for positive freedom, for isolating human personality by identifying the real self with a harmonious rational plan, collapses.[65]

Citizens of tolerant liberal regimes are likely to be shaped deeply by diversity: social pluralism penetrates to the core of the liberal personality, provoking the inner experience of value conflict and stimulating critical reflection. At the most

[63] MacIntyre, *After Virtue*, p. 153.

[64] Ibid. 204–5.

[65] Taylor's attempt to locate freedom by distinguishing 'authentic' desires and separating a 'true self' from internal obstacles to freedom, represents a turning back to the idea of freedom as 'self-dependency' which he is at pains to debunk elsewhere, see *Hegel and Modern Society* (Cambridge, 1979), 156.

obvious level, living in a pluralistic society widens the options that people typically have available to them, persons living in such societies must choose more often and are encouraged to reflect more deeply than those living in societies with few real alternatives.

The internalization of value pluralism is closely linked with normal liberal reflective capacities. Liberals such as Berlin and Rawls go so far as to portray the single-minded pursuit of a unified good as a form of irrationality. As Rawls puts it, 'there is no one aim by reference to which all our choices can reasonably be made'.[66] In subordinating everything to the pursuit of a single dominant end (becoming a major league football player, for example, or finishing a book),

fanaticism and inhumanity is manifest. Human good is hetero-geneous because the aims of the self are heterogeneous. Although to subordinate all our aims to one end does not strictly speaking violate the principles of rational choice . . . it still strikes us as irrational, or more likely as mad. The self is disfigured and put in the service of one of its ends for the sake of system.[67]

But Rawls goes too far. We may say that the 'internalization' of value pluralism and conflict is part of the liberal ideal of autonomy—part, perhaps, of being fully conscious of and sensitive to the moral complexity of our world. The inner experience of value pluralism is, as well, encouraged by citizenship in a vast, heterogeneous, liberal, 'extended republic'. Unless, however, the fanatical pursuit of a single end impairs the reflective capacities that distinguish persons, we should not label it as mad or irrational (at least not in legal or political terms).

Social pluralism compliments and supports the liberal capacity for reflective deliberation. The inner experience of value conflict, where Taylor wants to locate unfreedom, is an important spur to reflection. It could also help brake what could otherwise be a fanatical commitment to a perfectly consistent and comprehensive set of harmonious values. The inner experience of value conflict encourages a degree of

[66] Rawls, *Theory of Justice*, p. 560 and sect. 85 generally.
[67] Ibid. 554.

tentativeness in our commitment to any set of values, and this provides room for reflection, self-criticism, toleration, moderation, and an openness to re-evaluation and change. As Joseph Cropsey puts it, 'Men become dissatisfied with themselves when, and only if, what they are does not possess them exhaustively and to the exclusion of a power to scrutinize what they are.'[68] The liberal personality thrives not on a harmonious inner life, but on both 'internal' and 'external' value plurality, and a consequent unease or dissatisfaction.

The internalization of diversity and conflict allows the reflective self to maintain some distance from any single end, or the values of any particular community with which we happen to identify: each of our ends and the whole set of our ends can be seen as less than absolute, and not simply fixed or given. We cannot put aside all our ends and act from pure will or rationality. We can recognize, however, that we are not unreflectively, necessarily, or irrevocably tied to any particular end.

For liberals, the capacity to choose is more basic than what is chosen. As a consequence, liberals regard other choosers as like themselves in a morally decisive respect despite their disagreements on specific ends and goals, allegiances and memberships. We recognize an 'abstract' personhood in ourselves and others that allows us to pay our highest political allegiance to 'impersonal' rules of law and to liberal justice. Liberals forsake all-enveloping memberships in particular, homogeneous, local communities for memberships in many overlapping communities, and a regulating membership in an overarching, abstract, universalistic community of all persons —the Great or Open Society.

Contrary to what communitarians claim, the abstract, open view of the person, not detached from all commitments, but not inevitably, indissolubly, or unreflectively identified with any, is fully situated, or at home, in a pluralistic social environment. Indeed, as I shall argue below, the liberal personality is more fully situated, more at home, more equipped to thrive in a pluralistic society than the communitarian

[68] Joseph Cropsey, 'The United States as Regime and the Source of the American Way of Life', in Cropsey, *Political Philosophy and the Issues of Politics* (Chicago, Ill., 1977), 3.

self, whose identity is inextricably linked with particular allegiances, commitments, and goals.

The open society and open-mindedness are alike characteristically liberal. 'One who is riveted by fear of the unknown to one familiar life-form, or who has been so formed in suspicion and hate of outsiders that he can never put himself in their place' is, almost by definition, unreflective.[69] The liberal ideal excludes the bigot and the xenophobe. Toleration and broad-mindedness are liberal virtues by virtue of characterizing strong evaluators and persons capable of giving supreme allegiance to liberal justice. These attitudes cannot and should not be enforced by political means, but they do seem to be encouraged by life in a pluralistic liberal society. And we may call them liberal virtues in so far as they characterize persons and societies flourishing in a distinctly liberal way.

LIBERAL JUSTICE AND PERSONAL COMMITMENT

Central to both liberal justice and liberal autonomy is the capacity to reflect upon, criticize, and shape our identity-defining projects and commitments. This capacity entails a certain detachment from the commitment or allegiance being reflected upon, in order either to interpose an impersonal standard of justice or critically to examine our ends and values in light of alternatives.[70] One likely consequence of recognizing the plurality of and conflict among ultimate values will be a kind of detachment or moderation of commitment; 'few things touch me', as Montaigne put it, 'or, to put it better, hold me; for it is right that things should touch us, provided they do not possess us.'[71] We live, after all, in tolerant, open regimes, our fellow citizens lead very different lives from our

[69] Taylor, 'Negative Liberty', p. 204.
[70] Of course, it is one thing to gain critical distance for the sake of doing justice, another to gain it to reflect about the value of one's choices. One might, that is, deny that the reflective distancing required by liberal justice has anything to do with the critical reflectiveness of liberal autonomy. A point forcefully made to me by Charles Larmore. The logic of the distinction is clear enough, in practice (given that we are talking about diverse, tolerant, open societies) the two effects would seem to me to be difficult to isolate.
[71] Montaigne, 'On Husbanding Your Will', *Essays*, ed. Frame, p. 766.

own but we respect them as like us in a decisive respect from the point of view of political morality. The common perspective of tolerant liberal citizenship is a platform from which we can recognize the reasonableness of many choices we have not made, many options we have forgone. The consciousness and inner experience of value conflict is conducive to critical reflectiveness but also, perhaps, productive of a certain uneasiness or alienation from our own ends and purposes.

Some communitarians resist the limits liberalism imposes on personal commitments to projects and other people. Liberal reflectiveness, they say, undermines community ties and alienates people from their ends and from others. Michael Sandel argues that liberalism opens too wide a gulf between persons and their ends, goals, and commitments to others. Sandel seeks an alternative to, in particular, the liberal 'conception of the subject . . . the self as a subject of possession'. Sandel rightly argues that the idea of possession implies 'a distance' between myself and the characteristics or commitments I 'possess', between 'what is "me" and what is (merely) "mine".' And for the liberal subject, according to Sandel, all attributes, characteristics, and attachments are mere possessions:

For deontology insists that we view ourselves as independent selves, independent in the sense that our identity is never tied to our aims and attachments. . . . No transformation of my aims and attachments could call into question the person I am, for no such allegiances, however deeply held, could possibly engage my identity to begin with.[72]

Sandel would have us transcend liberal politics by permitting or encouraging 'constitutive' commitments, commitments that close the distance between the choosing self and its ends: as a 'desire or ambition becomes increasingly constitutive of my identity, it becomes more and more *me* and less *mine*'.[73] The constitutive theory of the self is intended to narrow the distance between persons and their commitments and to lower the boundaries among persons who share the same constitutive goals and commitments, making community more

[72] Sandel, *Limits*, p. 179.
[73] Ibid. 56.

central than liberalism allows. For selves 'constituted' by shared commitments,

community describes not just what they *have* as fellow citizens but also what they *are*, not a relationship they choose (as in a voluntary association) but an attachment they discover, not merely an attribute but a constituent of their identity. In contrast to the instrumental and sentimental conceptions of community, we might describe this strong view as the constitutive conception.[74]

Constitutive attachments are allegiances that 'go beyond . . . the "natural duties" I owe to human beings as such. They allow that to some I owe more than justice requires or even permits. . . .'[75] And so, for Sandel, the value of identity-constituting communities transcends and marks the limits of justice: 'As the independent self finds its limits in those aims and attachments from which it cannot stand apart, so justice finds its limits in those forms of community that engage the identity as well as the interests of the participants.'[76]

The communitarian claim that the impersonal requirements of liberal justice should give way to constitutive attachments has its roots in a broader opposition to universalistic moral requirements. Persons should not be expected, according to Bernard Williams, to assess their most important projects from the point of view of an impersonal utilitarian calculus because:

[a person] is identified with his actions as flowing from projects and attitudes which in some cases he takes seriously at the deepest level, as what his life is about. . . . It is absurd to demand of such a man, when the sums come in from the utility network which the projects of others have in part determined, that he should just step aside from his own project and decision and acknowledge the decision which utilitarian calculation requires. It is to alienate him in a real sense from his actions and the source of his action in his own convictions. It is to make him into a channel between the input of everyone's projects, including his own, and an output of optimific decision; but this is to neglect the extent to which *his* actions and *his* decisions have to be seen as the actions and decisions which flow from the projects

---

[74] Sandel, *Limits*, p. 150.
[75] Ibid. 179.
[76] Ibid. 182.

and attitudes with which he is most closely identified. It is thus, in the most literal sense, an attack on his integrity.[77]

The direct object of Williams's attack is utilitarian ethics, which is, in one way, considerably more demanding than liberal justice. The utilitarian injunction (act so as to maximize utility) requires us to forgo the advancement of our own projects and commitments whenever doing so would produce greater aggregate utility. Liberalism does not hold persons and their projects hostage to a maximizing calculus; instead it requires that each person must, in pursuing his projects, respect the equal rights of others. In another way, however, liberalism requires as much as utilitarianism: liberal justice requires persons to stand back from their projects and commitments and subject them to critical scrutiny from an impersonal, moral point of view. Liberal values, I have argued, ought to pervade our lives and condition all our other projects and commitments. But Williams denies that we can or should admit the pervasive reach of any impartial morality, not only utilitarianism. To require that impartial moral norms win out over ground projects,

cannot necessarily be a reasonable demand on the agent. There can come a point at which it is quite unreasonable for a man to give up, in the name of the impartial good ordering of the world of moral agents, something which is a condition of his having any interest in being around in that world at all. . . . [T]he Kantians' omission of character is a condition of their ultimate insistence on the demands of impartial morality, just as it is a reason for finding inadequate their account of the individual.[78]

Liberalism's defect, for Sandel and Williams, is its requirement of reflective detachment from our basic, self-defining commitments and projects.

We ought to reject any political or moral theory requiring less reflective distance or detachment than does liberalism. To see why, let us consider what a genuine alternative to liberalism would have to amount to. The 'constitutive' relationship between the self and its ends is deeply ambiguous, but let us

---

[77] J. J. C. Smart and Bernard Williams, *Utilitarianism: For and Against* (Cambridge, 1973), 116–17.

[78] Bernard Williams, 'Persons, Character, and Morality', in *Moral Luck* (Cambridge, 1983), 14; see also p. 18.

give it a strong interpretation: strongly or deeply constitutive attachments would be those that preclude the critical reflection on which liberalism depends. Even if communitarians would not endorse strongly constitutive attachments (or ground projects) they are what a communitarian would have to endorse to advance an alternative to liberalism.

To make a personal commitment an object of reflection, as liberals do, is, as Sandel notes, to 'establish a certain space between it and me . . . reflexivity is a distancing faculty'.[79] Liberal justice assumes that liberal citizens are able to reflect upon and critically evaluate their commitments to persons, groups, nationalities, causes, and so forth. A supreme political allegiance to 'impersonal' principles of justice might require that we part company with our friends or possibly even family if it should turn out that they have acted unjustly: liberal norms properly override and render subordinate all personal commitments, allegiances, and loyalties. At its strongest, liberal justice requires that one imagine oneself uncommitted to each particular value or allegiance in turn, for the sake of interposing impersonal liberal norms.

The strong interpretation of constitutive commitments does indeed pose an alternative to liberalism: it denies that any reflective distance at all can or should be established between the moral subject and its deep, defining, 'constitutive' goals and commitments. And this sometimes seems to be what communitarians want, as when Sandel says that we do not choose but 'discover' our attachments, that our commitments may be things that we 'are' and not what we 'have', that 'they go beyond the obligations I voluntarily incur', that they exist when 'to some I owe more than justice requires or even permits'.[80] Allegiances strongly 'constitutive' of personal identity are, like Williams's ground projects, placed entirely beyond the reach of critical reflection, beyond the scope of liberal justice: this occurs when devotion to particular causes or groups crowds out or supplants critical reflection. When personal identity is strongly constituted by particular commitments, the determinacy and closure of the communitarian self

---

[79] Sandel, *Limits*, p. 58.
[80] Sandel, 'The Unencumbered Self', *Political Theory*, 9 (1984), 81–96, and *Limits*, p. 179.

displace the critical reflectiveness and openness of the liberal self.

Sandel is not alone in tending to push strong evaluation toward a process that culminates or 'hits bottom' in a moment of pure discovery. Taylor also sometimes refers to certain attributes being 'essential to my identity', and of the process of reflection in terms of 'clairvoyance' or a striving 'to be faithful to something . . . a largely inarticulate sense of what is of decisive importance'.[81] And Williams speaks of the 'absurdity' of asking an agent to 'step aside' from 'projects and attitudes with which he is deeply identified'. All of this language suggests that the aim of deliberation is to uncover or clarify rather than to criticize and shape a deep core of individuality.

The capacity for reflective detachment from particular desires, projects, and commitments is what allows us to understand and conform with justice, and to devise and pursue a conception of the good life; these are what Rawls calls the two 'moral powers' of the liberal subject: the capacity for a sense of justice, and the capacity to adopt a plan of life.[82] By recognizing these capacities as the basis of our moral person-hood, we can recognize others as moral persons like ourselves, even if they do not share our desires, pursue our projects, or have our commitments. The capacity for reflective detach-ment helps us put a brake on our own pursuits and respect the equal rights of others.

Strongly constitutive attachments or deep ground projects, those placed beyond the reach of critical reflection, are very poorly suited to our pluralistic world. Nothing intrinsic to constitutive attachments or ground projects insures that persons so defined will respect the rights of others or abide by moral norms of any kind. Loyal Nazis may have been deeply constituted by their commitment to being 'good Ger-mans' but this hardly immunizes them from moral criticism or provides the stuff of good communities. Some people are, unfortunately, deeply committed to all sorts of unjust and vicious ends; in some cases those ends may be all that give them any interest in going on with their lives (a glimmer of hope for a new Reich or for a scientific breakthrough

[81] Taylor, 'Human Agency', pp. 38–40.
[82] Rawls, 'Constructivism', p. 525.

producing a Hitler clone). If some people cannot go on with their lives without projects that involve serious injustices, then they have no right to go on with their lives.

A high degree of sincerity, authenticity, depth of commitment, or persistence does not and should not immunize a person or group from moral criticism and possible intervention. Racial discrimination in the American South was bound up with deep traditions, conventions, and expectations, that constituted the identities of slave-owner and slave alike. The constitutive commitments of slave-owners and the Old South's traditions, conventions, and expectations were morally vicious. Discrimination was not privileged by depth of commitment, long practice, and widespread acceptance. Public justification is the work of articulable reasons, not of a plumb-bob testing the depth of a commitment or a timescale charting its duration.

To hold that commitments to one's nation, region, tribe, or even family can be constitutive of identity in a strong sense is to place them beyond critical reflection and choice. A strongly 'constitutive' attachment is the rock-bottom of my identity, I do not need to cite further reasons for such an attachment because it simply defines who I am. I cannot 'detach' myself from a strongly constitutive commitment or gain critical leverage upon it. To decide that no commitment should be granted this status is to reject illiberal communitarianism.

Moral agents should reflect critically on the moral quality of their actions from an impersonal point of view for the sake of conforming with liberal justice. Unless a community consists of a homogeneous and totally isolated group of persons, all sharing the same constitutive attachments and never bothering anyone else, it should not do without critically reflective moral capacities. As it is, our world is increasingly a *mélange* of ethnic, national, religious, and racial diversity.[83] There are no extensive political territories in the world without minorities. Humanity is ill-served by tribalism in any of its forms. The fact that a liberal public morality, when institutionalized and

---

[83] Katz explores the limits of communitarianism in Israeli politics, in 'Communitarianism and the Limits of Intercommunal Respect', Senior Thesis.

practised, helps people gain a critical distance on their local attachments is one of its greatest achievements.

The political centrality of liberal critical reflection does not presuppose the existence of what Sandel calls an 'unencumbered' or 'disembodied' self: an uncommitted *locus* of pure reflection buried deep beneath my particular commitments. Liberalism assumes that we can, and ought to, reflect on our particular commitments, which means gaining some distance on any commitment or allegiance. We must be able to imagine ourselves without the commitment being reflected upon if we are to test it by a public liberal standard of justice; we might be morally obliged to revise or renounce any commitment. But this does not mean that liberal citizens must (or even can) imagine themselves to be totally 'unencumbered' by a personal identity. To say that we must be able to reflect in turn upon each of our commitments (to my family, my church, my friends, my country, my university, and so on) does not assume that we can reflect on all of our commitments all at once.

An interpretation of constitutive commitments weaker than the one we have been considering leads us back to strong evaluation and the ideal of situated autonomy. A weaker sense of constitutive commitments denies that we can abstract from all our commitments all at once, but it allows that we can and ought to be able to reflect on each particular attachment in turn, no matter how deep, to interpose public standards of justice. Liberals need not deny the importance of understanding self, culture, and various community memberships as the raw materials of reflection.

Strong evaluation requires a relatively stable background of other commitments not (at the moment) being called into question. Critical reflection on some aspect of one's identity is possible because other aspects are not presently being questioned. If one questioned all of one's commitments all at once no progress would be possible and the self really would be 'disempowered' as Sandel suggests. A person need not, however, give up all his commitments in order to reflect critically on each one of them, though a lifetime of self-criticism might add up to a rather massive change.

If liberal reflection does not empty the self of all attachments and disempower it, neither does it isolate individuals from their social context. Liberals do not seek to 'get outside themselves' (metaphorically) because they undervalue their integrity, wish to flee from their projects, or because they aspire to be outsiders or strangers. Liberals seek a public rather than a self-centred point of view in order to give others their due and to live up to their moral duties and their capacity for reasonableness and autonomy. Liberal reasonableness and reflection do not provide metaphysical ladders for persons seeking to climb out of this world; rather, they define the proper aspirations of persons making their way in pluralistic society mindful that others have projects and lives of their own.

The aspiration driving the liberal project of critical reflection is neither a mere love of abstraction nor a devotion to contemplation for its own sake. It is, rather, the aspiration to act in a manner that can be publicly justified to ourselves and our reasonable fellow creatures. The point is not to purify or distil a wholly disembodied self or to leap for the perspective of the godhead. The point is to seek reasons that justify ourselves and our political arrangements here and now, to other persons whom we regard, and wish to treat, as reasonable and reasoning beings capable of sharing our reasons when they are good and of offering us better reasons when they are not. Our political project is not only to supply but to demand reasons of others, including public officials, and to accept good reasons from wherever they come.[84] And all this because we wish to do the right thing and treat others reasonably.

Without commonly acknowledged overriding principles of justice, men acting from different and opposing ideals of life would come constantly into conflict. We should not simply pursue our goals because they are 'ours' or those of our group any more than we can justifiably take what belongs to someone else because we really want it. Our actions must pass the public test of justice, the minimal burden that liberalism requires: respect for the equal rights of others to pursue their own good in their own way.

---

[84] On reason-giving as a 'publicly shared' and social point of view, see Rawls, *Theory*, pp. 516–17, and 'Constructivism', p. 570.

In a liberal society, coercive political arrangements require the support of articulable reasons capable of meeting objections and being fairly applied. This is, in part, because people really do disagree, and because we owe reasonable people the form of respect embodied in public justification. Communitarians sometimes suggest, however, that what we need are not good reasons but 'insight' and 'clarity' into each other.[85] 'Justice finds its occasion', says Sandel, not because people disagree but 'because we cannot know each other, or our ends, well enough to govern by the common good alone.'[86] But if we knew our ends better would we find that they are the same as everyone else's? Or would we find that like the plurality that governs the universe of moral value, people's goals and dreams really do differ?

I doubt that our communities would be better if uniformity replaced diversity and we did not, for that reason, need justice. What a desperately boring place the world would be if not for the challenges, arguments, and discoveries spawned by disagreement about what is good in life. Uncritical, unreflective, and narrow-minded people will have a hard time living up to the demands of liberal citizenship, and the timid may shrink from autonomy, but then societies composed of such people are unlikely to be very dynamic or exciting. Liberals cherish not conformists but dissenters because they force us to defend ourselves, and think about our beliefs, and so improve our understanding of personal and public morality.

Communitarian objections to liberal detachment and reflectiveness are driven in part by fear of the dislocation and isolation that could result from applying self-conscious criticism to all relationships and commitments. Sandel is straightforward: 'The morality of right . . . speaks to that which distinguishes us, the morality of good corresponds to the unity of persons and speaks to that which connects us. . . .'[87] Similarly, Williams's emphasis on personal integrity aims to seal the bond between persons and the projects which give their lives meaning and connectedness with others. Walzer's

---

[85] Sandel, *Limits*, pp. 32–3.
[86] Ibid. 183.
[87] Ibid. 133.

opposition to 'philosophical detachment' reflects the high value he places on political membership and participation.

Liberal rights place no obstacles before the common allegiance to shared ends. Liberal tolerance and pluralism incite people to reflect, to choose, to combine with others, to criticize, to renounce, to revise their ends, and combine again, in a never-ending project of self-definition and self-enactment. The dynamism of this process does entail a measure of distance from commitments and perhaps a degree of alienation. Some detachment is simply inseparable from the critically self-conscious life that liberal toleration spawns; a measure of unease is a price that must be paid for the diversity and progressiveness of the Great Society. Liberalism also respects the choices of those who withdraw from the current of criticism and change, so long as they conform to basic liberal norms.

We should limit our loyalties in the name of the basic, impersonal requirements of liberal justice. The liberal citizen may be required to renounce commitments to friends, country, or both, in the name of political morality. It all depends on what one's friends and country are up to. That does not mean that we must, as lonely individuals, step beyond the pale of all community attachments, it means rather that one community we always belong to is the community of reasonable persons. Liberalism requires that we regard our projects and commitments from the perspective of others, from 'outside' ourselves and our narrow circle, but not outside all communities or the human world.

Liberal citizens, as moral persons, must simply accept the possibility of dislocation that comes with the overriding commitment to liberal justice. Most of us have been members of groups, neighbourhoods, organizations, or political units, that have unjustly turned against outsiders or disfavoured members or unpopular minorities. Even the people we care for most may be swept up in injustice. Like Marshal Cain in *High Noon*, those with an overriding commitment to liberal principles must be prepared to stand aside from their friends and loved ones when they counsel actions incompatible with our own best understanding of what justice requires. Or we might, like Gordon Hirabayashi, decide we should leave quite innocent family members behind in the name of higher liberal ideals. What justice calls for in such limiting cases helps define the attitude appropriate to more normal circumstances; we teach children, after all, to think critically, to do what they think is right, and not to cave in to peer pressure. In the end, however, we should not exaggerate the solitariness of principled conduct: the best reasons of liberal justice are those that can be maintained publicly; we should not suppose that doing the right thing is going to often mean acting alone.

CONCLUSION

MacIntyre charges that liberals conceive of the self as a set of open possibilities, with no necessary attachments or fixed ends, and in this way denude the community of common virtues and ideals.[88] And yet, liberal autonomy (or even liberal autarchy) is not neutral with regard to the value of all ways of life. In times past, warriors, saints, and artists have been held up as ideals. The ideal liberal personality is characterized by reflective self-awareness, active self-control, a willingness to engage in self-criticism, an openness to change, and critical support for the public morality of liberal justice.

Liberal politics and the ideal of liberal autonomy discussed above call upon and encourage the development of a similar set of reflective capacities. Liberal politics calls upon every citizen to reason about the law for himself, to apply its norms in his own conduct, and to challenge official interpretations that are faulty. The liberal ideal of autonomy calls upon persons to take up a similar, critically interpretive attitude toward their own characters, commitments, and lives. Autonomous liberal persons do not simply accept their current projects as given, they do not adopt social norms and practices uncritically: they think for themselves about the best way of carrying forward their lives from where they are. Liberal politics and liberal autonomy are complementary: both converge on an ideal of character that is actively reflective, self-critical, tolerant, reason-giving and reason-demanding, open

---

[88] MacIntyre, *After Virtue*, p. 145.

to change, and respectful of the autonomy of others, a character disposed to enjoy and participate in the vast spectacle of
progress and diversity.

One might question the ultimate efficacy of strong evaluation. If our thought is conditioned by assumptions and pre-
suppositions as yet unrevealed, or by structural limitations on
our thinking beyond our awareness, then are we really autonomous? If our preferences are 'adaptive', or unwittingly
shaped by what we perceive to be available or not available,
are they genuine and worth respecting? If our most basic
judgments reflect the hegemony of some pernicious and
imposed system of belief, then all that follows is similarly
tainted and our apparent freedom is spurious. These worries
are real and vexing, but it is important to remember the liberal
emphasis on a Popperian attitude of self-criticism and openness to revision, even radical revision. Liberal ideals stress the
importance of self-conscious, self-critical awareness, and so
liberals should be relatively well positioned to detect
hegemonic belief systems. Liberals ought to support articulate
and defensible reasons, not the status quo.

For liberal-situated autonomy, reason, desire, and social
context are related and mediated by articulateness in a moral
language. Strong evaluation makes reflective choice an active
engagement. Moral dilemmas force us to reflect upon our own
character and deepest evaluations: in articulating our basic
values and coming to understand and evaluate our desires we
shape them and our character. The central role of articulation
in a shared moral language exhibits our situatedness as well as
our autonomy. The capacities called upon by strong evaluation complement those required by liberal justice. In Chapter
7 I shall argue that these active self-shaping subjects, free and
responsible and situated in a pluralistic social environment, are
equipped precisely to flourish in a liberal environment.

The status of the ideal of liberal autonomy is ambiguous. On
the one hand, autonomy would seem to have a favoured place
as a liberal ideal. It supports the energetic, self-critical, and
independent virtues of liberal citizenship, and would seem to
be a prerequisite of flourishing in a diverse, tolerant liberal
society. On the other hand, liberalism is generally anti-

paternalistic: it seeks to respect persons with basic reflective capacities and resists the political promotion of thickly textured common conceptions of the good life.

The ambiguity surrounding liberal autonomy could be resolved either by embracing some form of liberal neutrality, which really would try to treat autonomy like any other contested conception of the good life. Or it could be resolved by frankly embracing a robust form of liberal perfectionism, one that would promote liberal virtues such as autonomy without reservation. Charles Larmore and William Galston respectively embrace neutralist and perfectionist versions of liberalism. Their arguments are powerful, but both seem to me to, in opposite ways, embrace overly spare frameworks that neglect values that liberals should honour as best they can.

The ambiguity of autonomy should be preserved. Liberalism is not, as I argued in Chapter 2, neutral in its consequences: life in a liberal regime will tend to favour certain patterns of human flourishing, among them ones with a central role for autonomy. And liberal regimes sometimes directly and justifiably promote the self-criticism and openness to change that characterize autonomy. Political criticism and debate are exercises in a particular form of civic education, and public education itself has plenty of room for scientific but none for religious training. Explicitly or not, liberal regimes endorse and promote autonomy. But we still respect the non-autonomous: people have the right to lead lazy, narrow-minded lives, and so we minimize and soften interference with their choices. Equality of respect for persons is, perhaps, the more basic liberal concern, but the good of autonomy has, in a liberal political regime, a status that is independent and worth preserving: the first among equally respectable ideals of life.

The ambiguity of liberal autonomy reflects, I think, the broader tendency of liberal politics to pursue values that are in tension and the general fact of value pluralism. The pursuit of values in tension may be a sign of confusion. It seems to me, however, that we do well to hold together this particular pair of not entirely congruent principles, remembering that respect for the basic freedoms of all liberal persons has a kind of preeminence, but that freedom is animated and enhanced by the kinetic effects of the ideal of autonomy.

7

The Liberal Virtues

Communitarians charge that liberal regimes pay a high price for their central concern with diversity, individuality, impersonal law, and rights. What is lost, allegedly, is the possibility of a moral community, a common devotion to shared values, and citizen virtue, with the attendant risks of stability problems and legitimation crises. This chapter aims to show that liberal theory can provide an attractive vision of a distinctively liberal community and liberal virtues while remaining true to its core political convictions: the centrality of freedom and the supremacy of liberal justice. Liberals can reclaim a language which supposedly lies beyond the bounds of liberal politics, the language of virtue, citizenship, community, and human flourishing.

My aim is less empirical than normative, not a survey of attitudes but the evocation of possibilities and ideals. Liberal principles inform many of our political practices, and basic liberal values are affirmed by a large segment of the populace. Articulating the ideal state of affairs implicit in liberal theory and institutions is partly, then, an exercise in the critical interpretation of current politics. Liberal ideals provide a vision of what we ought to stand for as a people, and that vision is recognizably an extension of existing practices and attitudes.

There are many ways of living as a liberal. Submitting to liberal justice and acting in conformity with the rules and regulations of the liberal state is, let us say, the proper extent of our enforceable political duties. A common posture of outward conformity with liberal rights and rules is enough to describe a situation of liberal coexistence, and is compatible with many attitudes, traits, and personal commitments: with mutual indifference or even hostility overlaid by a common fear of reprisal or punishment for breaches of the liberal rules. Such attitudes were, very likely, characteristic of the 'primitive moments' of liberalism, as liberal tolerance emerged in the seventeenth century out of religious strife and civil war.[1] Liberal possibilities are not, however, exhausted by liberalism's primitive moments.

To stress the priority of liberal justice and the pedigree of the liberal virtues, we can try to draw liberal ideals out of the idea of a diverse polity composed of citizens who give their allegiance to liberal justice as a public morality. That is, these citizens do not simply act in outward conformity with liberal norms, they affirm liberal justice as a supreme moral commitment; they recognize and affirm the good reasons that justify and support liberal justice and support liberal political institutions. This is the best way of affirming liberal justice: a fully self-aware and critically reflective way, it comports with the liberal commitment to public justification and the constitutional citizen's engagement in critical interpretation. Substantive virtues and forms of human excellence are implicit in liberal justice, justification, constitutionalism, and citizenship.

Tendencies and institutions often associated with modern liberalism may support attitudes such as tolerance: urbanization, industrialization, and open mass markets, all serve to bring together large numbers of people from disparate backgrounds and throw them into a multiplicity of relationships structured, in Western societies, by liberal justice. As Voltaire observed:

Enter the Exchange of London, that place more respectable than many a court; you will see there agents from all nations assembled for the utility of mankind. There the Jew, the Mohammedan, and the Christian deal with one another as if they were of the same religion, and give the name of infidel only to those who go bankrupt.[2]

People have argued for centuries about whether market relations

[1] On liberal 'coexistence through mutual indifference', see Holmes, *Constant*, p. 245.
[2] Voltaire, 'Letters philosophiques', in *Mélanges* (Paris, 1961), pp. 17–18, quoted in Holmes, *Constant*, pp. 253–4.

have a positive overall effect on character and manners.[3] Commerce at least requires and facilitates the peaceful mixing of peoples from disparate cultural and religious backgrounds, peoples with different values, ends, and lifestyles. Markets do not require impartiality, benevolence, or broad sympathies, but they do at least seem to counteract and undermine the divisiveness of religious zealotry and the psychological narrowness and inflexibility of life characteristic of more isolated, closed, and homogeneous environments. Markets and urbanization help to lay the groundwork for the development of liberal virtues.[4]

We should not confuse the liberal character with *homo economicus* or assume that the pursuit of material gain is the overriding preoccupation of liberal citizens. Liberal citizens, I have argued, ought to subordinate their personal interests to public moral principles and many actually do so much of the time. Nevertheless, a more complete analysis would consider the ways that institutions related to liberalism, such as free markets, either support or subvert the liberal values.

At issue here are the character traits and virtues implicit in liberal justice. These can be culled from the character of a society composed of people who do not simply observe the norms of liberal justice, but who positively affirm them, and in doing so, participate in the liberal virtues. Such a society would be composed of people who fully exercise the first of what Rawls calls the two 'moral powers': the 'capacity to understand, to apply, and to act from (and not only in accordance with) the principles of justice'.[5] What can we say of a society whose citizens do not simply avoid what liberals consider injustice, but who understand liberal reasons and

[3] George Simmel argued that the divisiveness of competition is counteracted by the effort to serve the customer: 'Competition compels the wooer . . . to go out to the wooed, come close to him, establish ties with him, find his strengths and weaknesses and adjust to them . . .' in *Conflict and the Web of Group Affiliation*, trans. K. H. Wolff (Glencoe, Ill., 1955). And see also Albert O. Hirschmann's surveys of these debates in *The Passions and the Interests* (Princeton, NJ, 1977) and 'Rival Interpretations of Market Society: Civilizing, Destructive, or Feeble?', *Journal of Economic Literature*, 20 (1982), 1463–84.

[4] McClosky and Zaller argue that urbanization and secularization play important roles in encouraging support for capitalistic and liberal-democratic values, *American Ethos*, pp. 254–5.

[5] Rawls, 'Constructivism', p. 525.

affirm the positive value of acting justly? What would citizens be like who do not simply respect one another's liberal rights however grudgingly, but who possess the understanding and the attitudes that make them enthusiastic proponents of liberal rights and eager supporters of liberal institutions and practices? What sort of character, in other words, would be associated with a liberal form of personal excellence and a flourishing liberal community?

There are ideas usually taken to be central to liberalism that might seem to stand in the way of our exploration of liberal virtues. Liberal society is often thought of as at base characterized by disagreement, or by neutrality, or a sharp distinction between public and private spheres of life. Liberalism is, however, basically about agreement on values that are by no means neutral, and those public values have a private life. Let us focus briefly on these three misconceptions before turning directly to the liberal ideals of virtue and community.

PLURALISM AND LIBERAL UNITY

Liberals often regard 'disagreement' or conflict as the basic fact of social life, taking their cues from Hobbes. Liberal toleration of individual liberty is a necessity, we are told, because people disagree about what is good in life: people disagree about their religious commitments and other goals and ideals. And from the purportedly basic fact of disagreement, liberal political imperatives are characterized in negative terms: avoiding injustice and tyranny, keeping rules of law purposeless or noninstrumental. Or liberals emphasize the fundamental importance of keeping government 'neutral' or impartial between parties who disagree about what is good in life (as liberals like Dworkin, Ackerman, and Larmore have put it).[6] Or, sometimes, liberalism is taken to stand for nothing more definite than toleration and a 'spirit of accommodation'.

While the permanent fact of pluralism is the heart of the liberal political problem, conflict and disagreement are not the basic facts of liberal social life. It is wrong to think that liberal

---

[6] Dworkin, 'Liberalism', in *A Matter of Principle*, p. 191; Bruce Ackerman, *Social Justice in the Liberal State* (New Haven, Conn., 1980), 11; Larmore, *Patterns, passim.*

law is, can be, or even ought to be, in any strong sense purposeless, non-instrumental, or neutral with regard to conceptions of the good life, either at the level of society as a whole or at the level of individual lifeplans. Likewise, if liberalism stands for mere toleration or an indiscriminate spirit of accommodation, then it stands for everything, and it takes a stand for nothing.

These errors are related to the vulnerability of liberalism, as it is commonly understood, to the communitarian critique of liberalism. A political theory that appears to rest on the centrality of disagreement or conflict or self-interest, and that characterizes its basic political values in negative terms or in terms of neutrality or mere accommodation, has a kind of hard-headed quality to it; it modestly avoids reliance on contestable ideals. But to sap liberal politics of positive values in any of these ways is to underdescribe what liberalism stands for, even in its minimal cases, and it leads us to misunderstand what it means to be a liberal. When liberalism is underdescribed in these ways, a great gap looms between hard-headed, non-ideal cases of liberalism, and positive liberal ideals. When we underdescribe and misdescribe the authoritative public values of a liberal regime we also fail to see the extent to which liberalism shapes the lives of liberal citizens.

Even in its unidealized forms liberalism cannot really be neutral among public values—it stands for the supreme worth of certain public values: of individual liberty and responsibility, of tolerance of change and diversity, and of respect for the rights of those who themselves respect liberal values.[7] Liberalism requires the support of positive values to explain why respect is owed to persons and to justify their having the rights they do. Liberalism stands, above all, for the positive value of freedom, freedom to devise, criticize, revise, and pursue a plan of life, and it calls upon people to respect the rights of others whether or not they share the same goals and ideals.

Liberalism, as I argued in Chapter 2, rules out certain

---

[7] See Kant, *The Metaphysics of Morals*, Part 2: 'The Metaphysical Principles of Virtue', in *Kant's Ethical Philosophy*, trans. James W. Ellington, intro. Warner A. Wick (Indianapolis, 1986), and Shklar, *Ordinary Vices* (Cambridge, Mass., 1984), pp. 240–5.

conceptions of the good life altogether: any that entail the violation of liberal rights. And liberalism positively requires that everyone's scheme of values include certain features: respect for the equal rights of others, a willingness to persuade rather than coerce, the subordination of personal plans, projects, and desires to impersonal rules of law, and a contribution to the provision of public goods. The colouring of liberal values splashes pervasively over the vast canvass of a pluralistic liberal society. Some things are excluded completely, and everything is limited and conditioned.

Besides a set of positive values, liberalism represents a set of political institutions: a system of legal rules establishing order and giving substance and specificity to the ideal of equal freedom, representative institutions, and courts of law to adjudicate disputes, test the reasonableness of government actions, and enforce constitutional limitations even against the people's representatives. All liberal governments provide certain public goods—at a bare minimum, the apparatus of national defence, courts and police for justice (they are governments after all). In addition, encouragements to commercial activity, public schools, and poverty relief are almost always provided by liberal governments nowadays. These are not 'neutral' goods, but nearly all liberals would agree that some range of such goods should be provided by a coercive state. (And liberal societies also have semi-public institutions that help define and enforce liberal values, such as universities and the professions of journalism and law.)

So liberals have positive political values and political institutions and practices designed to embody and sustain these values. What liberals often fail to recognize is that these values, institutions, and practices exert a pervasive effect on the lives and the character of liberal citizens. Because liberalism is not neutral (either in its direct or its indirect consequences), and because liberal citizens may (and should) affirm and act from liberal values, we can speak of a distinctive liberal 'character'.

And yet, one might object, decidedly non-liberal groups do survive within polities structured by liberal values, such as the small, but not insignificant, groups of American Nazis. But let us consider what is required of groups like the Nazis if they are to live peaceably in a liberal regime. They must, first of all, respect the rights of those they hate or else suffer at the hands of the law. They must, that is, respect the property, the political rights, and freedoms of Jewish Americans. They may, occasionally, march in Jewish communities, but they must get permits, keep order, and otherwise respect the peace and quiet of these neighbourhoods. They can gather in uniforms, with broadsheets, slogans, music, and other paraphernalia, in legally rented private halls, as long as they do not make too much noise. Nazis must pay taxes to support the liberal institutions they detest, including public schools. The liberal polity requires that the Nazis be law-abiding Nazis and that is not easy. They cannot be 'gung-ho' Nazis, in fact they cannot *be* Nazis at all but only play at it.[8]

That a liberal society makes life hard on Nazis is not a matter for regret. But far less disagreeable and perhaps even admirable groups may find an open, pluralistic environment less than hospitable. Those who favour simple ways may be disorientated by the pace of change and movement. The devout are liable to object to the materialism and licence of a liberal society. Among those prepared to go along with the liberal settlement not all will readily embrace liberal virtues such as autonomy.

THE MIRAGE OF LIBERAL NEUTRALITY

It is, as I have already argued, impossible to sustain the claim that liberalism does not have important and non-neutral effects on which ways of life flourish and gain adherents in a liberal regime. More sophisticated versions of the neutrality thesis do not, however, argue for neutrality of consequences. Liberal neutrality, Larmore argues, 'is not meant to be one of *outcome*, but rather one of *procedure*. That is, political neutrality consists in a constraint on what factors can be invoked to justify a political decision'.[9]

The sophisticated neutralist would carefully restrict the

---

[8] Groups like the Nazis do raise serious problems, regarding the education of their children for instance. My point here is that liberal regimes importantly structure the lives and activities of such groups.

[9] Larmore, *Patterns*, p. 44.

kinds of reasons that are morally admissible grounds for government action, requiring that, 'The state should not seek to promote any particular conception of the good life because of its presumed *intrinsic* superiority—that is, because it is supposedly a *truer* conception'.[10] The liberal state may restrict ideals of life only 'for *extrinsic* reasons because, for example, they threaten the lives of others'.[11] The neutral state may not seek to 'foster or implement any conception of the good life that some people reject', for only then can it respect 'the equal freedom that all persons should have to pursue their conception of the good life'.[12] Governmental neutrality expresses equal respect for moral persons who are defined by their reflective capacity for a conception of the good life and not by the particular conception they choose.

A neutral justification for neutrality can be found, Larmore claims, in 'a universal norm of rational dialogue'.[13] When reasonable people disagree each should, out of concern with keeping the conversation going, 'prescind from the beliefs the other rejects', and 'retreat to *neutral ground*, with the hope either of resolving the dispute or of bypassing it'.[14] What moves both sides is simply a wish to keep the conversation going until they can find grounds for agreement that neither could reasonably reject.

The consistent neutralist will insist on neutral reasons 'all the way down', as it were, or all the way through the reasoned conversation of politics. But how neutral is reasonable conversation? Not very: some people will find head-bashing easier and more satisfying than reason-giving. And so, Larmore's ideal of reasonable conversation purports to be 'neutral only with regard to controversial conceptions', and not even 'completely neutral in this regard either, [but] it is very nearly so, and certainly neutral enough for practical purposes'.[15] Neutral enough for government work turns out to be not very neutral at all.

Liberal 'neutrality' stands for mutual respect among people committed at base to values that are by no means neutral. Larmore would not have us respect everyone, but only those who are reasonable. Among those who will not be

[10] Ibid. 43.   [11] Ibid.   [12] Ibid. 46.
[13] Ibid. 53.   [14] Ibid.   [15] Ibid. 55.

respected are 'fanatics and would-be martyrs' for whom 'civil peace is not so important', racists, and all those who reject 'the obligation of mutual respect'.[16] The bounds and nature of neutral respect are defined by liberal political norms and substantive criteria of reasonableness, criteria that are by no means neutral with respect to ideals of life. None of this is surprising since, as Larmore admits, 'neutrality' is 'too empty to generate any substantive political principles'.[17]

The closer we get, the faster the mirage of neutrality vanishes. Larmore finally advocates only what he calls 'the spirit of neutrality', or 'a higher neutrality; namely, that one should institute only the least abridgment of neutrality necessary for making a decision possible'.[18] Larmore's neutrality, like any political neutrality, is selective, and selective neutrality is not very neutral.

The commitment to political neutrality depends on the acceptance of a conception of social life in which citizens take seriously a public project of justification: these citizens wish to conduct a reasonable conversation about political morality with other people who share a basic interest in such a conversation, or in a process of public justification. It seems to me right to think of this commitment as the moral core of liberalism, but wrong to think that this core is in any important sense morally neutral.

The popularity of neutrality-talk is the consequence, I think, of two factors: a laudable concern to respect reasonable people who disagree widely over their conceptions of the good life, and a desire to facilitate agreement by describing liberalism modestly and uncontroversially. Neutrality builds on principles that are central to liberalism, but from them it erects an excessively strong ban on judgments about human ideals. Liberals properly deploy reasons that can be widely seen to be reasonable, and liberals believe in respect for all those who pass the threshold requirements of reasonableness. Liberals resist paternalism, and minimize interference with people's choices. These do not, however, add up to neutrality. Liberal restrictions on the reasons that can be offered to

----

[16] Ibid. 60.   [17] Ibid. 67.   [18] Ibid. 68.

support government actions are not strict enough to constitute a commitment to neutrality. Liberal ideals and virtues remain in the background, never quite out of view. Autonomy is, from a liberal perspective, not simply one ideal of life among others (though it will sometimes be treated as such). It is not to be regretted that liberal institutions help, in modest and gentle ways, to promote the ideal of autonomy, for that capacity helps make people more competent as liberal citizens and better able to flourish as persons in a liberal society.

THE PRIVATE LIFE OF LIBERAL VALUES

The distinction between public and private spheres of life, like the allied beliefs in the fundamentality of disagreement and in neutrality is apt to close off the possibility of liberal virtues. If liberal values are confined to a certain narrowly defined political sphere of our lives then it will be difficult to think about the ways in which those values shape our characters as a whole. Even so thoughtful a commentator as George Kateb describes a 'mode of restriction . . . characteristic of constitutional democracy: absolute prohibition of governmental intervention in certain areas of life, such as religion, speech, press, and assembly'.[19] Larmore, similarly, derides what he sees as a romantic 'cult of wholeness' that seeks to overcome the public/private distinction, and he bemoans the fact that 'liberal writers themselves have not always respected this separation of realms'.[20]

The metaphor of distinct spheres of public and private life has a certain usefulness, but it is also apt to be misleading, we need not reject it altogether, but we must rethink it or else fall prey to serious confusions about the reach of public values in a liberal polity. The public/private distinction reflects the liberal conviction that people may rightly be coerced by the state only for certain limited reasons, and in pursuance of rules publicly made according to certain procedures. This allows us to organize the conduct of our affairs so as to avoid, in general, unwanted public interventions or litigation. Nevertheless, it is

[19] Kateb, 'Procedures of Constitutional Democracy', p. 218.
[20] Larmore, *Patterns*, pp. 42, 106.

wrong to think that the influence of public values on private life and personal character is neutral, or merely negative or external.

The family and home life may be the paradigm of a private space, where intimate and familial relations are shielded from the interference of outsiders, including the state. But this simple picture is misleading. Public norms do not simply shield but penetrate and shape the relations of persons even in the sphere of family life. A husband cannot treat his wife and children however he wishes, their relations, even their most intimate relations, are structured by public values. And so husbands have been sued by their wives for rape, and domestic violence is a matter of intense concern.

Certain kinds of interventions in the most intimate sphere of family life are required by liberal norms, others are prohibited. Until recently, many states in the USA made it a crime even for married couples to use contraceptives. This has now been ruled unconstitutional by a Supreme Court invoking a right to privacy shielding these intimate personal decisions from state interference.[21] State bans on interracial marriages have also been struck down, and the right to read pornography in the privacy of the home has been protected. The courts have, as we have seen, refused to extend these liberal rights by including homosexual relations among the personal decisions and intimate activities protected by the right to privacy. Liberal politics structures private relations in a certain way: requiring some things, prohibiting others, and permitting freedom of choice between adults.

For liberals, the *ends* of politics are properly limited but pervasive at the same time. Liberal politics is limited because its ends and purposes are limited; that is, there are a limited set of ends or reasons that justify public intervention in our lives. But liberal politics is pervasive because public reasons, liberal norms of respect for the rights of others, override competing commitments and claim authority in every sphere of our lives. The undoubted crime of raping one's spouse vividly illustrates the unlimited reach of liberal norms and the fact that liberal politics has a private life.

---

[21] *Griswold* v. *Connecticut*; laws banning the distribution of contraceptives to unmarried couples were struck down in *Eisenstadt*.

Liberal politics does not insulate the private sphere from the public sphere; even in the absence of litigation, public values penetrate and partly constitute private relations. There is a closer relationship between liberal justice and the good of liberal citizens than liberals and their critics have often admitted. Liberalism embodies a set of substantive moral values, positive values that should secure the highest allegiance of liberal citizens, values that override or preclude many commitments, require some, and condition all other goals and projects, positive values that penetrate and pervasively shape the lives and characters of liberal citizens. Liberal political norms have a private life: they help shape and structure the private lives of liberal citizens. To a greater extent than liberals usually allow, freedom is a way of life.

THE LIBERAL VIRTUES

Let us begin, as we have before, with the idea of social pluralism. In the liberal community people disagree about goals, lifestyles, and religious beliefs. Such a community may, nevertheless, flourish in a liberal way and, if it does, it will have a discernible shape because liberal justice is not neutral among human goods or ways of life: it exerts the positive requirement that every citizen's 'good' includes certain features: a willingness to 'live and let live', to subordinate personal plans and commitments to impartial rules of law, and to persuade rather than coerce. Liberal justice could not be affirmed by a Protestant who believes he should fight to the death rather than live in peace with Catholics, and it could not be acknowledged as morally supreme by a citizen prepared to advance his interests through political means at the expense of the rights of others.

A 'live and let live' attitude reflects liberal convictions such as tolerance and personality traits that would help establish a stable liberal peace in a community whose members disagree about what is good in life. A liberal community whose members had this attitude toward one another would be better (as a community) than some others (one, for instance, characterized by mutual hostility held in check by mutual fear of reprisals or punishment). But a merely 'tolerant' community does not really stand out as one that is flourishing as a community. Liberal justice is compatible with forms of community and conditions of human character that fall below what could be considered 'excellent'.

Liberal values do not need to be in place for us to say of a society that liberal justice is 'in force' there, and neither the virtues nor the acts which would mark someone as possessing them are required by law. The liberal virtues will, nevertheless, distinguish a community flourishing in a distinctively liberal way from a community simply governed by liberal justice. Support for liberal justice is strained in societies comprised of large numbers of bigots who do not respect the dignity of minorities, or puritanical zealots who would abuse the right to privacy of other persons.

Liberal justice requires that we respect the rights of people with whom we disagree strongly over many particular values, allegiances, loyalties, and commitments. Differences of race, sex, religion, or ethnic background are all relegated to secondary, sub-political importance by liberal justice. In their political relationship, liberal citizens are members of what Popper has called the 'abstract society'.[22] Liberal citizens are called upon to respect not only members of their family, tribe, or race, but humanity in general. All persons, as possessors of abstract, impersonal reflective capacities, share a decisive moral equality in the eyes of liberal justice.

To survey the world of human affairs from the point of view of liberal politics is to survey it from a moral perspective. Liberal justice requires that we respect the rights of all persons. In their political capacity, liberal citizens regard others as essentially like themselves, or like themselves in a decisive respect, despite a myriad of other differences. Liberal politics represents, thus, an impersonal perspective which requires, in a sense, that we be capable of putting ourselves in the shoes of others, even those with whom we may disagree on nearly all of our substantive commitments; equal liberal respect breeds mutual respect.

The allegiance to liberal justice in a diverse society should

[22] Karl R. Popper, *The Open Society and Its Enemies, 1: The Spell of Plato* (London, 1966), 173.

encourage attitudes of tolerance and sympathy among people who disagree. As we come to realize that those who engage in lives different from our own are nevertheless like us in important ways, we may come to sympathize not only with these persons but also with their projects and commitments, with choices different from our own, with careers and lifestyles not seriously considered before. To sympathize with a variety of projects and commitments is to internalize the value conflict playing itself out in liberal society, as discussed in Chapter 6. Liberal citizens who acquire the capacity to sympathize with widely divergent ways of life acquire a range of 'live options' and become open to change. Live options incite self-examination, self-criticism, and experimentation. Live options multiply with mobility and leisure, the diffusion of knowledge, with the acceptance of 'off-beat' careers and of different sexual orientations, with the breakdown of gender-based stereotypes, and with the acceptance of divorce and remarriage. The liberal ideal of character is one with 'horizons' broad enough to sympathize with a variety of different ways of life.

The character that flourishes in a liberal, pluralistic social milieu, will have broad sympathies. The liberal citizen, capable of reasoning and acting from an impersonal standpoint in a pluralistic social milieu will also have a less exclusive or unreflective commitment to anything in particular. That is, liberalism may temper or attenuate the devotion to one's own projects and allegiances, by encouraging persons to regard their own ways as open to criticism, choice, and change, or simply as not shared by many people whom one is otherwise encouraged to respect. If a liberal pluralistic society is also, as I have suggested, an experimental and dynamic society, then people may also be encouraged to regard their commitments and ideals as contingent and vulnerable, as apt to become outmoded or trivial in an unpredictably changing world.

That broad sympathies and the acceptance of progress may lead to a certain attenuation in the more particular and local affections of pre-liberal societies is something communitarians seem reluctant to accept. Liberal justice itself requires a certain critical detachment from other, subordinate commitments, and the internalization of social pluralism leads toward a critical, experimental, open, autonomous ideal. Those in whom liberal sensibilities are highly developed will be friendlier and more open to outsiders or strangers, but also less exclusively committed to neighbourhoods, localities, and narrow allegiances. Liberal affections will be broader but less intense or deep than pre-liberal ones, liberal allegiances more open to critical analysis, choice, and change.

Even severe critics of liberalism have noticed the relative unattractiveness of 'pre-liberal' societies. As one such critic, commenting on the impact of British rule on life in 'idealized' Indian villages, put it,

sickening as it must be to human feelings to witness those myriads of industrious patriarchal and inoffensive social organizations dis-organized and dissolved into their units . . . we must not forget that these idyllic village communities, inoffensive though they may appear, had always been the solid foundations of Oriental despot-ism, that they restrained the human mind within the smallest possible compass, making it the unresisting tool of superstition, enslaving it beneath traditional rules, depriving it of all grandeur and historical energies.[23]

Rather than 'elevating man to be the sovereign of circum-stances', life in these closed, pre-liberal communities, Marx went on, perpetuated caste and slavery, 'subjugated man to external circumstances and . . . transformed a self-developing social state into never changing natural destiny . . .'.

Marx's comments prefigure Justice William O. Douglas's dissenting opinion in *Wisconsin* v. *Yoder*. Old Order Amish children must be consulted, argued Douglas, before the state allows their parents to keep them out of high school. An Amish child,

may want to be a pianist or an astronaut or an oceanographer. To do so he will have to break from Amish tradition. . . . If a parent keeps his child out of school beyond the grade school, then the child will be forever barred from entry into the new and amazing world of diversity that we have today. . . . If he is harnessed to the Amish way of life by those in authority over him and if his education is truncated, his entire life may be stunted and deformed.[24]

---

[23] Karl Marx, 'The British Rule in India', in *The Marx–Engels Reader*, 2nd edn., ed. Robert C. Tucker (New York, 1978), 657–8.
[24] 406 US 205 (1972), at 244–6.

Liberal persons are distinguished by the possession of self-governing reflective capacities. Further developing these reflective capacities leads one toward the ideal of autonomy and that ideal is the source of other liberal virtues. A political regime that makes the respect for rights its core value and which encourages the spread of diversity and toleration, provides ample opportunity and stimulation for the exercise of the capacities that enable people to channel and constrain their own projects so as to respect the rights of others, and actively to exercise their freedom of choice, to achieve self-mastery and self-control. To develop these powers is to cultivate aspects of the liberal form of excellence.

Striving for autonomy involves developing the self-conscious, self-critical, reflective capacities that allow one to formulate, evaluate, and revise ideals of life and character, to bring these evaluations to bear on actual choices and on the formulation of projects and commitments. To flourish as an autonomous person is actively to develop one's individuality. Autonomy implies the capacity to reflect critically and to act on the basis of these reflections; it implies the possession of what we might call 'executive' virtues: initiative, independence, resolve, perseverance, diligence, and patience.

The achievement of autonomy is recognizable in the disposition, as Oakeshott calls it, to experience the project of choosing in an ever-changing and uncertain world as an adventure rather than an ordeal.[25] The autonomous character is capable of affirming rather than bemoaning liberal modernity, with its many possible ways of life, the openness of all choices, and its protean ideal. The autonomous ideal contrasts sharply with MacIntyre's depiction of the modern individual as a drifting, aimless, passive creature, with a stunted or merely instrumental form of reason, with no place in a settled social context, a mere passive locus of open possibilities with no grounds for choosing.

We should not overemphasize what might in isolation be

thought of as the 'atomistic virtues'. Our discussion of strong evaluation and autonomy in Chapter 6 showed that one who excels as a liberal is one who is not simply able to reflect upon, criticize, and shape his own character. Autonomy arises with the understanding of the shared values and norms of a pluralistic and tolerant culture. There is no tension between being at home in a tradition or a set of social practices and the development of one's individuality. Autonomy is not a matter of discovering a deep, fixed core of individuality within the self, it is an actively critical and reflective way of comporting oneself within the complex matrix of a pluralistic culture, and of making its resources one's own. Cultural and social resources, when overarched by liberal political norms and attitudes, are not threats to autonomy but opportunities to explore.

Oakeshott is particularly good at emphasizing that a familiarity with the traditions and practices of one's society, an understanding of one's social inheritance, is not a constraint upon but really a condition of the meaningful development and exercise of individuality. To come to understand a social practice like a language or even a moral code is, for Oakeshott, to acquire a medium for the expression of one's individuality.[26] Of course, if law is to be liberty-empowering, as Oakeshott envisions, then it must be liberal in character. If social practices and moral norms are to promote rather than constrain liberty they must have certain substantive characteristics, they must embody attitudes of tolerance and openness to change rather than pressures to conformity.

Liberal citizens who act from and not only in accordance with liberal justice do not simply impose 'side-constraints' on self-chosen actions, rather, they seek to realize justice in their conduct as an independently valuable and regulative end. This overriding end will be shared by citizens who exhibit a liberal form of excellence. We must reject Sandel's suggestion that justice 'speaks to that which distinguishes' persons whereas an independent conception of the good 'connects' them to one another.[27] It is wrong to assume that only conceptions of the good can furnish persons with common ends capable of

[26] Oakeshott, *Human Conduct*, pp. 78–80.
[27] Sandel, *Limits*, p. 133.

constituting people's character and binding them to one another. Justice furnishes liberal citizens with ends capable of imparting a deep and noble unity to liberal community.

The point of publicly justified liberal politics is the realization of a common, substantive moral vision. Émile Durkheim understood the social unity that liberal justice could provide, a liberal unity that defeats charges of dissociation and detachment levelled by liberalism's critics:

Doubtless if the dignity of the individual derived from his individual qualities, from those particular characteristics which distinguish him from others, one might fear that he would become enclosed in a sort of moral egoism that would render all social cohesion impossible. But in reality he receives this dignity from a higher source, one which he shares with all men. . . . It is humanity that is sacred and worthy of respect. And this is not his exclusive possession. It is distributed among his fellows, and in consequence he cannot take it as a goal for his conduct without being obliged to go beyond himself and turn toward others. . . . Impersonal and anonymous, such an end soars far above all particular consciences and can thus serve as a rallying point for them. . . . [I]ndividualism thus understood is the glorification not of the self, but of the individual in general. Its motive force is not egoism but sympathy for all that is human, a wider pity for all suffering, for all human miseries, a more ardent desire to combat and alleviate them, a greater thirst for justice. Is this not the way to achieve a community of all men of good will?[28]

The rights of liberal citizen are grounded in public principles that justify and protect individuality in general. Liberal principles are not based on self-love but on respect for diversity, plurality, and the dignity of beings with the capacity for reflective and responsible choice. Liberal individualism properly understood is at base a moral commitment, depending upon a general and impartial perspective, not a self-centred one.[29]

Some of the liberal virtues are now before us: broad

[28] Émile Durkheim, 'Individualism and the Intellectuals', trans. and intro. by Steven Lukes, *Political Studies*, 17 (1969), 23–4.

[29] As Nagel puts it, 'altruism and related motives do not depend on taste, sentiment, or on arbitrary and ultimate choice. They depend instead on the fact that our reasons for action are subject to the formal condition of objectivity . . . on our ability to view ourselves from both the personal and impersonal standpoints, and to engage in reasoning to practical conclusions from both of these standpoints', *Possibility of Altruism*, p. 144.

sympathies, self-critical reflectiveness, a willingness to experiment, to try and to accept new things, self-control and active, autonomous self-development, an appreciation of inherited social ideals, an attachment and even an altruistic regard for one's fellow liberal citizens. The same virtues that contribute to individual flourishing in pluralistic liberal communities also contribute to the performance of liberal civic duties, the liberal virtues are both civic and personal virtues. The practice of liberal politics amplifies the liberal virtues: the rule of law teaches self-restraint, an appreciation for procedures and forms, and equality of respect.

By emphasizing the importance of a critical, questioning, challenging attitude toward official decisions, the practice of liberal politics helps develop reflective capacities, activity and independence of mind, and the autonomy of liberal citizens. Official acts, on the liberal constitutionalist's view, have no authority unless supported by the public moral principles that are objects of common interpretation. The authority to interpret the law is levelled so that every citizen has a right to interpret for himself the public moral principles of the liberal order. The faithfulness of a liberal democratic order to its public morality depends ultimately on the seriousness with which citizens themselves take their role as conscientious interpreters and reviewers of official acts. This is the significance of liberal theories of civil disobedience, which naturally culminate in a justification of rebellion against governments that become destructive of the proper ends of government, as the Declaration of Independence argued.

Every liberal citizen must, in order to remain true to liberal justice, give highest allegiance not to his or her own particular plans and projects, but to liberal public reasons and principles. Liberalism does not 'interiorize' the moral life, leaving politics and public life to the play of self-interest. Indeed, the liberal political space is pervaded by moral considerations: not only the judicial process but politics more broadly should be (and often are) guided by the interpretation of liberal moral principles. Liberal citizens must, furthermore, engage in public arguments if they wish to persuade others of the merits of their own interpretations of public norms. The liberal political arena, on the model I have explored, is a Forum of

Principle in which citizens should (and sometimes do) act as conscientious interpreters of public principles.

Liberal politics holds out the ideal of a community of interpreters, in which citizens are united by their devotion to a public morality. In the liberal community citizens address one another as fellow interpreters, sharing a commitment to self-critical reason-giving in place of sheer wilfulness, the narrowest personal interests, and arbitrary power. The attitudes nurtured by the workings of liberal politics—liberal sentiments of mutual respect and toleration, self-restraint, moderation, and autonomy—will have broader effects on the character of liberal citizens.

Of course, we should not overemphasize the amount of political participation that liberalism requires. Liberalism realizes that if men are allowed to be free they will often pursue narrow interests, it does not force on its citizens a conception of the good life with a very large political component, and it could undoubtedly be criticized, especially in its classical liberal form, for leaving too little to politics. There is, nevertheless, inevitably a participatory element in liberal practice, and ample opportunity for participation in the liberal ideal. Much of liberal politics will be informed by public moral principles; liberal citizens often recognize the authority of good reasons publicly given and defended; liberal political life should often have an elevating and educating effect.

We should also remember that liberal citizens will not learn justice only, or even mainly, from political participation as it is usually conceived of (voting, discussing candidates and political issues, campaigning, and so forth). From early on and throughout their lives, liberal citizens learn and apply public norms in their interaction with others. Children learn respect for rules and fair play from their parents and from childhood games. They criticize, discuss, listen to others, and take votes, they follow, debate, change, and help enforce rules, at home, in school, at work, in games, and with their friends. They gradually learn to restrain their impulses, to respect others as equals, and to direct and apply their energies with diligence. They learn to make judgments for themselves and hopefully acquire a measure of individuality and autonomy. They learn something about due process, and fairness, and respect for those who are different; they develop judicial, legislative, and executive virtues. All of this takes place without political control, though it is all importantly influenced by our political practices. It would be wrong, therefore, to view participation in campaigns and elections as the sole or even primary font of public virtue: private life goes a long way in helping to prepare us for our public duties.

Liberalism does not, I have argued, rely upon a strong distinction between public and private morality. 'Political' values penetrate and shape the private lives of liberal citizens; liberalism is a political culture and not only a set of rights and rules and offices. In their private affairs, then, liberal citizens ought to adopt a 'judicial' attitude toward their own projects, viewing them impersonally and imposing limits on them in the name of the rights of others. Our duty to respect the rights of others is as important in our personal as in our public lives, and since our personal dealings with others are bound to be more extensive, frequent, and earlier in life than our participation in politics, the practice of justice in personal affairs is likely to be the more important moral teacher.

If liberal autonomy and the practice of liberal politics emphasize activity, initiative, and moral duty, we can expect further effects on the character of liberal citizens. Like the democratic citizens Tocqueville observed, liberals will be willing to take initiatives on their own. And since nothing in the emphasis on individuality and choice would justify the supposition that liberal citizens will pursue self-gratification as a primary end, we should expect liberal citizens to be prepared to combine in voluntary associations for common ends both altruistic and otherwise. Autonomous liberal subjects will prize not isolated activity but the liberty to choose how to be associated, with whom, in what manner, and for what purposes. The public life of liberal subjects will not be confined to their political relationships, as critics of liberalism sometimes wrongly assume, but will include participation in the host of clubs and associations that do exist and flourish in liberal societies: the ubiquitous Kiwanis and Rotary, Chambers of Commerce, churches, environmental lobbies, retirement clubs, Masons, Elks, and Lions.

Liberalism stands first and foremost for basic political

guarantees and institutions such as rights and government by law. We can, I have argued, discern virtues connected fairly closely with active support for and participation in these rights and institutions, the same attributes that make it possible to flourish as a person in a diverse and tolerant liberal society. Public and private liberal virtues are interdependent and complementary, we can distinguish liberal virtues of private life that are judicial, legislative, and executive in character.

The judicial virtues are those that allow people to stand back from their personal commitments and projects and judge them from an impersonal point of view. Impartiality is the basic judicial virtue, which stands for a capacity to respect the rights of others and act justly, thus fulfilling the primary duties of liberal citizens. Another judicial virtue would be attachment to principle, and a reluctance to bargain and compromise where rights and liberal fairness are at stake. The judicial virtues are particularly requisite in a good judge, but all liberal citizens must, to some extent, cultivate these qualities if they are to treat those who lead different lives, whose interests may be in conflict with theirs, as persons equally worthy of respect.

The legislative virtues may be identified with the breadth of sympathies that develops after we come to respect the rights of persons with whom we disagree. These virtues include the ability sympathetically to survey different ideals in personal deliberation and the willingness to engage in dialogue with those who disagree. The legislative virtues share in judicial impartiality, but are inclusive rather than specific, engaged rather than detached, and more open to compromise and accommodation. The legislative virtues are characteristic, especially, of principled liberal legislators, but they will be possessed by all liberal citizens capable of realizing that democracy means not getting your way all of the time, and of electing fair-minded and impartial representatives.

The executive virtues empower one, having judged and reflected, to resolve, act, and persevere rather than drift, dither, and crumple at the first sign of adversity, to perform rather than reflect endlessly, to exercise an independence of thought rather than be swayed by the prejudices and pressures to conformity exerted by others. The executive virtues are especially required by the executive officers of the liberal state, but they will also be required by liberal citizens if they are vigilantly to oversee and review official acts, to rally to the defence of the regime, and to act themselves to correct sustained injustices within the regime. Citizens who cultivate executive virtues will also take voluntary initiatives in association with others to perform the many tasks not properly assumed by the liberal state.

Now these three sets of virtues are especially required by office-holders in each of the three branches of government, but citizens require these virtues as well. Citizens must be able to appreciate and assess the actions and perspectives of each of the three branches if they are to exercise competently their duty to engage in the oversight, criticism, and election of public officials. All three sets of virtues are required, furthermore, if citizens are to achieve the personal self-government required to flourish in a pluralistic social environment: they must be able to stand back from their own projects and judge them impartially, sympathize with and understand the projects of others, and decide, resolve, act, and persevere. Thus, analogous virtues are required for political and personal self-government in the liberal regime.

The virtues that make liberal self-government possible also make possible the government of our personal lives in a liberal society. We can say, following Plato, that the virtues that conduce to good government in the regime 'without' have their analogues in the qualities that control and direct the regime 'within'.[30] Impartiality, reflectiveness, self-criticism, the articulation and defence of moral reasons, forms of diversity, broad sympathies, and decisiveness, conduce to liberal forms of public and private excellence. The liberal virtues are at once political and personal, civic and private.

We can identify three 'degenerate' forms of personality and polity in which one-third of the virtues overwhelm the other two. An excess of judicial virtue would lead to detachment without engagement either with others or with one's own projects. An excess of the legislative virtues would lead to tolerance without discrimination, unprincipled accommodation, or to broad sympathies without personal resolve in a

---

[30] Plato, *Republic*, see Bks. 8 and 9.

particular direction. An excess of the executive virtues would lead to the headstrong pursuit of one's own projects without appreciation or proper regard for others.

It is impossible to stress the relative political importance of the three sorts of virtues without making substantive discriminations between different kinds of liberal justice, or different judgments about the overall ends of liberal politics, or the relative importance of the virtues contributed to good government by the three branches. Classical liberals, like Locke, Hayek, and Oakeshott stress the importance of the judicial virtues in politics. The aim of politics is mainly, for them, the protection of individual rights and the rectification of rights violations. The point or purpose of government as a whole is, for classical liberals, the fulfilment of basically judicial functions.[31] The social policy goals of more egalitarian liberals require information-gathering, monitoring, and administrative resources more readily available, at least according to some, to legislatures and executives than to courts.[32]

The virtues of an executive-dominated politics are promoted, though not exclusively, by those facing conditions of extraordinary (for us) instability. Social peace is the prerequisite of justice or any other social good; and, where chaos threatens, resort must be had to the focused energy of executive government. The politics of Hobbes and Machiavelli are dominated by the need for nearly unchecked executive energy, but even Locke and the Founders of the American republic were not insensitive to the ever-present possibility of circumstances calling for strong executive government.[33]

People are apt, depending on their dispositions and judgments, to become partisans of particular branches of the government. This is not surprising since, as I have argued, these offices call forth particular virtues the appeal of which is to some degree individualized and particular.

[31] See M. J. C. Vile, *Constitutionalism and The Separation of Powers* (Oxford, 1967), for a discussion of the seventeenth-century tendency to see all government in terms of judicial functions.

[32] See Donald Horowitz, *The Courts and Social Policy* (Washington, DC, 1977).

[33] See Locke's discussion of executive prerogative in the *Second Treatise*, ch. 14, pp. 421–7, and Hamilton, *Federalist*, no. 70.

LIBERAL COMMUNITY

I have discussed the liberal virtues, the qualities of a person who excels in a peculiarly liberal way, and we can now discern a liberal vision of the good community: a society whose members excel in the liberal virtues and which, as a consequence, flourishes in a distinctively liberal way. How might we characterize this flourishing liberal society? First, it would make room for individuality and social pluralism. It would be tolerant, open, and dynamic and its members would be prone to experiment with different lifestyles and commitments. It would probably pay for this diversity, tolerance, and experimentation with a degree of superficiality, the consequence of a lack of depth or persistence in commitments. There might be a certain amount of feigned or affected eccentricity. And with all the self-critical, self-shaping introspection, perhaps also a degree of self-absorption or even narcissism. Quiet obedience, deference, unquestioned devotion, and humility, could not be counted among the liberal virtues.

Liberalism holds out the promise, or the threat, of making all the world like California. By encouraging tolerance or even sympathy for a wide array of lifestyles and eccentricities, liberalism creates a community in which it is possible to decide that next week I might quit my career in banking, leave my wife and children, and join a Buddhist cult. Life in a pluralistic liberal society is a smorgasbord confronting us with an exciting array of possibilities. Society is open to change and diversity: less of a stigma attaches to unconventional lifestyles and to changes in lifestyle. The combination of diversity and openness to change constitutes an incitement to self-examination and invitation to experiment.

If all the world became liberal, all the world would become the same in certain important respects. Individuality, constrained by liberal norms, would flourish everywhere, but the diversity of forms of political organization would be eliminated, the differences between forms of social life would be reduced, and every sphere of social life would bear the peculiar tint of liberal values. It would be wrong to identify the spread of liberalism with the maximization of diversity or the liberation of unlimited experimentation: liberal norms rule out many experiments in social organization, require a common subscription to liberal rights, and encourage a uniformity of tolerance, openness, and broad-mindedness. If the spread of liberalism eliminates certain forms of diversity, it also extends the liberal community and liberal peace. In the history of the modern world, as has been argued, no two liberal regimes have ever gone to war with one another.[34]

Certain things of value may be lost in, or absent from, the forms of the good life that flourish in open, diverse, critical, experimental, uncertain, and ever-changing liberal societies. Stronger forms of community, deeper, unquestioning, untroubled forms of allegiance (to family, church, clan, or class) might embody genuine forms of the good life lost to societies that flourish in a liberal way. A lifelong, unquestioned devotion to a simple life in a small homogeneous community will hardly be available to one whose attitudes have been shaped by liberal individualism, social pluralism, tolerance, and critically reflective citizenship. Once a person recognizes the myriad possibilities of self-enactment that liberalism discloses, he forever regards his choices in a new light; in the very least what once may have been unquestioned components of a given identity or role become choices.

Everything chosen is one option among others; no 'choices' have the certainty and security of an identity unreflectively taken as given. One cannot choose to be simple or unworldly; by the time the issue arises it is too late. Once one's horizons are broadened to encompass a variety of possible ways of life, a range of 'live options', no act of will can narrow the vistas again. You could not really choose to be Amish after working for a few years in a Wall Street brokerage firm.

Will liberals, faced with live options and prone to critical reflection, have only shallow commitments to causes, projects, and ideals? If the spread of liberal pluralism brings security and a promise of peace, it also confronts us with the loss of old certainties, of a secure future on a well-trodden path. An identity is no longer simply given, it must be achieved and it is always open. Our standards of evaluation,

---

[34] See Michael Doyle, 'Kant, Liberal Legacies, and Foreign Affairs', *Philosophy and Public Affairs*, 12 (1984), 323–53.

aside from well-founded liberal norms of respect for persons, are never entirely fixed. Our potentialities and projects must be discerned, developed, and sustained in an uncertain and ever-changing world. What some people will experience as an adventure, others, like MacIntyre's drifting ditherer, will find unbearably burdensome.

Weakness of character, and failure to develop liberal virtues of autonomy, independence, and resolve, are not the only possible causes of dissatisfaction and disappointment in liberal modernity. The liberal ideal will not appeal to those who seek a final, definitive answer to the great question of how to live. Liberal justice itself provides a partial answer, but neither in ourselves nor in the world of human experience does there seem to be a fixed cognitive point, some final knowledge or wisdom, in which reflection terminates. Liberalism imposes burdens of choice on individuals in a pluralistic milieu without the assurance of complete and final right answers to the question of how to live.

It may be that a craving for certainty and stability is, among some people, ineradicable, and these will question the ultimate worth of liberal critical reflectiveness and autonomy. If there can be no secure possession of ultimate answers to the 'big questions' of life then it might seem rather pointless to engage in the arduous process of criticizing social conventions. If on the boundless sea there is no floor for anchorage or appointed destination then why set sail from the harbour? The critical search for good reasons might corrode the fixed points we have and yield only doubt, Hume's 'perpetual instability', and (perhaps) nihilism:

'A nihilist', said Nikolai Petrovich, 'that's from the Latin, nihil, nothing, as far as I can judge; the word must mean a man who . . . who accepts nothing.'

'Say, "who respects nothing,"' put in Pavel Petrovich.

'Who regards everything from a critical point of view,' observed Arkady.

'Isn't that the same thing?' inquired Pavel Petrovich.

'No its not the same thing. A nihilist is a man who does not bow down before any authority, who does not take any principle on faith, whatever reverence that principle may be enshrined in.'

'Well, and is that good?' interrupted Pavel Petrovich.

'That depends, uncle. Some people it will do good to, but some people will suffer for it.'[35]

But does the refusal to bow down before authority or to accept principles on faith lead to nihilism, as Arkady seems to assume? Liberal openness and critical thinking do not imply scepticism about the possibility of objective human goods or real moral values. Liberal openness and criticism do, however, imply doubt about our ability ever to identify the whole truth once and for all. 'We have an incapacity for proving anything which no amount of dogmatism can overcome. We have an idea of truth which no amount of scepticism can overcome.'[36]

It is hard to say how different people will come to grips with the perpetual openness to criticism and change. One possibility is found in Mill's confident depiction of those accustomed to questioning their values and having them questioned by others:

The steady habit of correcting and completing his own opinion by collating it with those of others, so far from causing doubt and hesitation in carrying it into practice, is the only stable foundation for a just reliance on it: for, being cognizant of all that can, at least obviously, be said against him, and having taken up his position against all gainsayers—knowing that he has sought for objections and difficulties, instead of avoiding them, and has shut out no light which can be thrown upon the subject from any quarter—he has a right to think his judgment better than that of any person, or any multitude, who have not gone through a similar process.[37]

Of course, having a right to think your opinion better than others and actually thinking it better are two different things. Nevertheless, to the extent that the truth of liberal norms can be publicly established, liberals will have good reason to be

---

[35] From Ivan Turgenev, *Fathers and Sons*, trans. Constance Garnett (New York, 1930), 24, and see Robert Eden's interesting discussion in *Political Leadership and Nihilism* (Tampa, Florida, 1983).

[36] Blaise Pascal, *Pensées*, no. 406, trans. A. J. Krailsheimer (Harmondsworth, 1965), 147.

[37] Mill, *On Liberty*, p. 21. And see Paul Feyerabend, 'Against Method: Outline of an Anarchistic Theory of Knowledge', *Minnesota Studies in the Philosophy of Science*, 4 (Minneapolis, Minn., 1970).

confident in their political convictions. As concerns political norms and associated values at least, liberal citizens have good reason for a Millian self-confidence; they have more and better reasons for self-confidence than those who have not subjected their political beliefs to critical reflection. To the extent that the truth of liberal justice can be defended in a public moral argument, we should expect liberal 'system-maintenance' values to be immune from corrosive scepticism without being insulated from criticism.

Even with regard to political beliefs liberals should never assume they are infallible; they should be committed to liberal norms in a certain way, a self-critically reflective way. This attitude is part of the best way of being committed to liberal justice, because liberal justice is a political morality whose justification depends on an openness to public criticism. In principle, liberal principles are not immune from criticism; in practice, liberal practices are strengthened by criticism because we have good reasons to support them. The very activities of reason-giving, reason-accepting, and public dialogue should help reinforce the liberal belief in the reasonableness of other persons, and so help invigorate and stabilize basic liberal political norms.

Liberals may well have the confidence appropriate to those who are committed to self-critical reason-giving, in a world in which there are good reasons for being liberals, and many reasonable ways of living as a liberal. Autonomous liberal persons have the raw materials for making reflective choices, but these choices will be less widely shared than basic political norms. Even if there is no final point of wisdom the grasping of which justifies critical reflection on personal commitments, progress is made by ruling out options that come to be widely seen as worthless. And, as many have argued, reflecting upon and actively exploring different conceptions of the good life itself helps constitute a good life.

Liberalism defines a framework of freedom and peace and a stance of reflective clear-mindedness from which to explore alternative conceptions of the good. The ideal of autonomy suggests a type of personality capable of finding in diversity and change the conditions of human flourishing, as Oakeshott puts it:

This is a disposition to prefer the road to the inn, ambulatory conversation to deliberation about means for achieving ends, the rules of the road to directions about how to reach a destination, and to recognize that

The road runs always to the sea
'Twixt duty and delight.

And since men are apt to make gods whose characters reflect what they believe to be their own, the deity corresponding to this self-understanding is an Augustinian god of majestic imagination, who, when he might have devised an untroublesome universe, had the nerve to create one composed of self-employed adventurers of unpredictable fancy, to announce to them some rules of conduct, and thus to acquire convives capable of 'answering back' in civil tones with whom to pass eternity in conversation.[38]

Millian confidence and Oakeshottian playfulness are only two among the possible responses to liberal openness and change. Some will find a world without more readily graspable absolutes to be full of despair and anxiety, or perhaps we all will at certain times.

We desire truth and find in ourselves nothing but uncertainty. We seek happiness and find only wretchedness and death. We are incapable of not desiring truth and happiness and incapable of either certainty or happiness. We have been left with this desire as much as a punishment as to make us feel how far we have fallen.[39]

And so, Nietzsche, 'no resting place is any longer open to your heart, where it has only to find and no longer to seek. . . .'[40]

Liberal pluralism, tolerance, change, and freedom do not stand for a moral void of arbitrary values and the will to power. But some will be unnerved, perhaps, by choice and flux and the need to carve out valuable personal projects. People have many reasons to doubt and criticize, however, and many reasons to be anxious about their lives, many quite unrelated to liberalism. There is no philosophical cure for doubt, but a number of practical treatments are available: a round of golf, a glass of beer, a summer barbecue. Liberalism does not provide solutions to all of life's cares, but neither does any other political system that we know of. If the virtues of

---

[38] Oakeshott, *Human Conduct*, p. 324.
[39] Pascal, *Pensées*, no. 401, p. 146.
[40] Nietzsche, from *The Gay Science* (285), in *Portable Nietzsche*, p. 98.

liberalism entail certain costs and losses, these seem to me well worth bearing.

CONCLUSION

Liberalism, I have argued, contains the resources to mount a positive response to its communitarian critics. Liberals have shared values, virtues, and a distinctive form of community, all of which are resources to be exploited in the face of communitarian criticisms. We might push this argument further by seeking additional virtues in institutions associated with liberalism, say, in science, in the optimistic faith in progress, or in the operation of a free market. I have tried to limit my concern to the virtues forming a core around liberal justice and constitutional institutions and ones fairly easy to discern in their penumbras.

Liberals typically stress the fact that people disagree radically about the nature of the good life and that proper rules of law should not impose one particular conception of the good on the whole society. But this simple picture is misleadingly incomplete. Personal commitments should not and often do not alone control the highest allegiances of liberal citizens. No one can rightly pursue his personal goals at the expense of the rights of others, and no one can rightly compete in a liberal market order by violating the rules that structure and constrain competition. Thus, liberalism acknowledges the primacy of social claims over individual claims, the primacy of a structure of rights and a system of proper law over individual desires, goals, and ends. When we add to shared liberal norms a capacity and willingness to participate in the public justification of liberal justice, then we approach the liberal ideal in which citizens share a public morality, take a hand in preserving valuable political arrangements, recognize in each other a common moral personality, and acknowledge an overriding duty to respect that personality.

The liberal arrangements I have described are, of course, ideals that we often fail to live up to, but these ideals are recognizable, none the less, in our actual practices and aspirations. We do sometimes approach liberal ideals, as when we support the civil rights of blacks, women, or of any minority or oppressed group on grounds of justice, or whenever we seek and offer good public reasons for legislation. As education, mobility, and toleration for diversity and change increase, our private lives may also approach the autonomous ideal. What should be clear, at least, is that liberalism properly understood stands for ideals of character far nobler than MacIntyre's unhappy and purportedly liberal trio, 'the Rich Aesthete . . . the Manager . . . and the Therapist'.[41]

A certain dissatisfaction and unease probably comes with the liberal's turf, and is not obviously unhealthy. If pluralists are right that moral values are many and in conflict, if there are many reasonable ways of participating in human goods, if choice and change are constant features of a good life, then a certain measure of critical unease seems necessary and even wholesome. Liberals are not typically overpowered by uncertainty or anxiety: many attachments and choices remain fairly stable, and most people find many good things worth enjoying and striving for.

Thinkers as diverse as Friedrich Hayek, Irving Kristol, and Jurgen Habermas argue that the legitimacy and stability of liberal regimes is parasitic on the lingering effects of a pre-capitalist or pre-liberal ethic.[42] An appreciation of the values and ideals grounded in liberal justice could help debunk the notion that liberal regimes are incapable of generating a common ethos capable of unifying a society. Political theory is not, of course, our only political beacon. We have seen more than enough of the political alternatives, in this century alone, to know that the liberal life is generally decent and good. In an era marked by the sudden transparency of the utter illegitimacy of an oppressive system that has, since the demise of fascism, ruled half the world and constituted the main alternative to free self-government, the purported crisis of legitimacy in liberal regimes does not stand out in especial starkness.

---

[41] MacIntyre, *After Virtue*, p. 29.
[42] Hayek, *The Constitution of Liberty* (London, 1976), 232–3; Irving Kristol, '"When Virtue Loses All Her Loveliness"—Some Reflections on Capitalism and "the Free Society"', *The Public Interest*, 21 (1976), 13; Jurgen Habermas, *Legitimation Crisis* (Boston, Mass., 1975).

Bibliography

A. BOOKS

ACKERMAN, BRUCE A., *Social Justice in the Liberal State* (New Haven, Conn., 1980).

ADAIR, DOUGLAS, *Fame and the Founding Fathers* (New York, 1974).

AGRESTO, JOHN, *The Supreme Court and Constitutional Democracy* (Ithaca, NY, 1984).

ANDREWS, WILLIAM G., ed., *Coordinate Magistrates: Constitutional Law by Congress and President* (New York, 1969).

ARISTOTLE, *Nichomachean Ethics*, trans. Martin Ostwald (Indianapolis, Ind., 1962).

——*Metaphysics*, trans. Richard Hope (Ann Arbor, Mich., 1968).

——*Politics*, trans. Carnes Lord (Chicago, Ill., 1984).

BACON, FRANCIS, *The Advancement of Learning* (London, 1974).

BARBER, SOTIRIOS A., *On What the Constitution Means* (Baltimore, Md., 1984).

BARRY, BRIAN, *The Liberal Theory of Justice* (Oxford, 1973).

BEDAU, HUGO ADAM, ed., *Civil Disobedience: Theory and Practice* (New York, 1969).

BELLAH, ROBERT, *et al.*, *Habits of the Heart* (New York, 1986).

BENTHAM, JEREMY, *Introduction to the Principles of Morals and Legislation*, ed. Wilfrid Harrison (New York, 1948).

BERGER, RAOUL, *Government By Judiciary* (Cambridge, 1977).

BESSETTE, JOSEPH, and TULIS, JEFFREY, *The Presidency in the Constitutional Order* (Baton Rouge, La., 1981).

BICKEL, ALEXANDER, *The Least Dangerous Branch* (New Haven, Conn., 1986).

BOORSTIN, DANIEL, *The Genius of American Politics* (Chicago, Ill., 1965).

BORK, ROBERT H., *Tradition and Morality in Constitutional Law: The Francis Boyer Lecture* (Washington, DC, 1984).

BOSWELL, JOHN, *Christianity, Social Tolerance, and Homosexuality* (Chicago, Ill., 1981).

BURKE, EDMUND, *Orations and Essays* (New York, 1900).

CARDOZO, BENJAMIN N., *The Nature of the Judicial Process* (New Haven, Conn., 1949).

CONSTANT, BENJAMIN, *Political Writings*, ed. Biancamaria Fontana, (Cambridge, 1988).

CORWIN, EDWARD S., *The 'Higher Law' Background of American Constitutional Law* (Ithaca, NY, 1979).

DAHL, ROBERT A., *A Preface to Democratic Theory* (Chicago, Ill., 1956).

DESCARTES, RENÉ, *Meditations On First Philosophy*, trans. Laurence J. Lafleur (Indianapolis, Ind., 1960).

DEVLIN, PATRICK, *The Enforcement of Morals* (London, 1965).

DEWEY, JOHN, *The Public and Its Problems* (Chicago, Ill., 1954).

DIAMOND, MARTIN, et al., *The Democratic Republic* (Chicago, Ill., 1966).

DICEY, A. V., *The Law of the Constitution* (Indianapolis, Ind., 1982).

DICKENS, CHARLES, *Tale of Two Cities* (New York, undated).

DIGGINS, JOHN P., *The Lost Soul of American Politics: Virtue, Self-Interest, and the Foundations of Liberalism* (New York, 1984).

DWORKIN, RONALD, *Taking Rights Seriously* (Cambridge, Mass., 1977).

——*A Matter of Principle* (Cambridge, Mass., 1985).

——*Law's Empire* (Cambridge, Mass., 1986).

EDEN, ROBERT, *Political Leadership and Nihilism* (Tampa, Fla., 1983).

ELY, JOHN HART, *Democracy and Distrust* (Cambridge, 1980).

EPSTEIN, RICHARD, *Takings* (Cambridge, Mass., 1985).

FAULKNER, ROBERT, *The Jurisprudence of John Marshall* (Princeton, NJ, 1968).

FEINBERG, JOEL, *Social Philosophy* (Englewood Cliffs, NJ, 1973).

FENNO, RICHARD F., *Homestyle: House Members in Their Districts* (Boston, Mass., 1978).

FINNIS, JOHN M., *Natural Law and Natural Rights* (Oxford, 1980).

FISHER, LOUIS, *Constitutional Dialogues: Interpretation as Political Process* (Princeton, NJ, 1988).

FULLER, LON L., *The Morality of Law*, 2nd edn. (New Haven, Conn., 1969).

——*The Principles of Social Order: Selected Essays of Lon L. Fuller*, ed. Kenneth I. Winston (Durham, NC, 1981).

Gallup Report, no. 253 (Oct. 1986).

GALSTON, WILLIAM, *Justice and the Human Good* (Chicago, Ill., 1980).

GLENDON, MARY ANN, *Abortion and Divorce in Western Law* (Cambridge, Mass., 1987).

GOOCH, G. P., *Political Thought in England: From Bacon to Halifax* (London, 1914/15).

GUNTHER, GERALD ed., *John Marshall's Defense of McCulloch v. Maryland* (Stanford, Calif., 1969).

——*Cases and Materials on Constitutional Law*, 11th edn. (Mineola, NY, 1980).

HABERMAS, JURGEN, *Legitimation Crisis* (Boston, Mass., 1975).

HAMILTON, ALEXANDER, JAY, JOHN, and MADISON, JAMES, *The Federalist Papers*, ed. Clinton Rossiter (New York, 1961).

HAMPSHIRE, STUART, *Freedom of the Individual* (London, 1965).

HART, H. L. A., *The Concept of Law* (Oxford, 1961).

——*Essays on Bentham* (Oxford, 1982).

——*Essays in Jurisprudence and Philosophy* (Oxford, 1983).

HAYEK, FRIEDRICH, *Law, Legislation and Liberty, 1: Rules and Order* (Chicago, Ill., 1973).

——*The Constitution of Liberty* (London, 1976).

——*Law, Legislation and Liberty, 2: The Mirage of Social Justice* (Chicago, Ill., 1978).

HERZOG, DON, *Without Foundations: Justification in Political Theory* (Ithaca, NY, 1985).

HIRSCHMANN, ALBERT O., *The Passions and the Interests: Political Arguments for Capitalism before its Triumph* (Princeton, NJ, 1977).

HOBBES, THOMAS, *Leviathan*, ed. C. B. Macpherson (Harmondsworth, 1981).

HOFSTADTER, RICHARD, *Anti-Intellectualism in American Life* (New York, 1963).

——*The Progressive Historians* (Chicago, Ill., 1979).

HOLMES, STEPHEN, *Benjamin Constant and The Making of Modern Liberalism* (New Haven, Conn., 1984).

HOROWITZ, DONALD, *The Courts and Social Policy* (Washington, DC, 1977).

HUME, DAVID, *A Treatise of Human Nature*, ed. L. A. Selby-Bigge (Oxford, 1968).

——*Essays: Moral, Political, and Literary*, ed. Eugene F. Miller (Indianapolis, Ind., 1985).

HUNTINGTON, SAMUEL, *American Politics: The Promise of Disharmony* (Cambridge, Mass., 1981).

IRONS, PETER, *The Courage of Their Convictions* (New York, 1988).

JAFFA, HARRY V., *Crisis of the House Divided* (Seattle, Wash., 1973).

JAMES I, King of England, *The Political Works of James I*, reprinted from the edition of 1616, with an intro. by Charles Howard McIlwain (Cambridge, Mass., 1918).

JOHANNSEN, ROBERT W, ed., *The Lincoln–Douglas Debates* (New York, 1965).

KANT, IMMANUEL, *Groundwork of the Metaphysic of Morals*, trans. H. J. Paton (New York, 1964).

——*Kant's Ethical Philosophy*, trans. James W. Ellington, intro. Warner A. Wick (Indianapolis, Ind., 1986).

KEEFE, WILLIAM J., *Congress and the American People* (Englewood Cliffs, NJ, 1980).

KELMAN, STEVEN, *Making Public Policy: A Hopeful View of American Government* (New York, 1987).

KINGDON, JOHN, *Congressmen's Voting Decisions*, 2nd edn. (New York, 1981).

KLUGER, RICHARD, *Simple Justice* (New York, 1976).

KOLKO, GABRIEL, *The Triumph of Conservatism* (New York, 1963).

KOVESI, JULIUS, *Moral Notions* (London, 1967).

KUHN, THOMAS, *The Structure of Scientific Revolutions*, 2nd edn. (Chicago, Ill., 1970).

LARMORE, CHARLES, *Patterns of Moral Complexity* (Cambridge, 1987).

LERNER, RALPH, *The Thinking Revolutionary* (Ithaca, NY, 1987).

LEVINSON, SANFORD, *Constitutional Faith* (Princeton, NJ, 1988).

LEWIS, C. S., *Studies in Words* (Oxford, 1960).

LINCOLN, ABRAHAM, *Collected Works*, ed. Roy P. Basler, 8 vols. (New Brunswick, NJ, 1959).

LOCKE, JOHN, *Two Treatises of Government*, ed. Peter Laslett (New York, 1963).

——*A Letter Concerning Toleration*, ed. James H. Tully (Indianapolis, Ind., 1983).

LOWI, THEODORE, *The End of Liberalism*, 2nd edn. (New York, 1979).

MAASS, ARTHUR, *Congress and the Common Good* (New York, 1983).

McCLOSKY, HERBERT and BRILL, ALIDA, *Dimensions of Tolerance* (New York, 1983).

——and ZALLER, JOHN, *The American Ethos: Public Attitudes toward Capitalism and Democracy* (Cambridge, Mass., 1984).

McDOWELL, GARY L., *The Constitution and Contemporary Constitutional Theory* (Cumberland, Va., 1985).

MACEDO, STEPHEN, *The New Right v. The Constitution*, 2nd edn. (Washington, DC, 1987).

MacINTYRE, ALASDAIR, *After Virtue* (Notre Dame, Ind., 1981).

——*Whose Justice? Which Rationality?* (Notre Dame, Ind., 1988).

MACKIE, JOHN, *Ethics: Inventing Right and Wrong* (Harmondsworth, 1979).

MADISON, JAMES, *The Papers of James Madison*, ed. W. T. Hutchinson *et al.*, 13 vols. to date (Chicago, Ill., and Charlottesville, Va., 1962–), vol. xi.

MILL, JOHN STUART, *On Liberty*, ed. David Spitz (New York, 1975).

MILTON, JOHN, *Areopagitica*, in *Complete Prose Works of John Milton*, ed. Douglas Bush *et al.*, vol. 2 (New Haven, Conn., 1969), 486–570.

MONTAIGNE, MICHEL DE, *The Complete Essays of Montaigne*, trans. Donald M. Frame (Stanford, Calif., 1985).

MORGAN, RUTH P., *The President and Civil Rights: Policy-making by Executive Order* (Lanham, Md., 1987).

MURDOCH, IRIS, *The Sovereignty of the Good* (Oxford, 1969).

MURPHY, WALTER F., *Congress and the Court* (Chicago, Ill., 1962).

——*The Elements of Judicial Strategy* (Chicago, Ill., 1973).

——and TANENHAUS, JOSEPH, *Comparative Constitutional Law: Cases and Commentaries* (New York, 1977).

——and PRITCHETT, C. HERMAN, eds., *Courts, Judges and Politics*, 4th edn. (New York, 1986).

NAGEL, THOMAS, *The Possibility of Altruism* (Princeton, NJ, 1970).

——*Mortal Questions* (Cambridge, 1981).

——*The View From Nowhere* (New York, 1986).

NEUSTADT, RICHARD E., *Presidential Power*, 2nd edn. (New York, 1980).

NIETZSCHE, FRIEDRICH, *The Portable Nietzsche*, ed. Walter Kaufmann (New York, 1968).

NOZICK, ROBERT, *Anarchy, State, and Utopia* (Oxford, 1980).

OAKESHOTT, MICHAEL, *Rationalism in Politics and Other Essays* (London, 1969).

——*On Human Conduct* (Oxford, 1975).

——*On History and Other Essays* (Oxford, 1983).

PANGLE, THOMAS, *The Spirit of Modern Republicanism* (Chicago, Ill., 1988).

PARFITT, DEREK, *Reasons and Persons* (Oxford, 1984).

PASCAL, BLAISE, *Pensées*, trans. A. J. Krailsheimer (Harmondsworth, 1965).

PELIKAN, JAROSLAV, *The Vindication of Tradition* (New Haven, Conn., 1984).

PITKIN, HANNAH FENICHEL, *The Concept of Representation* (Berkeley, Calif., 1972).

PLATO, *Euthyphro, Apology, Crito*, trans. F. J. Church, revised and introduced by R. D. Cumming (Indianapolis, Ind., 1956).

——*Republic*, trans. Allan Bloom (New York, 1968).

——*The Laws*, trans. Thomas Pangle (Chicago, Ill., 1988).

POPPER, KARL R., *The Open Society and Its Enemies, 1: The Spell of Plato* (London, 1966).

——*The Logic of Scientific Discovery* (New York, 1968).

RAWLS, JOHN, *A Theory of Justice* (Cambridge, Mass., 1970).

RAZ, JOSEPH, *The Authority of Law: Essays on Law and Morality* (Oxford, 1983).

——*The Morality of Freedom* (Oxford, 1988).

RIKER, WILLIAM H., *Liberalism Against Populism* (Prospect Heights, Ill., 1982).

RORTY, RICHARD, *Philosophy and the Mirror of Nature* (Princeton, NJ, 1979).
——*Consequences of Pragmatism* (Brighton, 1982).
——*Contingency, Irony, and Solidarity* (Cambridge, 1989).
ROSENBLUM, NANCY L., *Another Liberalism: Romanticism and the Reconstruction of Liberal Thought* (Cambridge, Mass., 1987).
ROSSITER, CLINTON, *Conservatism in America: The Thankless Persuasion* (New York, 1962).
ROSTOW, EUGENE V., *The Sovereign Prerogative* (New Haven, Conn., 1963).
ROUSSEAU, JEAN-JACQUES, *On The Social Contract, Discourse on the Origin of Inequality, Discourse on Political Economy*, trans. Donald A. Cress (Indianapolis, Ind., 1983).
——*The Government of Poland*, trans. Willmoore Kendall (Indianapolis, Ind., 1985).
SANDEL, MICHAEL, *Liberalism and the Limits of Justice* (Cambridge, 1982).
——ed., *Liberalism and its Critics* (Oxford, 1984).
SCHMITT, CARL, *The Crisis of Parliamentary Democracy*, trans. Ellen Kennedy (Cambridge, Mass., 1985).
——*Political Theology: Four Chapters on the Concept of Sovereignty*, trans. George Schwab (Cambridge, Mass., 1988).
SEIGAN, BERNARD, *Economic Liberties and the Constitution* (Chicago, Ill., 1980).
SHKLAR, JUDITH N., *Ordinary Vices* (Cambridge, Mass., 1984).
——*Legalism* (Cambridge, Mass., 1986).
SIMMEL, GEORGE, *Conflict and the Web of Group Affiliation*, trans. K. H. Wolff (Glencoe, Ill., 1955).
SMART, J. J. C., and WILLIAMS, BERNARD, *Utilitarianism: For and Against* (Cambridge, 1973).
SMITH, ADAM, *The Theory of Moral Sentiments*, ed. D. D. Raphael and A. L. Macfie (Oxford, 1979).
SMITH, ROGERS, *Liberalism and American Constitutional Law* (Cambridge., Mass, 1985).
SOLBERG, WINTON U., *The Federal Convention and the Formation of the Union of the American States* (Indianapolis, Ind., 1976).
STORING, HERBERT J., ed., *The Complete Anti-Federalist*, 7 vols. (Chicago, 1981).
——*The Anti-Federalist* (Chicago, 1985).
STRAUSS, LEO, *Persecution and the Art of Writing* (Ithaca, NY, 1989).
TAYLOR, CHARLES, *Hegel and Modern Society* (Cambridge, 1979).
——*Human Agency and Language: Philosophical Papers, 1* (Cambridge, 1985).

——*Philosophy and the Human Sciences: Philosophical Papers, 2* (Cambridge, 1985).

THAYER, JAMES BRADLEY, *John Marshall* (Boston, 1901).

TOCQUEVILLE, ALEXIS DE, *The Old Regime and the French Revolution*, trans. Stuart Gilbert (Garden City, NY, 1955).

——*Democracy in America*, ed. J. P. Mayer, trans. George Lawrence (New York, 1969).

TRIBE, LAURENCE H., *God Save This Honorable Court: How the Choice of Supreme Court Justices Shapes Our History* (New York, 1985).

TURGENEV, IVAN, *Fathers and Sons*, trans. Constance Garnett (New York, 1930).

UNGER, ROBERTO, *Knowledge and Politics* (New York, 1975).

VILE, M. J. C, *Constitutionalism and The Separation of Powers* (Oxford, 1967).

WALZER, MICHAEL, *Obligations: Essays on Disobedience, War, and Citizenship* (Cambridge, Mass., 1970).

——*Spheres of Justice: A Defense of Pluralism and Equality* (New York, 1983.

——*Interpretation and Social Criticism* (Cambridge, Mass., 1987).

WILDAVSKY, AARON, *The Politics of the Budgetary Process*, 4th edn. (Boston, Mass., 1984).

WILL, GEORGE F, *Statecraft as Soulcraft* (New York, 1983).

WILLIAMS, BERNARD, *Moral Luck* (Cambridge, 1983).

WOLIN, SHELDON, *Politics and Vision* (Boston, Mass., 1960).

YOUNG, S. DAVID, *The Rule of Experts* (Washington, DC, 1987).

YOURCENAR, MARGUERITE, *The Memoirs of Hadrian*, trans. Grace Frick (New York, 1981).

B. ARTICLES

ACKERMANN, BRUCE A., 'Why Dialogue?', *Journal of Philosophy* 86 (1989), 5–22.

ACTON, H. B., 'Political Justification', in Bedau, ed., *Civil Disobedience*, 220–39.

BARBER, SOTIRIOS A., 'Judge Bork's Constitution', in Walter F. Murphy and C. Herman Pritchett, eds., *Courts, Judges and Politics*, 4th edn. (New York, 1987), 641–5.

BATES, EDWARD, Attorney-General of the United States, 'Opinion of the Attorney General on the Suspension of the Privilege of the Writ of Habeas Corpus', *Opinions of the Attorneys General of the United States*, 10, ed. J. Hubley Ashton (Washington, DC, 1868), 74–92.

BENN, S. I., 'Freedom, Autonomy, and the Concept of a Person', *Proceedings of the Aristotelian Society, New Series* 76, 1975/6 (London, 1976), 109–30.

BERLIN, ISAIAH, 'Rationality of Value Judgments', C. J. Friederich, ed., _Nomos VII: Rational Decision_ (New York, 1967), 221–3.

BLOOM, ALLAN, 'Justice: John Rawls vs. The Tradition of Political Philosophy', _American Political Science Review_, 69 (1975), 648–62.

BORK, ROBERT H., 'Neutral Principles and Some First Amendment Problems', _Indiana Law Review_, 47 (1971), 1–35.

——'Foreword' to Gary L. McDowell, _The Constitution and Contemporary Constitutional Theory_ (Cumberland, Va., 1985), pp. v–xi.

BRUBAKER, STANLEY C., 'Reconsidering Dworkin's Case for Judicial Activism', _The Journal of Politics_, 46 (1984), 503–19.

CROPSEY, JOSEPH, 'The United States as Regime and the Sources of the American Way of Life', in Cropsey, _Political Philosophy and the Issues of Politics_ (Chicago, Ill., 1977), 1–13.

DOYLE, MICHAEL, 'Kant, Liberal Legacies, and Foreign Affairs', _Philosophy and Public Affairs_, 12 (1984), 205–35, and 323–53.

DURKHEIM, ÉMILE, 'Individualism and the Intellectuals', trans. and introduced by Steven Lukes, _Political Studies_, 17 (1969), 14–30.

EASTLAND, TERRY, 'The Politics of Morality and Religion: A Primer', in Carl Horn, ed., _Whose Values?_ (Ann Arbor, Mich., 1985), 5–21.

FEINBERG, JOEL, 'The Ideal of the Free Man', in James F. Doyle, ed., _Educational Judgments: Papers in the Philosophy of Education_ (London, 1973), 143–69.

FEYERABEND, PAUL, 'Against Method: Outline of an Anarchistic Theory of Knowledge', _Minnesota Studies in the Philosophy of Science_, 4 (Minneapolis, Minn., 1970).

FINNIS, JOHN M., 'Personal Integrity, Sexual Morality, and Responsible Parenthood', _Anthropos_, 1 (1985), 43–55.

FRANKFURT, HARRY, 'Freedom of the Will and the Concept of a Person', _Journal of Philosophy_, 67 (1971), 5–20.

FRIED, CHARLES, 'The Artificial Reason of Law or: What Lawyers Know', _Texas Law Review_, 60 (1981), 35–58.

FRISBY, MICHAEL K., 'House Democrats Prepare Bills to Counter High Court Rulings', _Boston Globe_, Friday 7 July 1989, p. 3.

GALSTON, WILLIAM, 'Defending Liberalism', _American Political Science Review_, 76 (1982), 621–9.

——'On the Alleged Right to Do Wrong: A Response to Waldron', _Ethics_, 93 (1983), 320–4.

——'Pluralism and Social Unity', _Ethics_, 99 (1989), 711–26.

GEERTZ, CLIFFORD, 'The Uses of Diversity', _Tanner Lectures on Human Values_, 7, ed. Sterling M. McMurrin (Cambridge, 1986).

GRAGLIA, LINO, A., 'Judicial Activism: Even on the Right, It's Wrong', _The Public Interest_, 95 (1989), 57–74.

GUTMANN, AMY, 'Communitarian Critics of Liberalism', *Philosophy and Public Affairs*, 14 (1985), 308–21.

HART, H. L. A. 'Are There Any Natural Rights', *Philosophical Review*, 64 (1955).

HIRSCHMANN, ALBERT O., 'Rival Interpretations of Market Society: Civilizing, Destructive, or Feeble?' *Journal of Economic Literature*, 20 (1982), 1463–84.

HOLMES, STEPHEN, 'Gag Rules or the Politics of Omission', in Jon Elster and Rune Slagstad, eds., *Constitutionalism and Democracy* (New York, 1988) 19–58.

JACKSON, ANDREW, 'Veto Message', 10 July 1832, J. D. Richardson, ed., *Messages and Papers of the Presidents*, ii (Washington, DC, 1896), 576–91.

JACOBSOHN, GARY J., 'Abraham Lincoln "On this Question of Judicial Authority": The Theory of Constitutional Aspiration', *Western Political Quarterly*, 36 (1983), 52–70.

KALT, JOSEPH P., and ZUPAN, M., 'Capture and Ideology in the Economic Theory of Politics', *American Economic Review*, 74 (1984), 279–300.

KATEB, GEORGE, 'Remarks on the Procedures of Constitutional Democracy', in J. R. Pennock and J. W. Chapman eds., *Nomos XX: Constitutionalism* (New York, 1979), 215–37.

KENNEDY, ELLEN, 'Introduction', to Carl Schmitt, *The Crisis of Parliamentary Democracy*. trans. Ellen Kennedy.

KINDER, DONALD R., 'Presidents, Prosperity and Public Opinion', *Public Opinion Quarterly*, 45 (1981), 1–21.

——and KIEWIET, D. RODERICK, 'Economic Discontent and Political Behavior: The Role of Personal Grievances and Collective Economic Judgments in Congressional Voting', *American Journal of Political Science*, 23 (1979), 495–527.

KING, MARTIN LUTHER, 'Letter from Birmingham City Jail', in Bedau, ed., *Civil Disobedience*, pp. 72–89.

KRISTOL, IRVING, '"When Virtue Loses All Her Loveliness"—Some Reflections on Capitalism and "the Free Society"', *The Public Interest*, 21 (1976), 3–15.

KYMLICKA, WILL, 'Rawls on Teleology and Deontology', *Philosophy and Public Affairs*, 17 (1988), 173–90.

LANE, ROBERT, 'Market Justice, Political Justice', *American Political Science Review*, 80 (1986), 383–401.

LEGGETT, WILLIAM, 'The Morals of Politics', *Plaindealer*, New York, 3 June 1837, reprinted in Joseph L. Blau, *Social Theories of Jacksonian Democracy: Representative Writings of the Period 1825–1850* (New York, 1954), 66–88.

LEVINSON, SANFORD, '"The Constitution" in American Civil Religion', *The Supreme Court Review*, 1979, ed. Philip Kurland and Gerhard Caspar (Chicago, 1980), 123–51.

MARX, KARL, 'The British Rule in India', in *The Marx–Engels Reader*, 2nd edn., ed. Robert Tucker (New York, 1978), 653–8.

MURPHY, WALTER F., 'The Art of Constitutional Interpretation', in M. Judd Harmon, ed., *Essays on the Constitution* (Port Washington, NY, 1978), 130–59.

——'Constitutional Interpretation: The Art of the Historian, Magician, or Statesman?', *Yale Law Review*, 87 (1978), 1752–71.

NAGEL, THOMAS, 'Moral Conflict and Political Legitimacy', *Philosophy and Public Affairs*, 16 (1987), 215–40.

NEVINS, ALLAN, 'The Case of the Copperhead Conspirator', in John A. Garraty, ed., *Quarrels That Have Shaped the Constitution* (New York, 1966), 90–108.

OAKESHOTT, MICHAEL, 'The Masses in Representative Democracy', in William F. Buckley, ed., *Did you Ever See a Dream Walking?: American Conservative Thought in the Twentieth Century* (Indianapolis, Ind., 1970), 103–23.

O'NEILL, ONORA, 'The Public Use of Reason', *Political Theory*, 14 (1986), 523–51.

RAWLS, JOHN, 'A Kantian Conception of Equality', *Cambridge Review* (1975), 84–99.

——'Kantian Constructivism in Moral Theory', *Journal of Philosophy*, 77 (1980), 515–72.

——'Justice as Fairness: Political, Not Metaphysical', *Philosophy and Public Affairs*, 14 (1985), 223–51.

——'The Idea of an Overlapping Consensus', *Oxford Journal of Legal Studies*, 17 (1987), 1–25.

——'The Priority of Right and Ideas of the Good', *Philosophy and Public Affairs*, 17 (1988), 251–76.

——'The Domain of the Political and Overlapping Consensus', *New York University Law Review*, 64 (1989), 233–55.

REHNQUIST, WILLIAM, 'The Notion of a Living Constitution', *Texas Law Review*, 54 (1976), 693–704.

RORTY, RICHARD, 'Postmodernist Bourgeois Liberalism', *Journal of Philosophy*, 80 (1983), 583–9.

——'Habermas and Lyotard on Post-Modernity', *Praxis International*, 4 (1984), 32–44.

——'The Priority of Democracy over Philosophy', in Robert Vaughn, ed., *The Virginia Statute of Religious Freedom: Two Hundred Years After* (Madison, Wis., 1988).

RUTLAND, ROBERT A., 'How the Constitution Secures Rights: A

Look at the Seminal Years', in Robert Goldwin and William Schambra, eds., *How Does the Constitution Secure Rights?* (Washington, DC, 1985), 1–14.

SANDEL, MICHAEL J., 'The Unencumbered Self', *Political Theory*, 9 (1984), 81–96.

SCANLON, T. M., 'Preference and Urgency', *Journal of Philosophy*, 72 (1975), 655–69.

——'Contractualism and Utilitarianism', in A. Sen and B. Williams, eds., *Utilitarianism and Beyond* (Cambridge, 1984), 103–28.

SCHAPIRO, MARTIN, 'The Constitution and Economic Liberties', in M. J. Harmon, ed., *Essays on the Constitution* (Port Washington, NY, 1978), 74–98.

SCHMITT, GARY J., 'Executive Privilege: Presidential Power to Withold Information from Congress', in Joseph Bessette and Jeffrey Tulis, eds., *The Presidency in the Constitutional Order* (Baton Rouge, La., 1981), 154–94.

STORING, HERBERT J., 'The Case Against Civil Disobedience', in Robert A. Goldwin, ed., *On Civil Disobedience* (Gambier, Ohio, 1968), 95–120.

——'The Constitution and the Bill of Rights', in M. J. Harmon, ed., *Essays on the Constitution* (Port Washington, NY, 1978), 32–48.

SUNSTEIN, CASS, 'Naked Preferences', *Columbia Law Review*, 84 (1984), 1689–732.

——'Interest Groups in American Public Law', *Stanford Law Review*, 38 (1985), 29–87.

THOMPSON, DENNIS F., 'Representatives in the Welfare State', in Amy Gutmann, ed., *Democracy and the Welfare State* (Princeton, NJ, 1988), 131–55.

WALDRON, JEREMY, 'A Right to Do Wrong', *Ethics*, 92 (1981), 21–37.

——'Galston on Rights', *Ethics*, 93 (1983), 325–7.

——'Theoretical Foundations of Liberalism', *Philosophical Quarterly*, 37 (1987), 127–50.

WALZER, MICHAEL, 'Philosophy and Democracy', *Political Theory*, 9 (1981), 379–99.

——'Flight From Philosophy', a review of Benjamin Barber, *The Conquest of Politics*, *New York Review of Books*, 36 (2 Feb. 1989), 42–4.

C. CASES

Abrams *v*. US, 250 US 616 (1919)
Bowers *v*. Hardwick 106 S. Ct. 2841 (1986)
Brandenburg *v*. Ohio 395 US 444 (1969)
Brown *v*. Board of Education 347 US 483 (1954)

Calder *v*. Bull 3 Dall. 395 (1798)
Champion *v*. Ames 188 US 321 (1903)
City of Cleburne *v*. Cleburne Living Center 473 US 432 (1985)
Cooper *v*. Aaron 358 US 1 (1958)
Craig *v*. Boren 429 US 190 (1976)
Dennis *v*. US 341 US 494 (1951)
Dred Scott *v*. Sandford 19 How. 393 (1857)
Edwards *v*. Aguillard 96 L. Ed. 2nd 510 (1987)
Eisenstadt *v*. Baird 405 US 438 (1972)
Ferguson *v*. Skrupka 372 US 726 (1963)
Fletcher *v*. Peck 3 L. Ed. 162 (1810)
Gitlow *v*. New York 268 US 652 (1925)
Griswold *v*. Connecticut 381 US 479 (1965)
Immigration and Naturalization Service *v*. Chadha 462 US 919 (1983)
Korematsu *v*. US 323 US 214 (1944)
Lochner *v*. New York 198 US 45 (1905)
McCulloch *v*. Maryland 4 Wheaton 316 (1819)
McLaurin *v*. Oklahoma State Regents for Higher Education 339 US 633 (1950)
Mathews *v*. Lucas 427 US 495 (1976)
Merryman, Ex Parte 17 F. Cas. 144 (1861)
Meyer *v*. State of Nebraska 262 US 390 (1923)
Milligan, Ex Parte 71 US 2 (1866)
Missouri ex rel. Gaines *v*. Canada 305 US 337 (1938)
Nebbia *v*. New York 291 US 502 (1934)
NRLB *v*. Jones & Laughlin Steel Co. 301 US 1 (1937)
Northern Securities Co. *v*. US 193 US 197 (1904)
Ogden *v*. Saunders 2 Wheaton 213 (1827)
Pierce *v*. Society of Sisters 268 US 510 (1925)
Plyler *v*. Doe 457 US 202 (1982)
Powell *v*. McCormick 395 US 486 (1969)
Schenck *v*. US 249 US 47 (1919)
Stanley *v*. Georgia 394 US 557 (1969)
Sweatt *v*. Painter 339 US 629 (1950)
Texas *v*. Johnson 88–155, Dec. 21 June 1989
US *v*. Carolene Products 304 US 144 (1938)
US *v*. Darby 312 US 100 (1941)
US *v*. E. C. Knight 156 US 1 (1895)
US *v*. Nixon 418 US 683 (1974)
Webster *v*. Reproductive Health Services 57 LW 5023, Dec. 3 July 1989
West Virginia State Board of Education *v*. Barnette 319 US 624 (1943)
Whitney *v*. People of State of California 274 US 357 (1927)

Wickard *v*. Filburn 317 US 111 (1942)
Williamson *v*. Lee Optical of Oklahoma 348 US 343 (1955)
Wisconsin *v*. Yoder 406 US 205 (1972)

D. UNPUBLISHED WORKS

BICK, M. M., 'Conceptions of the Self and the Community: Rawls and Sandel', M. Phil. Thesis, Politics (Oxford, 1984).
BRAND, DONALD A., 'In Defence of Sovereign Immunity', presented at the Program for Constitutional Government, Harvard University, Cambridge, Mass., 6 Oct. 1989.
GALSTON, WILLIAM A., 'Comment on Stephen Macedo, "The Politics of Justification"', presented at a symposium on The Politics of Justification, Institute for Humane Studies, George Mason University, Fairfax, Va., 21 Apr. 1989.
GUTMANN, AMY, 'A Liberal Public Philosophy', presented at the conference on Liberalism and the Good, Georgetown University, 3–5 November 1988, Washington, DC.
KATZ, ROBERT ALAN, 'Communitarianism and the Limits of Intercommunal Respect: A Moral Argument with Historical Illustrations Drawn from the Case of Israel', Senior Thesis, Government (Harvard, 1987).
MEESE, EDWIN, III, Address before the District of Columbia Chapter of the Federalist Society Lawyers Division, 15 Nov. 1985, Washington, DC.
——'The Law of the Constitution', speech given at Tulane University, 21 Oct. 1986, New Orleans, La.

Index